The Allocator's Edge shows just how much the investable universe has expanded and provides a practical path to true diversification. What Phil Huber prescribes is not (yet) the conventional wisdom, but it will be. A decade from now, Phil's philosophy and quest for safer, more reliable portfolios will be mainstream—and the investor/RIA of the future built upon it. *The Allocator's Edge* is bold in vision, full of accumulated wisdom, and immensely practical, giving allocators advice they can implement today to bring greater financial security to those they care for. If you are managing money for others, read this book.

— Ross Stevens, Founder and CEO, Stone Ridge Holdings Group

Phil Huber does a wonderful job explaining the current predicament financial advisors face in meeting the needs of their clients and offers a clear explanation of alternatives available. His articulation and display of the need for alternatives is handcrafted for any advisor to copy and paste to make the case for their clients. Phil's description of the past, present, and future of alternatives is an effective manual for anyone looking to understand where to go. I highly recommend having *The Allocator's Edge* on your reference bookshelf.

— Ted Seides, Founder, Capital Allocators, LLC

Phil Huber has written an important book on an important topic. We know that building good portfolios is getting harder, and Phil gives us a toolkit and a roadmap for getting the job done.

— Brian Portnoy, Ph.D., CFA, Founder, Shaping Wealth

With language easy enough for a novice investor to understand and a depth of insight for experienced investors to value, Phil Huber has created the modern, comprehensive guide to alternative investing. For anyone looking to expand their investment palette beyond stocks and bonds and learn not just what alternatives are available but how to deploy them in a portfolio, *The Allocator's Edge* is essential reading.

— Corey Hoffstein, Chief Investment Officer, Newfound Research

The Allocator's Edge really hits the mark as a primer in understanding why alternatives are important and sets a solid foundation for how to incorporate non-traditional exposures in portfolios. I would certainly recommend this to analysts, financial advisors, or other investors looking to be more conversant and comfortable with this third "bucket"—one I believe will be critical to delivering clients' desired outcomes over the next decade.

— Shannon Saccocia, Chief Investment Officer, Boston Private Wealth

The Allocator's Edge has always been about unlocking the power of uncorrelated risk premia. As democratization and access to product grow, all investors need to arm themselves with requisite knowledge. Phil Huber has put together an excellent set of guiding principles to help today's allocator navigate and harness the complexity premium.

— William J. Kelly, Chief Executive Officer, CAIA Association

Phil Huber has a breadth of knowledge across investing that I'm envious of. I can't believe how much this book covers, and how high quality the analysis across each section is. If I were a financial advisor or institutional allocator seeking to expand my knowledge of alternative investments, this is the book I'd pick up first.

— Ali Hamed, Co-Founder and General Partner, CoVenture

With low interest rates and elevated equity valuations, traditional portfolios are increasingly at risk of being bodyslammed. Phil Huber provides readers a ringside seat to the modern alternative investment landscape, covering everything from farmland to digital assets. This comprehensive guide extends beyond the why and into the how, with concrete and actionable takeaways for financial advisors and asset allocators to bring their portfolios into the 21st century.

— Meb Faber, Chief Executive Officer & Chief Investment Officer, Cambria Investment Management

Phil Huber has created a clear roadmap for investing for the next decade—his book is that rare combination of insightful and entertaining.

— Matt Kadnar, Partner and Portfolio Manager, GMO

Grab your highlighter and get ready to learn. *The Allocator's Edge* offers the sophisticated investor a comprehensive look into the world of alternative investments. Phil Huber clearly articulates the essential concepts in an approachable manner that makes this book a valuable resource to allocators, advisors, and investing enthusiasts.

— Peter Lazaroff, Chief Investment Officer, Plancorp

With equity capital markets near all-time high valuations and interest rates close to all-time lows, it appears the traditional 60/40 portfolio that has served investors well for decades will be challenged to generate the rates of return needed going forward. In *The Allocator's Edge*, Huber provides investors a practical guide on how to incorporate alternative investments into a portfolio framework to bridge this gap.

— Chris Schelling, Director of Alternatives, Venturi Private Wealth, and Author, *Better than Alpha*

Do you think stocks are expensive? Do you shudder at bond yields? If you're nodding your head, then this book is for you. In *The Allocator's Edge*, Phil Huber unpacks the misunderstandings and misconceptions that often accompany alternative investments. From private equity and hedge funds to catastrophe bonds and non-traditional lending, Phil explains alternative strategies in a way that can teach a financial professional and also make sense to the layman.

—Michael Batnick, Director of Research at Ritholtz Wealth Management, and co-host of the Animal Spirits podcast

THE
ALLOCATOR'S
EDGE

Every owner of a physical copy of this edition of

THE ALLOCATOR'S EDGE

can download the eBook for free direct from us at Harriman House, in a DRM-free format that can be read on any eReader, tablet or smartphone.

Simply head to:

ebooks.harriman-house.com/allocatorsedge

to get your copy now.

THE ALLOCATOR'S EDGE

A modern guide to alternative investments and the future of diversification

Phil Huber, CFA, CFP®

HARRIMAN HOUSE LTD
3 Viceroy Court
Bedford Road
Petersfield
Hampshire
GU32 3LJ
GREAT BRITAIN
Tel: +44 (0)1730 233870

Email: enquiries@harriman-house.com
Website: harriman.house

First published in 2021.
Copyright © Phil Huber

The right of Phil Huber to be identified as the Author has been asserted in accordance with the Copyright, Design and Patents Act 1988.

Hardback ISBN: 978-0-85719-793-1
eBook ISBN: 978-0-85719-794-8

British Library Cataloguing in Publication Data
A CIP catalogue record for this book can be obtained from the British Library.

For my wife, Christie,
and our daughter, Hannah.

You are my world.

To that, there is no alternative.

ABOUT THE AUTHOR

Phil Huber, CFA, CFP®, as both a wealth management practitioner and an investment industry thought leader, is uniquely qualified in understanding the merits of alternative investments as well as the myriad challenges that accompany their use in the portfolios of wealthy individuals and families.

Phil is the Chief Investment Officer for Savant Wealth Management, where he helps oversee the firm's investment and portfolio-management related functions. As co-chair of the firm's Investment Committee, Phil leads the research efforts that he and his team perform on asset managers, investment strategies and portfolio construction techniques.

Phil has been featured in a number of notable media outlets, including *The Wall Street Journal*, *The New York Times*, *InvestmentNews*, *CityWire RIA Magazine*, and Bloomberg TV. In 2018, 2019, and 2020, he was named one of Investopedia's Top Financial Advisors. He also produces his own investing blog, *bps and pieces* (bpsandpieces.com).

He has been involved in the financial services industry since 2007. Phil joined Savant as part of a merger with his prior firm, Huber Financial Advisors, where he worked for twelve years and last served as the firm's Chief Investment Officer. Prior to his days at Huber Financial, Phil was employed at a global asset management company where he worked closely with financial advisors to develop investment strategies for their clients.

He holds a bachelor's degree in finance from the Kelley School of Business at Indiana University and is a CERTIFIED FINANCIAL PLANNER™ professional. Phil also is a CFA® charter holder and a member of the CFA society of Chicago.

Phil and his wife Christie live in the northwest suburbs of Chicago where they enjoy reading, yoga, and spending time with their daughter Hannah. He is also a lifelong, diehard professional wrestling fan.

CONTENTS

FOREWORD BY CLIFF ASNESS

It is hard to write an unbiased non-self-serving foreword to a book when a) you already think quite highly of the author, b) you think the author thinks quite highly of you, and c) the author's recommendations line up fairly well with your own (with an admitted nod to Upton Sinclair). Luckily for me "unbiased" is not a requirement for a foreword and I will thus make no attempt to temper my praise with manufactured critique added solely for credibility. Be forewarned.

My summary of Phil's wonderful book can be broken into three parts.[1]

1. What's the situation?
2. What do you do?
3. Why is doing it hard and how might we make it less hard?

So, what's the situation? Well, I won't rehash all the evidence Phil presents (or people like me have been screaming about for a while!) but valuations on both stocks and bonds are very expensive today. That means (almost but not quite by definition[2]) that they have done really well for a while, but sit at substantially lower expected medium- to long-term expected returns right now. That doesn't mean it's a certainty they'll underperform

---

1 By the way, Phil starts each chapter with a great set of quotes, all implicitly about investment but rarely explicitly about investing. Please make sure you glance at them as you read the book as they are both fun and informative.

2 It doesn't have to be so for stocks. For example, you can get to a very high P/E by price going up or earnings falling through the floor. So it's theoretically possible to be at very expensive valuations without having had abnormally high returns. But that's not the case today. Stocks are very expensive versus history and have indeed done very well.

their historical norms going forward. Expectations are just that—they aren't ex post realizations. And it's not without controversy. I have colleagues who've written papers on the difficulty in statistically "proving"[3] this as you just don't get enough non-overlapping long-term periods.[4] But, the point estimates (i.e., if you had to make one guess from the data) go the way intuition would suggest. That is, more expensive starting valuations lead to lower expectations of future return and vice versa. Again, it's difficult to prove that beyond a reasonable statistical doubt, but it has been historically true and fits our economic intuition (at least mine)—two things that are enough for me to give it serious consideration.

What's more, one thing that makes today fairly unique is *both* stock and bond markets are very expensive versus history at the same time. That means that *portfolios* (e.g., like the classic 60/40 stock/bond portfolio) of U.S. or global stocks and bonds taken together are actually more expensive than their component parts. In the past when one of these was quite expensive (e.g., stocks in the 1999–2000 technology bubble) the other (e.g., bonds in the 1999–2000 technology bubble) was often cheap, and thus the portfolio, even without any tilts or timing towards the cheaper one, was not as extreme as today. Today, both major asset classes have done very well versus history for quite a long time, leaving both of them quite expensive, and thus the portfolio of stocks and bonds even more expensive vs. history. As a result, at least in Phil's and my opinion, the expected going forward return on this diversified portfolio of stocks and bonds is extremely low versus history.

Phil then shows that it doesn't seem that most real-world investors actually believe this! Rather, their estimates for the future currently seem higher than historical experience. To those seduced by Phil's (and my) reasoning, that may appear backwards (and we think it is!). However, for many, having experienced at least a decade of superb returns on both stocks and bonds (with some big bumps along the way of course) the intuition runs the exact opposite way. They expect the good times to continue to roll on and on.

So, what do you do? Well, I really should say "what do you do if you believe Phil and Cliff?" but let's consider that implied from now on. Well,

---

3 "Proving" here means a really small chance you're wrong. Sadly, you never really prove anything in statistics you just reduce the chance you are mistaken.

4 For one paper on this statistical difficulty see J. Boudoukh, R. Israel and M. Richardson, *Financial Analysts Journal* 75:1 (2019).

you're faced with substantially lower expected return on traditional assets today vs. history. Many organizations and individuals have return goals, and financial obligations, that makes this a real problem looking ahead. One thing you could do is just accept it. Stay the course, realize you'll likely make less than-hoped-for for a while, perhaps quite a long while (the alternative is making a ton less for a little while but that's kind of scary), but not make any big errors. Not a crazy plan but Phil (and I) are interested in how we can perhaps do better.

One option is to stay with traditional stocks and bonds but add a ton more alpha than you used to assume you could, either through security selection or market timing. Nice work if you can get it! This isn't a screed about perfect efficient markets and the impossibility of either of these attempts. That would be pretty hypocritic of me. But it is a warning that both of these are a zero-sum game that you were, I assume, already engaged in if you believe in it. Why anyone can suddenly get much better at this now that traditional assets are offering less is anyone's guess but it doesn't seem like the best plan to us.[5]

So, Phil lands on the recommendation to diversify away from traditional stocks and bonds. OK, that sounds great. But into what? Phil goes through multiple options that all can fall under the rubric of "alternative." Some have done even better than traditional markets (e.g., crypto), some have kept up, but many (e.g., liquid alts that put significant weight on the "value factor"—something I know a bit about) have lagged what seems like an ever upwards, ever anti-cheap assets stock and bond market. Phil is non-partisan across these. If they pass a basic reasonableness test, including that they are getting more investable for more people all the time, he likes them, at least for a small part of the whole. He advocates a broad portfolio of many different types of alternatives, and taking a slice of what's normally allocated to traditional stocks and bonds and allocating it to that alternative portfolio. We all might do it slightly differently. I for one am more cynical than Phil about privates (e.g., the dampened reported volatility might make them look better than the really are), more clueless about crypto (I'm kind of cynical, but not in a knowledgeable way, more in an old-man harrumphing kind of way), even more clueless about farmland (like House Greyjoy my family

---

5   Admittedly, some of Phil's suggestions to come, like liquid alts, are a form of indeed pursuing more alpha going forward.

sigil might be "we don't sow"[6]), and even more bullish than he on liquid alts which have taken a pounding for a while leaving many of them the rare things that look cheap not expensive today versus their history (massive Upton Sinclair alert). No matter. As a whole, it's hard to argue with Phil's non-denominational diversified portfolio of diversifiers. I'll leave the details to Phil (you do have to read the book!) but he shows that such a portfolio of diversifiers has great potential to help the situation that investors in a more traditional portfolio find themselves in.

So, it's simple right? No it ain't. In fact it's ridiculously hard. Phil discusses why it is so hard and how might you make it less hard.

Here I picture Phil as Colonel Nathan R. Jessup screaming at us all "You can't handle diversification!" OK, more accurately, though not as pithy, he's (not screaming but politely explaining) that diversification, particularly away from assets that have (note the tense, people assume "have" is the same as "will" way too much in investing!) done great, is in fact much harder to handle than those in an ivory tower might think. Of course, he has some concrete ideas how to help get there (and stick there which is also very hard!).

At one point Phil says "Most allocators intuitively like the idea of uncorrelated returns, but most balk at the actual experience of owning uncorrelated return streams." This certainly fits my experience! As Phil discusses, diversification is, by definition, being different than the norm. When the norm does very well, being different will, also mostly by definition, hurt you, at least relative to your "norm"ish peers. That's not easy to live through! It's not easy even if you're doing it precisely because you strongly believe it will lead to doing better than the norm long term. When it doesn't work it's going to hurt, and hurt more than many anticipate when and if they allocate to these alternatives to begin with. Diversifying away from the norm means almost by definition you'll be trailing when most people you know are doing great. You'll have your moments, including hopefully the most important one (the long term). But, it's really hard to stick with through the lean years. And I do mean years with a plural. Everything in investing seems to go on longer than we all expect, and it seems (and this is probably a tautology in some equilibrium fashion) many of us throw in the towel at exactly the wrong time. We suffer for years and then can't take it, leaving

---

6 Actually my family did officially vote on a motto about 15 years ago. For those curious it was "are you going to finish that?"

(in my case sometimes within minutes of the low!) at the near exact point it finally starts to work and work and work. If that's going to be the case it is truly better not to have diversified at all but, rather, have simply accepted the lower expected returns on traditional assets and held the line there.[7]

Of course Phil is not without suggestions on how allocators can weather these difficulties and actually see diversification through. I won't spend a lot of time on them here. Again, you have to read the book! But one thing Phil says that I particularly love is "Great investments (and by extension great portfolios) are nothing if not paired with equally great investors." I think that's just staggeringly true.[8] An example (where the portfolio creator and the investor are one and the same) is Warren Buffett (isn't he an example of everything?). My colleagues wrote a paper on Buffett's investing success.[9] They found his success came a large part from picking the "right" investing styles over his career (for those keeping score at home it's buying cheap, high quality, low volatility/beta stocks) and, taking advantage of the lower volatility/beta, applying modest leverage. But they also found one other thing that's really neat. A big part of his success came from not backing off during some periods of tremendous relative or absolute difficult performance. And he did that when he was plain old Warren Buffett not the WARREN FREAKING BUFFETT THE GOAT we know today. It's just one example where doing something ex ante good, like the styles Buffett tilts towards, must be paired with staying power. I can't promise you Phil will turn all us readers into Warren Buffett but if you read his book I think it helps you at least move in that direction.

In summary, Phil tells us stocks and bonds have done great, but are now poised to do less great over the next X years, just when people now expect them to do even greater. He tells us we should diversify into some alternatives and makes a very reasonable recommendation about which to include. Perhaps most importantly, he coaches us about how hard it's going to be, how important it is to stick with it, and offers some concrete ideas

---

7   Phil notes in the book that alternatives also often get a shorter leash than other investments. First, I'm here to testify that is true! Second, while true, it's perhaps also why there's the most to gain here. Doing things that are easy rarely leads to a long-term edge. For instance, "easy" makes them easy to arbitrage away. Doing things that are hard is not sufficient for generating such an edge (there can indeed be hard but stupid things) but does seem necessary.

8   And it makes me a very thankful man for the investors I've (mostly) encountered in my career.

9   A. Frazzini, D. Kabiller and L. H. Pederson, *Financial Analysts Journal* 74:4 (2018).

how to make it happen. He offers a mantra for the whole project—SHARP. It stands for sensible + humble + autonomous + resolute + persevering. Personally, I think he's forcing it a bit with resolute and persevering being pretty similar, and he wussed out on adding an "E" to make it "SHARPE," but it's really great stuff![10]

Phil tells us diversifying properly is vital, today more than ever. But, that sticking with it is a harder battle than you might think, yet a battle worth waging, and when it comes to waging it he's got your six.

Read the book.

Cliff Asness
Managing and Founding Principal,
AQR Capital Management

---

10   This coming from me who prefers my own acronym MAGFANTs (Microsoft, Apple, Google, Facebook, Amazon, Netflix, and Tesla) to the more well know FANGs. It's my foreword and I'll be a hypocrite if I want to be.

INTRODUCTION

Trade-Offs All the Way Down

For AS LONG as I can remember, I have been fascinated—nay, obsessed—with asset allocation.

I know what you're thinking—this guy needs more hobbies.

And you'd be right, but that's neither here nor there...

My infatuation with asset allocation stems from my strong conviction that diversification—true diversification—is indistinguishable from magic. I mean, think about it. To put different investment ingredients together in a blender and have the resulting smoothie taste great *and* be less filling than the sum of the parts?

The direct parallels between asset allocation and our everyday lives captivate me. Whether in markets or in life, we continually walk a tightrope of trade-offs in the decisions that we make. Want to be physically fit? You need to balance the trade-offs between a healthy diet and exercise against your desire to watch TV and eat the things you enjoy. Want to have a successful career? You need to balance the trade-offs of a higher salary and recognition from your peers against your willingness to work long hours and spend time away from your loved ones.

This brings us to the myriad trade-offs we must make as investors: return objectives, risk tolerance, income needs, liquidity preferences, tax considerations, and so on and so forth. The deeper you go, the more you realize that it's trade-offs all the way down.

For the last several decades, traditional asset allocation techniques have proved sufficient in helping investors achieve their most important financial goals. It is my belief that while the conventional core building blocks of portfolios—stocks and bonds—will still be necessary going forward, they are no longer sufficient.

To that end, I have spent an inordinate amount of time over the last decade-plus of my career researching modern approaches to asset allocation and leading-edge portfolio construction techniques. I believe that most investors have historically been limited in terms of the types of diversification they can access, but that is changing.

My raison d'être with *The Allocator's Edge* is to reach other forward-thinking financial advisors and investment professionals involved in the asset allocation process who believe we can do better than the status quo. Some will be resistant to change, while others will keep an open mind. Either way, I'm confident those who bring an unwavering commitment to doing what's necessary to improve their clients' odds of achieving their most important financial goals will walk away from this book more confident than before in that very possibility.

The road to success in this new era will not be paved with the familiar and comfortable. It is no secret that old habits die hard. But excellence in asset allocation requires a continuous evolution of ideas. We now live in an era where alternatives can stand on equal footing with stocks and bonds as a third pillar of diversified portfolios. The evidence and rationale are too compelling to ignore.

Writing instructor David Perell encourages authors to write at the intersection of what they know, what excites them, and what others want. I'm confident I've got the first two covered and it is my hope that in picking up *The Allocator's Edge* you possess the third intersection of this Venn diagram.

When I set out to write this book, I had four main priorities with the end reader in mind. I wanted it to be:

- Interesting
- Accessible
- Comprehensive
- Actionable

If after reading *The Allocator's Edge* you feel that all four of those boxes have been checked, that's about the best compliment I could receive.

A Two-Asset World

Most investors live in a two-asset world. You want the prospect of high returns with commensurate risk? Buy stocks. You want safety and income with the accompanying lower expected returns? Buy bonds. Find yourself stuck somewhere in the middle? Buy some combination of the two. It is impossible to pinpoint exactly when and how it happened, but somewhere along the way, the specific combination of 60% stocks and 40% bonds became the de facto standard in asset allocation.

The last thirty-plus years have been defined by a secular decline in interest rates, providing a once-in-a-generation tailwind for fixed income investors coming off the heels of the inflationary environment of the 1970s. Or, as writer Morgan Housel puts it, "The most underrated investing traits are patience and having your career coincide with a 30-year record decline in interest rates."

There's good news and there is bad news. Let's just rip off the Band-Aid and get the bad news out of the way first. There is a high probability that the 60/40 portfolio that worked tremendously in the past will ultimately fall short in meeting the return targets and objectives of investors in the decades ahead. There are two main culprits to blame here: high valuations of the "60" and paltry interest rates on the "40."

Let's start with equities. There is a wealth of evidence supporting the notion that starting valuations matter a great deal to long-term returns. The mean-reverting nature of valuations links high (low) starting multiples with lower (higher) than average returns. For U.S.-domiciled investors with an embedded home bias, this challenge is particularly acute as our domestic stock market in 2021 ranges from slightly rich to obscenely expensive, depending on your preferred valuation metric. Figure A shows the cyclically adjusted price-to-earnings ratio (CAPE) for the S&P 500 throughout history. It has recently reached levels seldom seen in its history.

Figure A: S&P 500 Shiller CAPE Ratio (1901-2021)

Source: Author.

This tells you nothing about what might happen in the next year or two, as valuations alone are a blunt timing tool. But it certainly doesn't paint a pretty picture for the next seven to ten years. The story in international markets is not nearly as bad, but market multiples abroad are by no means a screaming buy.

Let's move on to fixed income now. As of March 2021, the 10-year Treasury rate sits at around 1.5%. That is materially higher than the low of 0.52% reached in 2020, but still historically low. Assuming realized inflation of roughly 2%, investors are set up for negative expected real returns from an asset that has historically acted as ballast against equity volatility and generated mid-single digit returns in the process. One doesn't have to make an interest rate forecast to confidently declare that the halcyon days of fixed income are all but over.

Figure B shows the 10-year Treasury rate from 1962 to 2020. You can see that the rate in 2020 is historically low and that the rate has been on a downward trend since the 1980s.

Figure B: Historical 10-Year U.S. Treasury Rate (1962–2020)

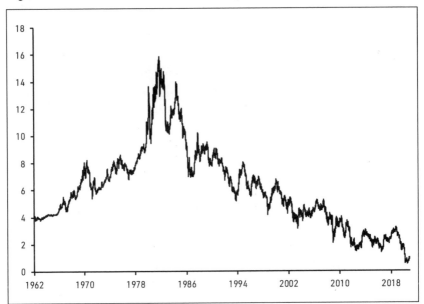

Source: Author.

The result of these two forces colliding is dramatically lower expected real returns for traditional 60/40 portfolios. According to AQR, the expected medium-term real returns for a U.S. 60/40 portfolio is a measly 1.4%—less than one-third of its long-term average since 1900.

Don't get me wrong. I think almost all investors should own stocks. I also think most investors should own *some* bonds. These core portfolio pillars are not going anywhere anytime soon and both serve valuable roles in a portfolio. But we can do better. The goal is not to replace stocks and bonds, but to augment them.

Three Choices

With conventional portfolios stuck between a rock and a hard place, allocators can choose one of three paths to confront today's challenges on behalf of their clients:

1. Do Nothing

This is the path of least resistance. And it is likely the road that most will take, as inertia is a force to be reckoned with. Maintaining the status quo will feel comfortable, but the price of admission for that comfort will come in the form of falling short of investors' objectives. Return targets are unreasonably high, yet capital market expectations are stubbornly low. Something's got to give.

2. Take More Equity Risk

This choice might solve the return side of the equation but requires a very long horizon and will incur some bumps along the way. Investors will likely have to incur cringeworthy levels of volatility and drawdowns that will keep them from sleeping well at night. And we must remember the equity risk premium is promised to no one—that's why it's a risk premium. History has demonstrated several lengthy dry spells. In theory, this approach might work. In practice, the odds are slim.

3. Think and Act Differently

Investing differently than others is easier said than done. There is peer risk, career risk, and a whole host of other considerations to factor in. Choosing this path takes courage, but it is where the opportunity lies ahead.

The Opportunity

What do I mean when I say we need to think and act differently?

I promised there was good news as well. A net positive for investors is that the investable universe has grown by leaps and bounds, providing a more diverse toolkit with which to build portfolios.

The solution to the dilemma facing traditional asset allocation is to embrace additional sources of return that lie outside the conventional orthodoxy. A wide range of exposures once considered un-investable are now increasingly democratized thanks to the confluence of technological advancements and financial innovation. From niche asset classes to strategies designed to intelligently exploit structural market inefficiencies and behavioral biases, investors today can enhance their portfolios by including valuable, diversifying return streams sourced from non-traditional risk premia.

The effective implementation of alternative investments in the context of a diversified portfolio is simultaneously the biggest opportunity and the biggest challenge facing financial advisors, asset allocators and other sophisticated investors today.

———————

There are no easy answers to the dilemma we face as asset allocators. But there are worthwhile solutions. And as we all know, nothing worthwhile is ever easy.

If you have been on board conceptually with alternatives, but have struggled with implementation and client adoption, worry no more.

If you are a natural skeptic—and you absolutely should be—then this is an opportunity to objectively reassess the portfolios of the families and institutions you serve.

The new paradigm suggested in this book involves a sizable and wholesale shift, both in dollars and in mindset. Succeeding unconventionally is unnatural and challenging for all of us, but I am confident that the long-term outcome is one of more robust and rewarding portfolios that can deliver across a wider spectrum of goals and objectives.

It's time to stop being complacent.

It's time to start getting creative.

It's time for us to sharpen the Allocator's Edge.

HOW TO USE THIS BOOK

THE ALLOCATOR'S EDGE is designed to arm financial advisors, institutional allocators, and other professional investors with the tools and techniques required to seize the opportunity in alternative investments on behalf of the people and entities they serve.

The book itself is divided into three parts, taking us from *why* to the *what* to the *how*. It is not imperative to read each chapter in succession, but it is highly encouraged.

Part I of *The Allocator's Edge* defines the challenge—and the opportunity—that allocators face. The traditional portfolio construction methods ubiquitous today are no longer enough to meet the reasonable risk and return targets of most investors. The three chapters in this section seek to answer the following three questions about alternative investments in today's investment landscape:

- Why will traditional portfolios be challenged going forward? (Chapter 1)
- Why have many investors struggled with the adoption of alternatives to date? (Chapter 2)
- Why is the opportunity in alternatives today more compelling than it was yesterday? (Chapter 3)

Part II of *The Allocator's Edge* is an exploration into an array of diversifying return streams that, while individually risky, can collectively lower overall portfolio risk when used in conjunction with stocks and bonds. Used strategically over a long horizon, a diversified mix of these non-traditional assets and strategies can put allocators in a position to deliver better, and more consistent, outcomes for investors.

The chapters in Part II progress through the past, present, and future of alternative investments. Each chapter takes a deep dive into a particular segment of alternatives, seeking to understand their history and potential role(s) in a portfolio. Despite the chronological structure of Part II, these chapters can be read out of order depending on what topics pique your interest.

Chapter 4 examines the roles of private equity, hedge funds, real estate, and natural resources (commodities and gold) as the historical cornerstones of alternative investing. We see the tangential relationships between these mainstays of institutional portfolios and some of the modern alternatives discussed in the subsequent chapters of Part II. Specifically, chapters 5–8 address alternative risk premia, insurance-linked securities, real assets, and non-traditional credit, respectively.

Chapter 9 closes out this section with a survey of the future investable universe. The nascent asset classes covered here, each intriguing and promising, are candidates for portfolio eligibility at some point in the future but are maybe not quite ready for "prime time."

As you read chapters 4–9, you may find yourself wanting concrete suggestions on what specific investments could be used to implement the strategies being discussed. While not a recommendation of any fund or manager, Appendix 1 provides a sample list of investment options by category. This is meant to function as a jumping-off point for additional due diligence.

Part III of *The Allocator's Edge* is where we leave the realm of conceptual, roll up our sleeves and answer questions related to portfolio design, implementation, and communication.

Chapter 10 attempts to reconcile the challenge of matching the right investments to the appropriate investment vehicles. There is a lot of nuance in understanding which asset classes can or should go into different fund structures.

Chapter 11 provides a blueprint for crafting recipes (portfolios) from the various ingredients (assets) covered in Part II, with an emphasis on the practical implementation considerations faced by financial advisors.

Chapter 12, the concluding chapter, focuses on the skills required of tomorrow's allocators in delivering outstanding investment experiences for clients. Great investments are nothing if not paired with equally great investors. Half of the battle that allocators face is effectively educating and communicating alternative investments with their end clients. We wrap things up by gaining new perspectives to match our new portfolios.

If you're like me, bullet point summaries can be a helpful device to distill the key takeaways of a chapter or as a quick refresh without having to reread in entirety. As such, each chapter includes a section at the end called *The Allocator's Cheat Sheet* that contains a handful of bullet points that cover the high notes.

The best allocators understand the importance of managing expectations for stakeholders and clients. As such, it is worth mentioning what this book is not, to better calibrate expectations for you the reader. *The Allocator's Edge* is NOT:

- **A treatise on the tax treatment of alternative investments**: I am not a CPA or a tax professional. There are some general comments on the taxation of alternative investments throughout the book, but more specifics are beyond the scope of this book.
- **An instruction manual for building portfolios**: It is my strong belief that non-traditional investments will be an essential part of well-functioning portfolios for the indefinite future, but I am somewhat agnostic to the specifics of their construction. Different strokes will apply to different folks. I am confident, however, that there are enough details and examples shared to help inform the decision-making of each reader in a way that makes the most sense for their organization and constituents.
- **A mile deep on every alternative asset class**: I would have loved going even deeper on many of the topics covered within, but the comprehensive nature of this book only allows for so many layers to be peeled back. My hope is that the contents of this book will follow the first rule of show business—always leave them wanting more! For those looking to take a dive into the deep end of the pool, Appendix 2—the Research Rabbit Hole—is a curated compilation of the best books, podcasts, white papers, articles and blog posts canvassing each topic discussed in the book.

With that out of the way, *The Allocator's Edge* awaits. Let's get started!

PART I

THE ALLOCATOR'S DILEMMA

CHAPTER 1

Hindsight is 60/40—The Impaired
Vision of Traditional Portfolios

"What got you here won't get you there."
— ***Marshall Goldsmith***

*"The first step towards getting somewhere is to decide that
you are not going to stay where you are."*
— ***J.P. Morgan***

W E BEGIN CHAPTER 1 by challenging the conventional wisdom of
traditional asset allocation methods.

Conventional asset allocators instinctively look backwards, sticking with
what has worked in the rear-view mirror but not paying attention to the
road ahead. With impeccable acuity, they can see that a balanced portfolio
of stocks and bonds was just about the best diversification strategy money
could buy for the last 40 years. To say their hindsight is 20/20 would be an
understatement.

Their hindsight is better than 20/20. It's 60/40.

The practice of asset allocation, at least as we know it today, can be
traced primarily to the inaugural "Stocks, Bonds, Bills, and Inflation: The
Past and Future" study, published by Roger Ibbotson and Rex Sinquefield
in 1976. This landmark paper detailed the return histories of stocks, bonds,
one-month T-Bills and inflation. The latest chart of Ibbotson data for the
returns of these assets from 1926 to 2020 is shown in Figure 1.1.

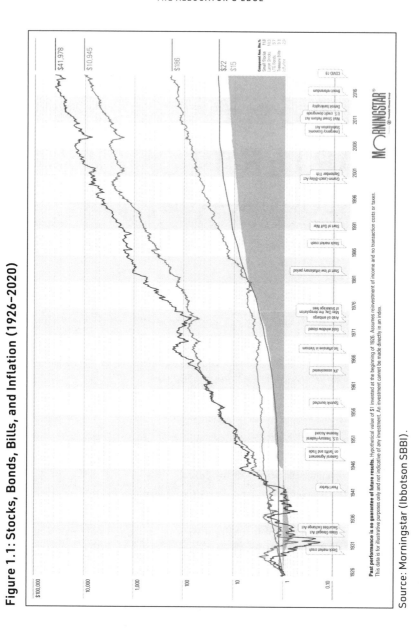

Figure 1.1: Stocks, Bonds, Bills, and Inflation (1926–2020)

Source: Morningstar (Ibbotson SBBI).

The long-term risk premium generated by stocks is on full display, but stocks have experienced massive declines at multiple points along the way. Few possess the intestinal fortitude to ride the ups and downs of an all-stock portfolio throughout the duration of their investing lifetime, so a countervailing force is needed.

[Bonds have entered the chat]

The quest for uncorrelated return streams has always been the "holy grail" of investing. The combination of unrelated assets—each with independent return drivers—delivers the magic that is diversification. Said differently, diversification allows the whole to be greater than the sum of the parts.

For the last 40-plus years, bonds have been the peanut butter to stocks' jelly. On their own, bonds have generated meaningful returns. Used in conjunction with stocks, they have offered low to negative correlation and positive returns when needed most—during crisis periods when equities suffer.

This successful one-two punch has led many to a default posture of (roughly) balancing the two asset classes. We can't pinpoint its inception, but somewhere along the way 60% stocks and 40% bonds became the standard. Not quite an even split, but pretty darn close—with a slight nod given to stocks for their higher expected returns.

The 60/40 portfolio has become synonymous with balanced asset allocation. Stocks for growth, and bonds for income and diversification. As simple and easy as it gets. I'll be referencing '60/40' throughout the book, but please treat it as shorthand for any balanced allocation to stocks and bonds. This includes variants like 70/30 and 50/50 that while not 60/40 in name, should be thought of in concert.

The reason 60/40 is so canonical is quite simply because it has worked tremendously for investors for over four decades. The pleasant journey it has provided and its increasing ease of implementation have made it a perennial favorite among investors. But don't take my word for it. Let's go to the tape.

60/40: By the Numbers

Investor Michael Batnick compiled several historical statistics supporting the 60/40 portfolio's reign at the top of the asset allocation food chain over the last 50 years. It is important to note that this example uses a U.S.-only version of the balanced portfolio. While many 60/40 investors deploy some level of global diversification, they often still retain significant home bias. For U.S.-based investors, this positioning has only served to strengthen returns in the most recent decade. Over the last 50 years, the U.S.-only 60/40 has delivered:

- Positive returns in 82% of rolling one-year periods, 93% of rolling three-year periods, and 99% of rolling five-year periods.
- Only one calendar-year decline greater than 20%, but ten calendar-year gains of over 20%.
- An average annualized return of over 10%.

The rolling returns of a 60/40 portfolio from 1976 to 2020 are shown in Figure 1.2.

Figure 1.2: Rolling Returns of a 60/40 Portfolio (1976–2020)

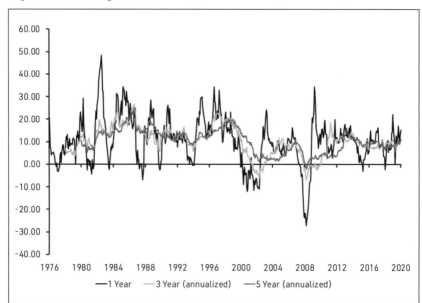

Source: 60% S&P 500 Total Return Index, 40% Bloomberg Barclays US Aggregate Bond Index.

After reading those numbers, you might be wondering what the concern is. I mean, why fight an uphill battle against something that has behaved in such a consistent and rewarding fashion?

Because past is not prologue and the conditions that made the 60/40 ripe for success in prior decades—namely high and falling interest rates—are no longer intact.

The remainder of this chapter is a guided tour of the assumptions and issues underlying the rocky foundation of the ubiquitous 60/40 portfolio.

"Past Performance is Not Indicative of Future Results"

This simple phrase, heard ad nauseum in every mutual fund commercial that airs on CNBC, goes in one ear and out the other for many investors. We hear it so often that we fail to take it seriously until we learn its meaning the hard way. Knowing how susceptible we are to the siren song of past performance, it's no wonder why investors remain so enamored with the 60/40 today.

The 2010s were not kind to broad diversification and thoughtful portfolio construction. Most diversification strategies only served as a drag on returns, leading to investor frustration. A simple 60/40 portfolio of U.S. stocks and bonds outkicked its coverage by a mile over the past ten years.

The Sharpe ratio for both U.S. stocks and bonds over the last ten years is shown in Figure 1.3. These recent numbers are juxtaposed with the average Sharpe ratio for each going back to 1925, as well as the 25th and 75th percentile numbers over that period. Clearly both asset classes have recently earned better risk-adjusted returns than almost any other time in history.

Figure 1.3: Rolling 10-Year Sharpe Ratio of Stocks and Bonds (1973–2020)

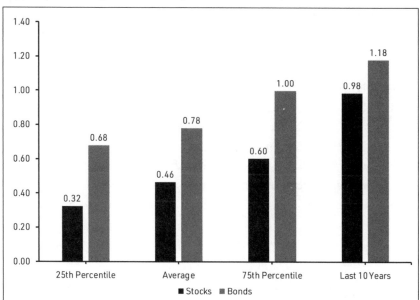

Source: Stocks: S&P 500; Bonds: Bloomberg Barclays Intermediate Govt/Credit.

Figure 1.4 combines stocks and bonds into a 60/40 blend, showing the Sharpe ratio of the balanced portfolio relative to its own history going back to 1973. To no surprise, the last decade has provided better than average returns and a relatively smooth ride.

Figure 1.4: 60/40 Portfolio Ten-Year Sharpe Ratio (1973–2020)

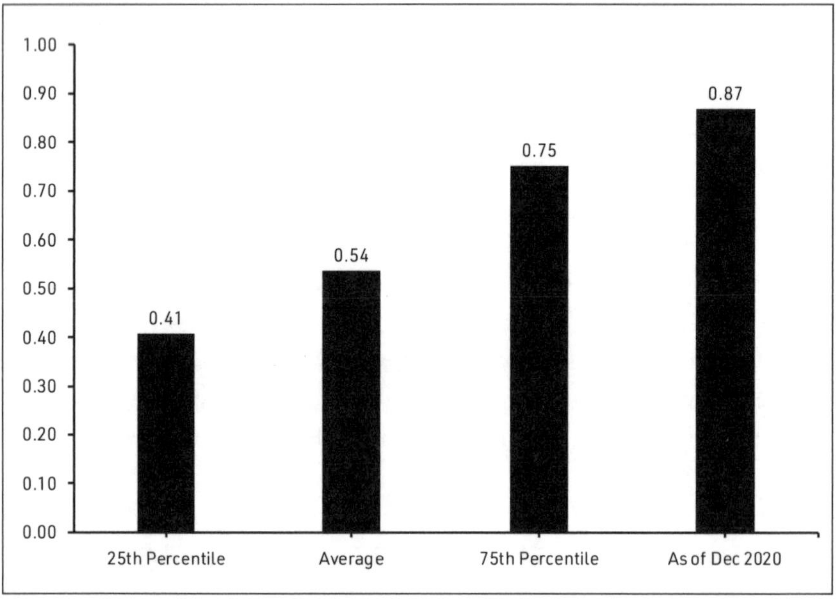

Source: Author.

Multiple generations of investors have yet to live through an era in which bonds didn't provide robust returns and meaningful equity diversification. Yet if we travel back in time to the early 1980s, after inflation and interest rates had peaked, we see a much different picture for investors that had just lived through the prior 20 years. The period from 1962 through 1981 was one of extremely high inflation by historical standards in the U.S., eating away at the real returns of both stocks and bonds. This is illustrated in Figure 1.5.

Figure 1.5: Historical Ten-Year Treasury Rate (1962–2020)

Source: FRED, DFA Returns Web.

The phrase "Lost Decade" often gets associated with the S&P 500 during the 2000s. Bookended by the bursting of the Tech Bubble on the front-end and the Global Financial Crisis on the back end, this ten-year stretch saw negative returns to the US Large Cap stock index over the full period.

One would imagine that a balanced portfolio of stocks and bonds has avoided a lost decade like this. In nominal terms that would be correct, but when adjusted for inflation the story changes. Investment manager GMO explored the returns to a 60/40 portfolio going back to the beginning of the 20th century and found several lengthy periods where it was flat or negative in real terms. This is shown in Figure 1.6, where the shaded areas correspond to rough patches experienced by 60/40 portfolios.

Figure 1.6: 60/40 Portfolio Returns—Including Shaded Periods with Poor Returns (1900–2020)

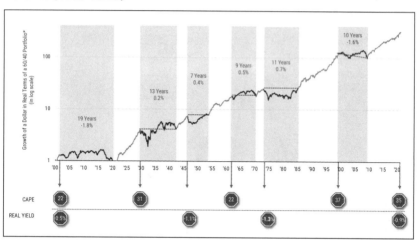

Source: GMO. To maximize the length of the data set, GMO used U.S. Treasuries for the bond allocation and the S&P 500 for the stock portion.

This lookback exercise reinforces that the experience of the last 40 years is more of an outlier than what we should expect going forward. Upon closer examination, a pattern begins to emerge. Elevated stock market valuations and/or low real bond yields are present at the onset of each of these episodes. Pricey stocks are not that uncommon. And while it has been some time, we've seen miniscule bond yields before too. What makes today so unique is that we have not previously seen such elevated valuations and such low bond yields simultaneously in our lifetimes.

A Negative Stock-Bond Correlation is No Guarantee

Despite being less risky, there is no ironclad rule requiring bonds to be uncorrelated, or negatively correlated, with stocks. This is not physics. In fact, there have been multiple extended periods of time in which correlation between stocks and bonds has been meaningfully positive. This relationship between these asset classes can be tenuous when certain variables manifest. Figure 1.7 shows rolling three-year correlations of stocks and bonds, and we can see that there were positive relationships between the two for much of the 20th century.

Figure 1.7: Three-Year Correlation of Stocks and Bonds (1928-2018)

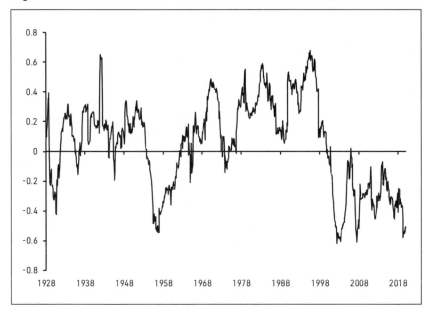

Stocks: IA SBBI US Large Stock TR USD; Bonds: IA SBBI US IT Govt TR USD.

The level of diversification that bonds will offer against stocks will largely be determined by the prevailing economic conditions—i.e. growth and inflation.

If fixed income loses its luster and is incapable of fulfilling its role as a diversifier to stocks, allocators will have no choice but to seek out investments that can.

How Reliable are Bonds as a Tail Hedge?

It's worth taking a step-back and refreshing ourselves on why bonds tend to do well during equity drawdowns in the first place. When the economy is on shaky ground and equities are falling, investors typically forecast central bank action in the form of interest rate cuts to stimulate activity. Falling rates provide a cushion not just in bond price appreciation, but also by pushing up the present value of stock earnings via a declining discount rate. Historical downturns have seen the Fed lower rates by an average of ~500 bps.

Asset manager GMO analyzed the six bear markets for global stocks in the last 30 years and compared the changes in ten-year Treasury yields and the corresponding capital gain or loss experienced by ten-year Treasury notes over the same timeframe. The results are shown in Table 1.1.

Table 1.1: U.S. Treasury Performance During Equity Bear Markets

Bear Market	Start	End	MSCI World Return	Yield Change for 10-Year U.S. Treasury Note	Capital Gain/ Loss of 10-Year U.S. Treasury Note
First Gulf War	7/16/90	9/28/90	-21.3%	0.4%	-2.4%
LTCM	7/20/98	10/5/98	-20.3%	-1.3%	10.7%
TMT	3/27/2000	10/9/02	-49.8%	-2.6%	21.9%
GFC	10/31/07	3/9/09	-57.8%	-1.6%	13.6%
Euro Crisis	5/2/11	10/4/11	-22.0%	-1.5%	13.7%
Covid-19 Crisis	2/19/20	3/23/20	-34.0%	-0.8%	7.8%
		Average	-34.2%	-1.2%	10.9%

Source: GMO.

GMO found that in five of these six bear markets (all except the First Gulf War), the ten-year Note provided a meaningful cushion against equity losses, averaging double-digit gains. The caveat is that all those capital gains came with the implicit assumption that the Fed would cut rates to help stop the economic bleeding. In each of those cases, such a course of action was possible, but in 2021 it is not.

With that cushion now depleted, there is little juice left for the Fed to squeeze through interest rate cuts. Instead, global central banks have been forced to resort to new and unconventional policy measures that in some cases lack major historical precedent. The unproven nature of today's policy toolkit has led many to wonder if bonds' days as a depression hedge are numbered.

Tastes Great? Less Filling?

For decades now, bonds have had the distinction of tasting great (high returns) AND being less filling (low risk). While that combination may still ring true for Miller Lite fans, bond investors no longer have that luxury. Quite the opposite, in fact. Bond investors today are forced to sip on the low yields (Tastes Bad!) and growing interest-rate sensitivity (More Filling!) being offered by core fixed income.

One of the redeeming qualities of bonds is that the math is much easier than it is for stocks. The possible return scenarios over the life of the bond are straightforward to calculate, particularly the upside. For high-quality bonds, starting yield is often a pretty good approximation of your long-term return.

Figure 1.8 from PGIM Investments compares the average yield of the 10-year U.S. Treasury over the last four decades to the average annual return of the Barclays Aggregate Bond Index. As yields continued their march downward, the bond index returns came down right alongside them. With the ten-year Treasury hovering between 1–2%, it leaves little hope for anything but a marginally positive return from core fixed income over the next decade.

Figure 1.8: Bonds' Annualized Returns by Decade

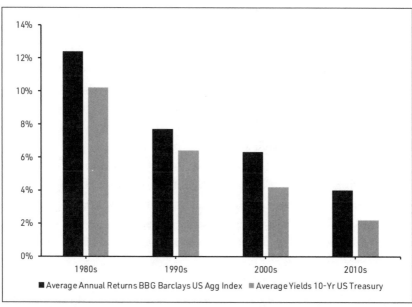

Source: Bloomberg Barclays, PGIM Investment and US Treasury Department. Analysis conducted by PGIM Investments, as of 12/31/20.

What the future holds for interest rates is anyone's guess. Forecasting the direction and magnitude of interest rate movements is a fool's errand. Assuming there actually is a zero bound on short-term Fed policy rates in the U.S., there is little additional room for additional price appreciation. Perhaps longer-term rates in the U.S. will dip below zero, joining the chorus in Europe, Japan, and much of the developed world. Regardless, there appears to be an asymmetry between the seemingly capped upside and a highly uncertain downside.

The downside scenarios come in two flavors, according to GMO—Purgatory and Hell. The former, which implies an eventual normalization of interest rates, would incur more short-term pain. The latter, Hell, assumes rates fail to normalize and the realized returns on bonds become structurally lower. In this latter case, we would be spared the violent repricing accompanying Purgatory in the short run, but the calculus would shift over the long run. This type of long slog would bring major negative implications for savers and investors, raising the odds of a retirement shortfall by a massive margin.

The sad reality is that starting yields have a mathematical relationship that is quite strong with corresponding future long-term bond returns. And without overstating the obvious, that starting point today—no matter where you look across the yield curve—is a far cry from where things stood 10, 20, 30, 40, or 50 years ago.

As of June 2020, 20% of developed market government bonds had a negative yield. Ninety percent had yields lower than 1%. I'll repeat that once more with feeling—*90% of government bonds in advanced economies had yields below 1%.* With nearly half the 60/40 portfolio anchored to those low yields, there are some incredibly wild assumptions that must be made to allow for returns even in the same ballpark as those in the past.

To make matters worse, low-rate environments have a history of remaining that way for a stubbornly long time. The Bank of Japan's policy rate first went to zero in September of 1995. The European Central Bank cut to zero in June of 2014. The United States initially embarked on their zero-interest rate policy (ZIRP) in December of 2008. Despite a series of rate hikes that began in late 2015, we now find ourselves back where we were before.

For decades, a 60/40 portfolio comfortably yielded more than 4%—padding the balanced portfolio's total return and supporting the notion that it was sufficient to generate 5% *above* inflation after accounting for capital appreciation. The last time 60/40 yielded 4% was February 2009, and today that number sits well below 2%. This is shown in Figure 1.9.

Figure 1.9: Trailing 12-Month Yield of a 60/40 Portfolio

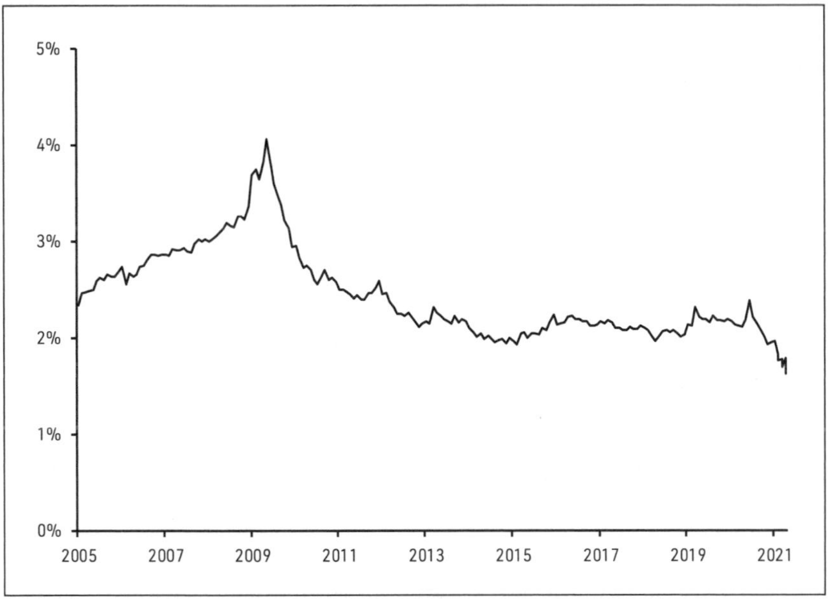

Source: 60% SPY ETF, 40% AGG ETF; rebalanced monthly.

The "I" Word

Inflation is one of the most talked about and yet least understood concepts in financial markets and macroeconomics. It's a phenomenon we debate ad nauseum with very little evidence and knowledge of how and when it will manifest. Sure, we can explain and identify it ex-post, but that's not much use.

Elevated inflation is a structurally challenging environment for stocks and bonds to thrive in. Research from hedge fund Bridgewater Associates decomposed the excess returns from stocks and bonds into distinct periods of rising and falling inflation. What they found is that virtually all the excess returns from both asset classes came when inflation was falling. The data is shown in Table 1.2.

Table 1.2: Excess Returns Over Cash (Since 1970)

	Stocks	Bonds	60/40
Rising Inflation	-1.5%	0.4%	-0.7%
Falling Inflation	8.5%	3.5%	6.5%

Source: Bridgewater Associates.

To be clear, high and rising inflation is not a prerequisite for disappointing returns to a 60/40 portfolio, but it certainly is its Kryptonite. A path to address or avoid the problems caused by inflation requires investors go to where the problem does not exist.

What About Stock Valuations?

We have talked at length in this chapter about bonds and their severely limited potential in the years ahead. But the majority of a 60/40 portfolio is comprised of stocks. As of 2021, stocks in the U.S. are trading at historically expensive multiples. What that says about equity returns over the next 12 months is anybody's guess. It has been said many times before that valuations are a blunt market timing tool. Yet over longer periods of time, starting valuations do have a tighter relationship with future realized returns, as illustrated in Figure 1.10. And the picture painted right now is not a pretty one.

Figure 1.10: S&P 500 Forward P/E and Subsequent One-Year and Five-Year Returns

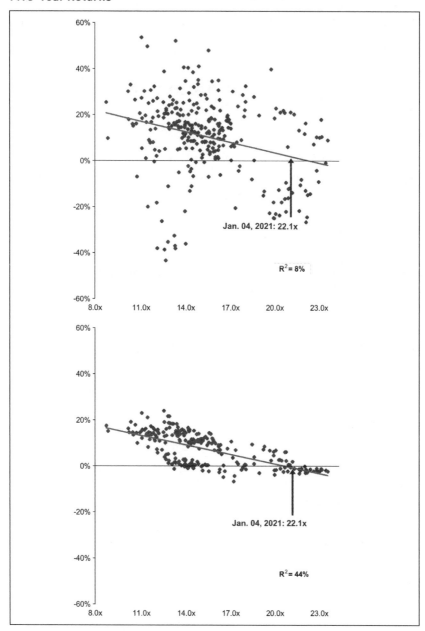

Source: FactSet, Standard & Poor's, Thomson Reuters, J.P. Morgan Asset Management. Returns are 12-month and 60-month annualized total returns, measured monthly, beginning December 31, 1995. R^2 represents the percent of total variation in total returns that can be explained by forward P/E ratios. Data as of January 4, 2021.

Valuations do not even need to mean revert or come down from their currently elevated levels for future equity returns to disappoint. Dividend yields, an important component of total return, are nothing to write home about at current levels.

The Equity Risk Premium is Not Guaranteed

The lion's share of 60/40's struggles in years to come will derive from the bond portion's limited ability to do much heavy lifting. But that doesn't mean that the stock side of the equation should get away scot free. Given enough time, equities usually compensate investors for the risks they bear. But usually is not the same as always, as we will discuss in this section.

From 1927 through the end of 2019, the U.S. Equity Risk Premium (as represented by the Fama/French Total U.S. Stock Market Index minus the One-Month US Treasury Bill) has been negative for:

- 30% of one-year observations
- 21% of five-year observations
- 15% of ten-year observations

Think about that for a second. Fifteen percent of the time, you would have been better off owning T-Bills over ten years than investing in the U.S. stock market. Your ability to earn a positive return over the risk-free rate in a decade-long stretch has a lot to do with how lucky, or unlucky, your start and end dates are.

The fact that such long periods of time can pass without anything to show for it is exactly why it is called the equity *risk* premium in the first place! No one is handing out guarantees of free money here. History does show—at least in the U.S.—that longer horizons such as 20 or 30 years reduce the odds of a negative or disappointing outcome, but they do not eliminate it entirely.

Any time you reference the historical consistency of the long-term equity risk premium over time, you will inevitably be met with the reply of: **Now Show Japan**. This is because it is the most well-known exception to the rule. Japan's stock market experienced one of the biggest booms and bubbles of all-time in the 1980s. At one point, it represented 44% of the MSCI World Index. On December 31st, 1989, the four largest companies in the world were Japanese banks. And then the bubble burst, with Japanese stocks getting cut in half (and then some) in the early 1990s.

It wasn't until 2020 that the MSCI Japan Index recovered to its 1989 peak in local currency terms. Even in US dollar terms, the Japanese equity market did not recover until 2017—nearly 30 years later.

Does this mean the U.S. is destined to be Japan? No. But it does remind us to prepare for a landscape that can look much different than today.

Figure 1.11 shows Japanese equity returns (MSCI Japan, in local yen currency), for the period 1990–2020.

Figure 1.11: Japanese Equity Returns, Local Currency Growth of $100 (1990–2020)

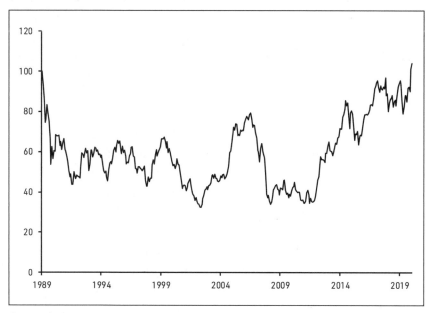

Source: Author.

Japan is one example. Other countries have seen—and will see—multiple decades lapse without meaningful benefits accruing to shareholders. Diversifying globally across stock markets will help mitigate the risk of any one country being a dud, but it won't remove the risk entirely of disappointing decades in stocks.

Collective Error

Very few are willing to challenge the dominance of 60/40 type portfolios today. Why look a gift horse in the mouth? Owning such a portfolio has been a winning proposition for much of its history. The past decade has been even more generous to 60/40 owners, providing not only the higher than usual returns we all crave, but with a side dish of lower than normal risk. A potent combination if there ever was one.

And why should investors argue with, or try to fight, what's been working? After all, if markets have proven us anything over the years it's that they are relatively efficient over time. Even the staunchest contrarians would admit that simply going against the grain of the crowd at all times is surely a losing proposition. Profiting from contrarianism requires two things: you being right and the market being wrong. And if the market is *usually* right, then it would not auger well for a default stance of swimming against the tide. Pleasant-sounding as it may seem, a "Constanza Portfolio" of acting in opposition to your natural instincts may not end well, despite the short-lived success it offered *Seinfeld's* George.

While the "wisdom of crowds" concept holds water, it is occasionally punctuated by moments of the "madness of crowds" and what can be described as collective error. As Eric Peters of One River Asset Management describes, "sometimes the catalyst for an event is the uniform belief that it can't happen—a widely held assumption that something is impossible shifts behaviors in ways that all but manifest the impossible outcome."

So, what are today's impossible outcomes? I can think of a few:

- Runaway inflation that cannot be contained by developed market central banks and governments around the globe.
- The U.S. stock market echoes the experience of Japan—multiple decades of a negative equity risk premium.
- Treasuries cease behaving as risk-off, safe haven instruments during times of crisis.
- The U.S. dollar will be dethroned as king, making room for another global reserve currency.
- Conventional asset allocation will no longer work the way it has in the past.

Long-term optimism is a deserved outlook that will likely be rewarded over a long enough time horizon. As investor Morgan Housel states, "Optimism and pessimism can coexist. If you look hard enough, you'll see them next to each other in virtually every successful company and successful career. They seem like opposites, but they work together to keep everything in balance."

A default setting of optimism pairs well with a dose of pessimism and a routine of asking "what if…?" no matter how unpleasant the consequences may sound. What if inflation creeps up faster and higher than we think is possible? What if the U.S. stock market isn't always the runaway train that it has been over the last ten years? What if interest rate volatility rears its ugly head? Or worse yet, what if rates stay structurally tethered to the lower bound for much of our remaining lifetimes?

What Does the Future Hold for 60/40?

With limited room to fall and no theoretical limit on how much rates can eventually rise, investors are presented with asymmetric trade-offs for traditional portfolios. Exactly how financial advisors and asset allocators can thread this needle will be addressed in the subsequent chapters.

Some of the 60/40 allocation's shortfalls can be addressed through intelligent portfolio construction decisions within the 60 and the 40, respectively. But those choices, assuming they pan out, may not move the needle nearly enough. *The math is the math.*

There is a vast discussion we could have around the myriad ways one can slice and dice a 60/40 portfolio—active versus passive, value versus growth, large versus small, domestic versus international, total return versus income, long duration versus short, rebalanced versus buy and hold. The permutations are almost infinite. They are all important decisions that can strongly affect investor outcomes over time. But alas, these worthy conversations are beyond the scope of this book and are already the benefactors of much spilled ink and a litany of documented research.

Less trafficked and debated, particularly in the wealth management community where I ply my trade, are the nuances and merits of the heterogenous and oft-mislabeled and misunderstood arena of alternative investments. It is this universe that will be the central focus of this book.

Any approach to balanced asset allocation should aim to get the most out of the full menu of assets available, rather than be wholly beholden to any one asset class. With interest rates near zero (or below) in many places across the globe, it is increasingly clear that bonds cannot be exclusively relied upon as the sole diversifier of equity risk. Understanding the nature of this new dynamic and its potential effects across asset classes and investment strategies will be critical to future success.

It might seem trivial to expend much energy trying to eke out a few extra basis points of return or a few less basis points of risk, relative to a vanilla, easy-to-understand portfolio like a 60/40 allocation. But we must remind ourselves of two things:

- First: the future does not have to look like the past.
- Second: small, incremental progress can transform into a large, cumulative advantage when stretched and compounded over a multi-decade horizon.

Behavior change takes time. Investors make decisions either by necessity or by choice. Adoption of innovation can move at a snail's pace. The first index fund from Vanguard—initially ridiculed as "Bogle's Folly" when it was launched by Vanguard founder, the late great Jack Bogle—took decades to become mainstream. Today, index funds are the default option for millions of investors globally and represent trillions of hard-earned dollars being put to work.

Much as innovation has allowed investors to implement low-cost, diversified portfolios with the click of a button, recent innovations have broadened the spectrum of possibilities for investors to build more durable and resilient portfolios.

This chapter has covered the necessity component of the pending behavior change facing allocators today. Throughout the remainder of this book, we will examine and tackle the choice side of the coin.

Stop Admiring the Problem

Rusty Guinn, investor and co-founder of *Epsilon Theory*, recalled a conversation with a friend about what was driving his business success. The friend's answer?

"I banned admiring the problem."

The friend elaborated:

"I figured out that we kept banging our heads against the wall on the same problems over and over. We approached them from every direction. We threw all our resources and ideas at describing them. We knew everything there was to know about them. And after we were done admiring the problem, we were no closer to solving them than when we started."

The time has come to stop admiring the problem and do something about it. We know interest rates are historically low. We know the odds of 60/40-esque portfolios delivering the returns of yesteryear are miniscule. We know the returns they *are* priced to deliver are insufficient to investors who plan on living long, full lives. We know that taking on substantially more equity risk to address the shortcomings of bonds is not the answer for most people.

We know what got us *here* won't get us *there*.

The days of admiring the problem are over. The time to solve the problem starts now and my hope is that the remainder of this book makes a dent in contributing to that endeavor.

Since the turn of the century, asset allocation has been relatively easy. In fact, it's been almost too easy. The days of a simple and easy 60/40 portfolio are now numbered. The investment landscape is constantly evolving, and it is imperative that investors evolve along with it.

The challenges facing traditional portfolios are deep but not insurmountable. To those who dare to be different and are willing and able to absorb the commensurate career risk and social non-conformity—I encourage you to read on. We can overcome the hurdles in front of us and that process starts with a reimagining—and a subsequent rebuilding—of portfolios in the years ahead.

In the remaining two chapters of Part I, we will unpack the nuance behind the word "alternatives" and why adoption, particularly outside of the institutional investor community, has been mixed.

We will then unpack the impacts that evolution and innovation have had on the current and future investable universe. Hindsight may be 60/40, but allocators now have the option of avoiding the rear-view mirror and building portfolios designed for tomorrow, not yesterday.

THE ALLOCATOR'S CHEAT SHEET

- Our collective hindsight is quite fond of the 60/40 portfolio.
- The recent experience of the 60/40 has been higher than average returns and lower than average risk. Future results face an uphill battle of elevated stock market valuations and historically low bond yields.
- Bonds are not structurally uncorrelated, or negatively correlated, to stocks. We have seen episodes in the past in which stocks and bonds have declined in concert.
- The double-edged sword of low yields and extended duration create asymmetric risks to the downside for bonds.
- High and rising inflation is the Kryptonite for traditional stock-bond portfolios.
- The equity risk premium is not written in stone, and overconcentrating a portfolio in stocks is not advisable to risk-sensitive investors.
- The portfolios that got us *here* won't get us *there*. The good news is that investors are better equipped to build better portfolios than ever before if they are willing to embrace thinking differently than their peers.

CHAPTER 2
Alternatives—The Most Loaded Word in Investing

"Words are loaded pistols."

— *Jean-Paul Sartre*

"You keep using that word. I do not think it means what you think it means."

— *Inigo Montoya, The Princess Bride*

I N CHAPTER 1, we reviewed the history of the 60/40 portfolio, namely the factors that led to its ubiquity today and the harsh reality of why it is likely insufficient going forward. Enough ink was spilled "admiring the problem." What comes next is how we arrive at an answer to the question:

If not 60/40, then what?

The answer is that we look to *alternative* assets.

"Alternative" triggers visceral reactions among investors—some positive, many negative.

High fees, complexity, derivatives, illiquidity, tax headaches, lack of transparency, black box—these are just a handful of the thoughts and images that might be conjured in people's minds when *alternative* is uttered.

The term itself can serve as a psychological barrier between investors and investments they otherwise might be interested in were it not for how they were framed.

This chapter will dissect the strong connotations of alternative investments and address techniques we can use to simplify and unpack the meaning behind the most loaded word in investing.

The Rise of Alternatives

Many of yesterday's "alternatives" are now commonplace in the model portfolios of financial advisors—real estate investment trusts (REITs), high yield bonds, emerging markets, gold, Commodities, MLPs, TIPS. These asset classes, which are relatively liquid and inexpensive to access today, weren't widely available to retail investors two or three decades ago. Few could classify them as true alternatives today. If anything, they could be considered the low-calorie option: Diet Alts.

The growth of interest in and use of alternative investments in recent years, particularly in the institutional investor community, has been staggering.

Institutional investors

Assets in alternatives, according to Preqin, have gone from $1 trillion in 2000 to over $8 trillion in January 2021, when you combine private equity, private credit, and hedge funds. Preqin predicts those numbers will reach $14 trillion by the year 2023. Institutional investors, such as pensions and endowments, have been leading the charge, with data from Pew Charitable Trusts showing an increased allocation to private equity and hedge funds jumping from 11% in 2006 to 26% a decade later.

Retail investors

Following in the footsteps of institutional investors, financial advisors and retail investors made their first earnest attempt at employing alternatives at the tail end of the aughts. The advent and proliferation of liquid alternatives—or liquid alts—can be traced to the insatiable appetite for capital preservation-oriented strategies in the aftermath of the GFC.

The collapse in equities and other risk assets during the tumult of 2008–09 spurred a torrent of interest in alternatives, and subsequently asset flows. These liquid alts aimed to replicate many of the underlying strategies pioneered and pursued by less liquid hedge funds and attempted to deliver them to the masses in 1940 Act registered vehicles such as mutual funds, closed-end funds (CEFs) and exchange-traded funds (ETFs) sponsored by big, brand-name asset management firms. Relative to the illiquid private partnerships they were seeking to disrupt, liquid alts sold themselves on their ability to provide a roughly similar experience with the convenience of lower fees, daily liquidity, 1099 tax reporting, increased transparency, and SEC regulatory oversight.

If Wall Street marketing departments are good at one thing, it's capitalizing on investor demand. Pre-GFC, liquid alts were little more than an afterthought; a drop in the bucket of the fund industry at large. That drop would eventually turn into a tidal wave of asset flows, with the category reaching assets of roughly $740 billion in 2019, according to Cerulli. While double the size of where things stood in 2009, that number is roughly flat since 2014 in light of a continued equity bull market and general disappointment in the investment results of liquid alts. Wilshire Associates estimates that investors redeemed around $25 billion from liquid alts in 2019 alone, prior to the COVID-19 Crisis that unfolded in 2020 and brought market volatility back with a vengeance.

While many advisors served a quick tour of duty in alternatives—with some vowing never to return—interest is still strong, with nearly half of advisors surveyed by Cerulli using alternatives in their client portfolios.

The rub here is that the average allocation to alternatives was about 4% of the total portfolio—hardly enough to move the needle. Wealth managers understand the need for the diversification that alternatives can provide in a zero-rate world that challenges 60/40 portfolios, but struggle with the trade-offs related to cost and complexity that their clients might not see the value in.

It may strike some as odd that there is such a contrast in the use of alternatives between institutional and retail investors. But these two have many differences related to sophistication, objectives, constraints, time horizon, access, tax sensitivity, and liquidity needs. Furthermore, much of the retail investor cohort is serviced by financial advisors who are faced with the task of responsibly overseeing and managing the needs and wants of dozens (if not hundreds) of end clients as opposed to one large pool of capital.

A Loaded Word

As institutional investors continue to eat up alternatives with a spoon, it is worth taking a deeper look into what is driving a more tepid reaction among retail investors and their advisors.

To gain better insights into what's happening between the ears of professional investors and those they serve, I conducted what can only be described as the most rigorous and scientific of all experiments: I asked Twitter.

I posed the following open-ended question to my followers:

When you hear the term "alternative investment," what is the first thing you think of?

These are a few of the responses to my little word association game:

- Complexity
- Fees
- Misunderstood
- Opaque
- Illiquid
- Unnecessary
- Diversification
- Scam

With the strong rhetoric and passionate opinions expressed, it is little wonder alternatives can be so polarizing and why widespread adoption has been an uphill battle.

Why is the A-word such a lightning rod within the investment industry? Much of the consternation surrounding alternative investments stems not from their underlying characteristics, but from how they are misunderstood, misused, and misrepresented.

The Education Gap

One of the chief impediments to broader adoption of alternative investments among non-institutional investors is the significant knowledge gap for both advisors and their end clients. A greater emphasis on education could go a long way in dispelling some of the myths and misconceptions advisors and their clients have about alternatives.

For advisors looking to gain expertise in alternatives, it can feel like learning a new language. The sheer amount of jargon and the alphabet soup of acronyms and abbreviations is daunting for novices, leaving us susceptible to stepping on unseen hazards on what author Brian Portnoy describes as a "linguistic minefield."

This "education gap" is displayed in Figure 2.1, from a Morningstar and Barron's study. Relative to their institutional counterparts, advisors are less confident in the benefits of alternatives while also expressing less clarity about their inner workings.

Figure 2.1: Top Reasons for Hesitating to Invest in Alternatives

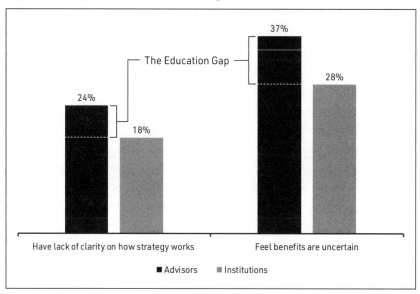

Source: Morningstar and Barron's "Alternative Investment Survey of U.S. Institutional and Financial Advisors," 2015.

The modest allocations to alternatives by advisors are not due to lack of demand or interest from their clients. A Natixis survey found that nearly 60% of individuals reported that market volatility had them looking for investments other than stocks and bonds. Seven in ten expressed interest in strategies that can enhance diversification and about two-thirds wanted investments less tied to the broad market. Interestingly, 15% of those surveyed didn't know if they owned alternative investments, indicating that advisors have room to improve their clients' understanding of what they own and why they own it.

While great strides have been made in advisor education over the past decade by some of the leading asset managers and research shops, the focus has been too much on the "what" of alternatives at the expense of the "why" and the "how." Until those two circles are squared, this education gap is likely to persist.

Buyer Beware

Another contributing factor to the sub-par implementation of alternatives is the presence of bad actors—some unscrupulous and others just naive. Unfortunately, the actions of a few can lead to poor perceptions and generalizations of the whole. Skeptics of alternatives might describe them as investments that are "sold, not bought." As an advocate and proponent of alternatives, I naturally disagree, but I can also appreciate the sentiment having been witness to some less than ideal marketing and sales tactics from purveyors of alternatives throughout the years.

Perhaps the most seductive (and common) is the "invest like Yale" approach, which plays into our desire for exclusivity and sophistication. [1] The allure of investing just like the world's top university endowments is too loud a siren song for many to resist. The good news is that you don't need to be Yale (or any endowment for that matter) to succeed with alternatives. You just have to be humble about what is (and isn't) realistic.

The other pitch invokes what I call the "magic bullet" approach. We've all seen the late night infomercial touting the all-in-one kitchen gadget. It can chop, grate, blend, grind—it does it all! Some salespeople have pitched alternative assets as a magical elixir that can cure whatever ails investors. Capital appreciation, income generation, low correlation, inflation protection—this [fill in the blank] alternative does it all! But alas, no such portfolio magic bullet exists. If it sounds too good to be true, it probably is.

---

1   Sadly, David Swensen, the famed investment manager and Chief Investment Officer at Yale, died at the age of 67 after a long battle with cancer in May of 2021.

While not emblematic of the general experience of alternative investments, as we all know a few bad apples can spoil the bunch. As the saying goes: Fool me once, shame on you. Fool me twice, shame on me. To separate the wheat from the chaff in alternatives, investors are better off filtering out those that engage in either of the above red flag tactics.

The Three Dirty Words in Finance

Another area of alternatives aversion stems from what AQR's Cliff Asness facetiously dubbed the three dirty words in finance: leverage, shorting and derivatives, or LSD. These alternative investing tools alter the perception and feelings of the end user—leading them to see or hear things that may not exist.

Leverage

Leverage is frequently used in alternatives to take lower-risk strategies with solid risk-adjusted returns and make them matter more. Since this can amplify outcomes in both directions, we should approach the use of leverage with prudence and moderation. Problems associated with leverage in alternatives generally arise when used in excess, and when combined with volatility and/or illiquidity.

While some of the biggest corporate failures like Bear Stearns and Lehman Brothers were compounded by excessive leverage, we often lose sight of its positive use cases. For many, the American dream of home ownership is made possible through the use of leverage.

Shorting

Short sellers usually aren't the most popular people at cocktail parties. As a *New York Times* column suggests, "there is something discomfiting about the idea of getting fantastically rich off someone else's misfortune, which is what happens when a 'short' trade succeeds."

Some investment mandates contain long only provisions that prohibit short selling, but even some unconstrained investors are simply flat-out opposed to shorting. Perhaps they feel it is un-American to place wagers on the decline or failure of a business. This bias was particularly acute in the depths of the GFC and even more recently with the GameStop-Reddit fiasco. Making millions from a *big short* might make you a legend within trading circles, but certainly not in the court of public opinion.

Despite its mixed reputation, there are many legitimate uses of short selling in alternative investment strategies. Engaging in short selling allows for the hedging of unwanted exposures, the ability to make relative value bets and the provision of liquidity. Short selling also plays an important role in markets by improving price discovery and holding management teams accountable. Last, but not least, the existence of short sellers reinforces a system of checks and balances in financial markets that might not otherwise uncover outright frauds such as Enron, WorldCom, Luckin Coffee and Wirecard.

Derivatives

A frequently cited quote from Warren Buffett in a 2002 Berkshire Hathaway annual letter describes derivatives as "financial weapons of mass destruction." But if you continued reading that letter, you would find that Buffett also said: "Indeed, at Berkshire, I sometimes engage in large-scale derivatives transactions in order to facilitate certain investment strategies." Does this make Uncle Warren a hypocrite? Of course not! Buffett is saying that derivatives are not inherently bad, but can be quite dangerous in the wrong hands or used irresponsibly.

From futures and forwards to swaps and options (and their lovechild swaptions!), the universe of derivatives is vast, and they frequently appear within alternative investments. Payoff structures from derivatives can be either linear or non-linear and can range from incredibly simple to insanely complex. Despite their complexity, the use cases are abundant in alternatives and beyond. Employers grant compensation in the form of stock options. Multinational corporations hedge their currency risk with FX forwards. Banks swap fixed rate payments for floating rate to manage interest rate sensitivity. An auto manufacturer might hedge the price of aluminum to fix input costs, while an airline might hedge its fuel risk to manage its largest expense.

As Peter Parker was cautioned by his Uncle Ben prior to becoming Spider-Man, "with great power comes great responsibility." Leverage, shorting and derivatives—individually or collectively—are capable of being used irresponsibly and causing damage. But that does not mean they cannot be valuable arrows in an investor's quiver. Each have their fair share of heroes and villains, but these "three dirty words" of finance do not deserve a blanket negative reputation. If properly managed, these tools can improve risk-adjusted returns, hedge unwanted risks, increase liquidity, exploit market inefficiencies, and reduce the significant concentration risk in investor portfolios.

Too Rich for My Blood

Another meaningful hurdle for investor adoption of alternatives is cost. Investors need to reconcile the inherently higher expenses of alternative investments in a Vanguard-dominated world. As low-cost indexing reigns supreme, investors have grown accustomed to rock-bottom expenses for core stock and bond exposures. With market beta effectively free, anything on top of that gets an extra layer of scrutiny—and rightfully so. Where this trend towards lower costs goes too far is taking what is a very important thing that matters (fair fees) and implying that it's the only thing that matters.

A singular focus on fees and costs may invariably lead to the omission of truly diversifying and value providing investments. Better investment outcomes can result from enhanced returns, reduced risk, improved diversification, heightened investor discipline, or the achievement of non-monetary objectives aligned with the end-user's values and preferences. Any new investment introduced to an existing portfolio should be measured by its ability to provide more in benefits to one or more of the aforementioned areas, relative to any additional cost it brings to the portfolio as a whole.

A focus on overall portfolio expenses and implementation costs as opposed to the individual holdings is strongly advised. Lines get blurred, and improper inferences made, when apples are compared to oranges. That is not to say that there aren't some obscenely costly alternative investment products out there—there absolutely are. Too many, to be frank. But an investment's fees are often best measured relative to peers in a similar category and/or passive fund options, if there are any. While there are some firms charging exorbitant fees for liquid alts, there are also a handful of asset managers leading the charge to deliver uncorrelated alternatives at more reasonable fee levels, including AQR, Vanguard, BlackRock, and GMO, among others.

All else equal, low cost is better than high cost. That goes without saying. But all else is rarely equal in the world of investing. Cost is an important factor in making investment decisions, but it's not the only factor. All incremental costs need to be weighed against the expected benefits and all cost savings should be accompanied by an understanding of what you're forgoing.

Implementation Roadblocks

On the financial advisor side, one limiting factor to larger allocations to alternatives is not lack of interest, but rather lack of experience and the perceived barriers to entry and implementation hurdles that might be involved. Few advisors are equipped to overcome the additional regulatory, organizational, and capital hurdles that alternatives have historically been associated with. Advisors don't know what they don't know and can be prone to paralysis by analysis if overwhelmed with all the moving pieces involved. The lack of resources and support introduces an additional wrinkle for advisors at smaller organizations that lack the in-house personnel or expertise.

Alternatives that are private and illiquid in nature can prove time intensive and laborious to financial advisors and asset allocators that lack the requisite experience in this space. Contrasted with traditional mutual funds and ETFs where each dollar invested is put to work immediately, private market funds present myriad challenges related to gaining exposure, achieving a diversified allocation, and maintaining that allocation over time.

While there is much room to improve, the growth and development of alternative investment platforms is encouraging. These platforms—such as iCapital and CAIS—are built specifically for wealth managers to address their concerns around education, account minimums, manager selection and due diligence, document management, commitment pacing, performance reporting and onboarding operations.

Great Expectations, Bad Experiences and Acquired Tastes

Author and marketing guru Seth Godin wrote about his experience of taking a friend to a local Italian restaurant and the friend ordering a hamburger and French fries rather than any of the regional specialties and handmade pastas on the menu. To the friend, the word "restaurant" meant a place where they can get a burger and fries. Seth writes, "If you look at many 1-star reviews (of books, of music, of restaurants) this is precisely what you're going to see. A mismatch of expectations. A mismatch that is blamed, completely, on the person who created the work, not the critic."

We don't know if we're going to enjoy an experience until we experience it. But our expectations going in play a big role in the outcome. Just ask anyone who has accidentally grabbed grapefruit juice out of the fridge in the morning thinking it was orange juice. Even if you like grapefruit juice (which for the record is disgusting) it won't matter if you were expecting O.J. Negative surprises are the by-product of misaligned expectations.

A 2019 survey by Natixis of 9,100 investors globally highlights just how overly optimistic, and perhaps unrealistic, our expectations can be. The financial advisors surveyed had fairly conservative return expectations of 6% above inflation for a diversified portfolio. The individual investors surveyed, on the other hand, had average expectations of 12% above inflation. The average gap between individual investor and professional expectations globally was 113%. The expectation gap between professionals and individuals varied by country but was consistently positive across the globe. See Table 2.1.

Table 2.1: Investor Real Return Expectations for a Diversified Portfolio (%)

	Individual Investors	Expectation Gap	Finance Professionals
Argentina	11	70	6
Australia	12	85	6
Canada	10	78	6
Chile	13	88	7
Colombia/Peru	14	137	6
France	10	79	5
Germany	9	72	5
Hong Kong	13	164	5
Italy	11	134	5
Singapore	11	96	6
Spain	13	232	4
Switzerland	12	119	5
UK	11	152	4
US	11	73	6
Average	12	113	6

Source: Natixis Investment Managers 2019 Global Survey of Individual Investors.

It's hard enough developing return expectations for traditional portfolios, let alone for asset classes and strategies that investors have yet to experience first-hand or that have limited historical data sets to analyze. When expectations are lofty, and our subsequent experiences run counter to those desires, bad outcomes are likely to follow. This predicament is just one reason why alternatives have been an acquired taste for most investors.

Bad experiences for investors often manifest in the form of return-chasing behavior. Human nature causes us to pile into investments because they've just experienced a great run, only to abandon ship when things turn south, underperforming the very funds we invest in. The behavior gap, as it is often referred to, is as evident in alternatives as it is in traditional asset classes. According to Morningstar's 2020 "Mind the Gap" study, "it also appears that investors have timed their investments poorly, pumping money into the funds in 2013, only to see three straight years of lackluster returns, and then pulling out assets in 2018, missing out on decent returns in 2019." It appears the less familiar investors are with an asset class, the shorter a leash it gets when inevitable performance challenges surface.

Thoughtful level setting between advisors and their clients around what to expect from alternatives is unlikely to turn someone into an overnight aficionado, but it might go a long way in fostering more patience and discipline with alternatives instead of swearing them off altogether.

Unloading Alternatives

If we comprehend why alternatives is such a loaded word, and how that can influence portfolio construction and asset allocation decisions, is there anything we can do to unload it? In my opinion, there is. We must:

- Embrace the grey
- Kick the bucket
- Keep it simple

Embrace the Grey

As investors, we are constantly being asked to pick tribes, exude confidence, and pack things into tidy little compartments. The reality is that though we may like things to be black and white, many shades of grey (although perhaps not 50) permeate the investment world. Ideas and concepts that at first blush we perceive to be diametrically opposed are often separated by a much thinner line in reality.

In this vein, the delineation between traditional and alternative is far from black and white. Traditional and alternative investments are often not that dissimilar to each other in practice, once we isolate the factor that makes the alternative asset *alternative*. For example:

- **Liquidity, or lack thereof**: the underlying economic risks facing public and private markets are quite similar. The time commitment involved is what separates the two.
- **Perceived novelty**: Bitcoin is fast becoming a portfolio staple for the millennial crowd, but their parents' generation are less familiar with digital gold.

- **Old wine in new bottles**: Catastrophe Reinsurance has been around for centuries. The ability for your average investor to allocate to it has not. Innovative fund structures have democratized this diversifying asset class.
- **Unconventional implementation**: Value investing in equities is as old as the hills. Tools like leverage, shorting and derivatives allow investors to extract the value factor (and other classic investment styles) in their purest form, without the associated market risk.
- **Unfamiliar terrain**: the classic example of emerging markets is an area that investors were once unaccustomed to allocating to that has since become widely adopted.

Kick the Bucket

A by-product of our black and white thinking is our affinity for placing assets in buckets. Stocks go into the equity bucket. Bonds go into our fixed income bucket. And everything else goes into our alternatives bucket. The problem with the alternative bucket is that there is much less homogeny amongst the components relative to those in the equity and fixed income sleeves. A catch-all term like alternatives welcomes all comers for what they are not—namely stocks and bonds—rather than what they are.

Complicating matters further, one investor's traditional is another investor's alternative. Let's take Real Estate Investment Trusts (REITs) as an example. I conducted a Twitter poll asking how they should be categorized given the choices of Equities, Real Assets, and Alternatives. None of the three options presented received a majority of the votes.

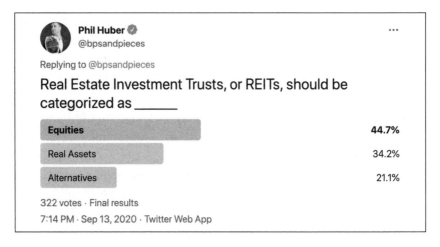

The lack of agreement among investors demonstrates that labels can be misleading and the more we subscribe to them as investors, the more prone we become to losing sight of what we own and why we own it. Just ask anyone who owned a substantial amount of high-yield bonds as part of their fixed income bucket in 2008–09. As famed physicist Richard Feynman describes, there is a "difference between knowing the name of something and knowing something." You can have the most colorful and vibrant pie chart in the world, but a portfolio is more than just slices of a pie. The whole should be treated with more regard than the individual components.

This may prove too ambitious and is unlikely to pick up steam any time soon, but a progression towards eliminating the term "alternatives" from our lexicon may benefit investor outcomes in the end. I won't hold my breath though.

While proper taxonomy in investing is a necessary evil, allocators can take things a step further by having a checklist that all investments must pass regardless of their nature. For example, the investment should be:

- Economically intuitive
- Well supported empirically
- Likely to persist in the future
- Reasonably priced and accessible

If all these boxes are checked, allocators can have greater confidence in their decisions. Another framework for evaluating any investment— traditional or non-traditional—would be to answer the following questions:

- What types of assets are being bought and sold?
- How are investment returns generated?
- What is the role of the strategy within a portfolio?

The responses to these inquiries should carry much more weight in influencing asset allocation decisions than what bucket something belongs to. While there is no perfect solution to the bucket problem, we will revisit the topic in Part III of this book with some ideas and suggestions on how to address it.

Keep it Simple

Valuable and diversifying asset classes routinely get discarded to the "too complex" pile for reasons related to illiquidity, ambiguous classification, unfamiliar tools and techniques, novel wrappers, or career risk. This is unfortunate because many alternative investments are complex in implementation only. Conceptually, they are often quite simple and intuitive. The challenge facing allocators lies in creating conceptual models that get investors more comfortable with embracing investments they currently deem too complex.

———————

The life of an allocator is not easy these days—faced with the unenviable task of trying to make lemonade out of the lemons that the 60/40 toolkit offers in today's world. Even with an expanded pond from which to fish in, allocators and advisors understand that the journey is just as important as the destination for end clients, and that the introduction of alien components to a portfolio may introduce some behavioral speed bumps along the way.

Investors and clients have every right to be skeptical of alternatives. It is human nature to be uncomfortable with the unfamiliar. While institutional allocators dived headfirst into alternatives, the mainstream individual investor is still uncertain. For this gap to narrow, the onus rests with the advisors serving these investors to help them make thoughtful decisions around the role of non-traditional investments in helping them achieve their objectives.

Professional allocators must come to grips with the following concepts to make well-informed decisions around the use of so-called alternatives:

- How to think about liquidity
- The ability to simplify complexity
- Proper framing of costs vs. benefits
- Sourcing, sizing, and setting expectations
- Getting comfortable with being uncomfortable

For allocators who wish to introduce or increase alternative allocations within their portfolios, the obstacles are significant but not insurmountable.

Part III of this book will navigate these implementation and communication challenges in greater detail.

The next chapter will take a journey through the evolution of asset allocation and how the overlapping themes of innovation, democratization, and codification have influenced our ability to build better portfolios.

THE ALLOCATOR'S CHEAT SHEET

- The word alternative, regardless of the source of its use, tells you more about what something isn't rather that what it is.
- Institutional allocators have served themselves a full helping of alternatives, with some even going back for seconds. The appetite among financial advisors and individual investors is not quite there ... yet.
- Our collective emotions around alternative investments are colored by our past experiences and expectations, the additional expenses and implementation hurdles imposed by them, and the further education needed to get comfortable with them.
- We can unload alternatives by embracing the shades of grey that separate traditional and alternative, rethinking how we bucket alternatives in our asset allocation constructs, and simplifying an inherently complex playing field for our end users.

CHAPTER 3

How Investors Got to Now—
The Evolution of Asset Allocation and
the Democratization of Alternatives

*"Innovation is the ability to see change as an
opportunity—not a threat."*

— *Steve Jobs*

"The future is already here—it's just not evenly distributed."
— *William Gibson*

"Life, uh, finds a way."
— *Dr. Ian Malcolm,* Jurassic Park *(1993)*

T HE LACKLUSTER PROSPECTS of 60/40 portfolios and the myriad
obstacles historically associated with non-traditional investments place
asset allocators in a challenging environment.

The good news is that there are new opportunities for investors to access
alternative investments. The confluence of technological advancements
and financial innovation has dramatically broadened the opportunity
set. Investors today can augment their core portfolios with valuable and
diversifying return streams sourced from non-traditional risks.

The Only Constant is Change

For as much as we shined a light on the headwinds facing 60/40 portfolios in chapter 1, the implication is not that alternatives are only necessary in today's environment due to low interest rates or elevated stock valuations.

Sure, those realities make the introduction of additional diversifiers somewhat timely. But the notion of evolving portfolios with the times and continually seeking incremental improvement should be timeless. In other words, even in a hypothetical world of normalized yields and fairly priced stocks, there would still be a compelling case to broaden portfolios to alternatives for reasons of diversification and an expanded menu of assets that gives more flexibility and choice to investors.

Our ability to give alternatives a role in all portfolios today exists because of our evolved understanding of the drivers of risk and return, and our increased knowledge of what types of asset classes and strategies work over time. This ability also exists because innovation and technology have allowed for: lower barriers to entry for historically hard-to-access alternatives; more liquid and systematic approaches that aim to deliver the beta of once alpha-driven categories at a lower cost; and more investor-friendly vehicles.

In short:

- We're getting smarter
- Technology is getting better
- Markets and portfolios adapt to changing conditions

The inevitable end results of these overlapping factors are the evolution of asset allocation and the democratization of alternative investments.

We're Getting Smarter

Investors a century ago lacked the data, analysis, technology, and insights we have at our fingertips today. In many respects, investors of yesteryear were feeling around in the dark.

Fast forward to today's world and a lot of the heavy lifting has been done for us. Researchers and practitioners are continually "articulating, extracting, and assembling investment risk" for use in portfolios.[2] This is akin to the centuries long (and still ongoing) process undertaken by scientists to identify the chemical elements that make up our physical universe.

It's easy to get lulled into thinking that all 118 chemical elements were created or discovered at the same time, but the periodic table has undergone continuous and well-documented expansion over time, supporting innovation and embracing change. In the early 18th century, the rich and colorful table we know today would be barely recognizable with only 13 discovered elements in 1718. The late 18th and early 19th centuries saw a flurry of new elements added to the mix, with a total count of 53 by 1825. An early version of the periodic table we're all familiar with today surfaced in the 1860s and counted 63 listed elements at the time. As the science of chemistry became more formalized and our knowledge of atoms, protons, neutrons, and electrons deepened, the periodic table rounded itself out. As recently as 2016, four new elements were added.

The Periodic Table of Investment Assets

The investable universe is far vaster than most investors realize. If we took the average investor's perception of the investable universe and translated that into a periodic table, it would likely resemble one of the early iterations from centuries ago rather than the reality of today.

The taxonomy of diversification can be visualized similarly by creating a different kind periodic table, with investments as the elements.

In doing so, we can assign primary and secondary objectives to each investment, so that we can better understand the risk and return drivers of our portfolios.

---

2 A. Litowitz and B. Portnoy, "The Art And Science Of Knowing What You Own," Magnetar Capital (September 5, 2019).

Figure 3.1: The Periodic Table of Investment Assets

Mm (P) — Cash						
St (P, Y) — Short Term	**Lg** (Y, P) — Investment Grade Corporates					
It (Y, P) — Intermediate Term	**Jk** (Y, G) — High Yield Corporates					
Lt (Y, D) — Long Term	**Bk** (Y, G) — Bank Loans	**Mu** (Y, T) — Municipal Bonds	**Rp** (G, D) — Risk Parity	**Rt** (G, Y) — REITs	**Va** (G, D) — Value	**Py** (G, D) — Profitability
Tr (Y, P) — Treasuries	**Ab** (Y, G) — Asset Backed Securities	**Sd** (Y, P) — Sovereign Debt	**Ta** (G, D) — Tactical Asset Allocation	**Lp** (G, Y) — Energy MLPs	**Sz** (G, D) — Company Size	**Sy** (G, D) — Company Size
Tp (I, P) — TIPS	**Na** (Y, G) — Non-Agency MBS	**Ed** (Y, G) — Emerging Market Debt	**Rr** (I, D) — Real Return	**Rn** (G, Y) — Renewable Energy	**Gd** (D, I) — Gold	**Bd** (Y, G) — Business Development Co.
Ag (Y, P) — Agency MBS	**Cm** (Y, G) — Commercial MBS	**Cl** (Y, G) — Collateralized Loan Obligations	**Td** (G, Y) — Target Date	**Gi** (G, Y) — Global Listed Infrastructure	**Ct** (D, I) — Commodities	**Nr** (G, D) — Natural Resource Equities

Ls (G, D) — Long/Short Equity	**Sb** (D, G) — Short Bias	**Ma** (D, G) — Merger Arbitrage	**Gm** (D, G) — Global Macro	**Sp** (D, G) — Style Premia	**Tf** (D, G) — Trend Following	**Re** (D, Y) — Reinsurance
Mn (D, G) — Equity Market Neutral	**Ed** (D, G) — Event-Driven	**Ca** (D, G) — Convertible Arbitrage	**Fx** (D, Y) — Currency Carry	**Rv** (D, G) — Relative Value	**Vr** (D, Y) — Variance Risk Premium	**Dl** (Y, L) — Direct Lending

Legend:

- **Y** Income/Yield
- **P** Capital Preservation
- **I** Inflation Protection
- **G** Growth
- **D** Diversification
- **L** Illiquidity Premium
- **T** Tax Efficiency

								G **Mg** Mega Cap
						G **Us** Domestic Equity	G **Lg** Large Cap	
						G **Dm** Foreign Developed Markets	G **Mc** Mid Cap	

G ... D **Mo** Momentum	G ... D **Qt** Quality	G ... Y **Dv** Dividend Yield	G ... D **Ew** Equal Weight	G **Em** Emerging Markets	G **Sc** Small Cap
D ... G **Lq** Liquidity	G ... D **Lv** Low Volatility	G ... D **Gr** Growth	G ... D **Fw** Fundamental Weight	G **Fm** Frontier Markets	G **Mi** Micro Cap
Y ... G **Cv** Convertible Bonds	G **En** Energy	G **In** Industrials	G **Cs** Consumer Staples	G **Fi** Financials	G **Co** Communication Services
Y ... G **Ps** Preferred Stock	G **Mt** Materials	G **Cd** Consumer Discretionary	G **Hc** Health Care	G **Tn** Information Technology	G **Ut** Utilities

Y ... P **Ml** Marketplace Lending	G ... L **Pe** Private Equity	G ... L **Vc** Venture Capital	G ... L **Pi** Private Infrastructure	I ... L **Ti** Timberland	D ... I **Cb** Collectibles
Y ... D **Nc** Niche Credit	G ... L **Dd** Distressed Debt	G ... L **Pr** Private Real Estate	I ... L **Fa** Farmland	G ... D **Da** Digital Assets	D ... I **Ar** Fine Art

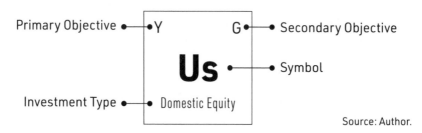

Primary Objective → Y   G ← Secondary Objective

Us → Symbol

Investment Type → Domestic Equity

Source: Author.

Imagining portfolios through the lens of a periodic table helps demonstrate the breadth of the investable universe. It also reinforces that the ways different investments influence and interact with one another matters more than the individual line items themselves. With more raw materials to work with, we are presented with an even greater number of potentially useful ways to combine them.

Markets are continually evolving, which means our methods and techniques for harnessing them and capturing their rewards need to adapt as well. As the investable universe continues to expand, failing to take advantage of the opportunities offered is likely to result in portfolios that are inefficient, concentrated, or both.

Imagine how limited our understanding of the world would be if chemists had stopped at 63 elements in the 1860s. Is it likely we'll discover another 100 elements or another 100 asset classes? Probably not. But we should always keep pushing the frontier further west in search of a better tomorrow.

The Codification of Investment Returns

The building blocks that comprise risk and return have been largely codified thanks to our enhanced ability to process enormous amounts of data, and then examine, analyze, and interpret historical results. Long ago, before the influence of academia and the proliferation of reams of historical data for us to dissect and pore through, investing was an art. Competition was scarce (at least relative to today) and few investors possessed the skills to understand companies and their pricing to make good investments.

Harry Markowitz advanced our understanding of the concepts of risk and diversification in the context of maximizing returns. In 1952's "Portfolio Selection," Markowitz writes: "Investors diversify because they are concerned with risk as well as return. Variance came to mind as a measure of risk." The idea of an efficient frontier which minimizes variance for a level of expected returns set the stage for William Sharpe's Capital Asset Pricing Model (CAPM), which relates the expected excess return of a security over the risk-free rate to the expected return of "the market" through the lens of beta (β). The simple elegance of CAPM masked the underlying and more complex reality. Despite being an early milestone in the decomposition of risk and allowing for a better appraisal of stock picking ability, its shortcomings left more work to be done.

Enter Professors Eugene Fama and Kenneth French. These two gentlemen—Gene at the University of Chicago and Ken at Dartmouth—related the expected returns of stocks to the expected return of the market, as well as company size and value, as measured by book-to-price. According to their model, the premiums associated with smaller companies and those with higher book-to-price multiples went a long way in explaining the cross section of expected stock returns.

Following Fama and French's seminal work, it was off to the races in the asset management industry to develop and market products that fit neatly into this framework. In 1992 the now ubiquitous nine-square grid known as the Morningstar Style Box™ was unveiled, allowing investors and advisors to analyze the investment style of stock funds (Figure 3.2).

Figure 3.2: Morningstar Style Box

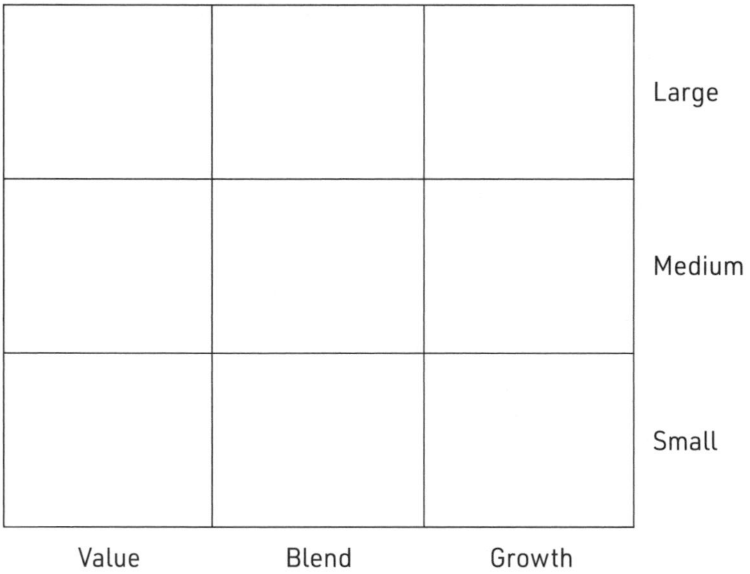

			Large
			Medium
			Small
Value	Blend	Growth	

Source: Morningstar.

While the asset management industry continued to slice and dice fund mandates to meet allocators' ever-growing need for precision, academics continued their quest to identify and translate the drivers of expected returns across and within assets. Subsequent attempts to improve on the Fama-French Three-Factor model include the addition of momentum (Jegadeesh/Titman in 1993 and Carhart in 1997), and profitability (Novy-Marx in 2013). Soon, we would have a veritable Factor Zoo with data-seeking researchers and practitioners finding over 400 patterns in historical data.[3] The clear majority of these would prove to be nothing more than noise—random occurrences with little to no theoretical backing or statistical significance.

The continued decomposition of risk and return led to a transformation in how we look at portfolios, moving away from an asset class mindset towards a factor-based approach. While asset classes provided convenient labels, factors brought us closer to the essence of what was driving returns. As Andrew Ang of BlackRock notes, factors are to asset classes what nutrients are to food.

As allocators increasingly spoke the language of factors, the industry adapted. The aforementioned Morningstar Style Box™, having always been a blunt tool for analysis, benefitted from being recognizable to even the most novice of investors. But Morningstar realized that its two dimensions did not tell the full story and in late 2019 introduced a Factor Profile tool as a complement to further explain an equity fund's exposure to sources of return (Figure 3.3).

Figure 3.3: Morningstar Factor Profile

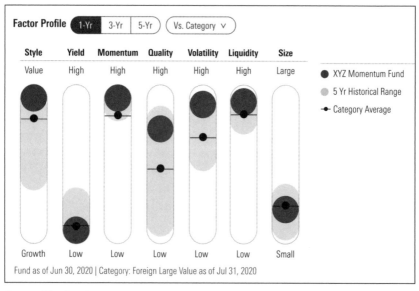

Source: Morningstar.

---

3   C. Harvey and Y. Liu, "A Census of the Factor Zoo," SSRN: ssrn.com/abstract=3341728 (February 25, 2019).

Commensurate with the shift from asset class labels to factors was the realization that yesterday's alpha is often tomorrow's beta. Before the advent of the benchmark indices like the Dow Jones Industrial Average or the S&P 500 to gauge relative performance, investors had no means by which to determine whether their own stock selections or those of a hired manager were of any value. Absent such a benchmark, any returns above the risk-free rate could then be perceived as success and a testament to stock picking skill.

Some of the early discovered betas were linked to broad asset classes like stocks and bonds. Subsequent betas were introduced for (at the time) exotic asset classes like commodities, real estate, and emerging markets. Stylistic betas followed, allowing for apples-to-apples comparisons of managers with tilts to factors like size or value. Per AQR research, "each new beta becomes a yardstick investors can hold up against their existing investments to see whether their managers are adding or subtracting value."[4] It was only a matter of time before alpha began to shrink in alternative asset classes as hedge fund betas for strategies like merger arbitrage and trend following began to emerge. Figure 3.4 illustrates the idea that most of what was once deemed alpha was really just undiscovered beta.

Figure 3.4: The Evolution from Alpha to Beta

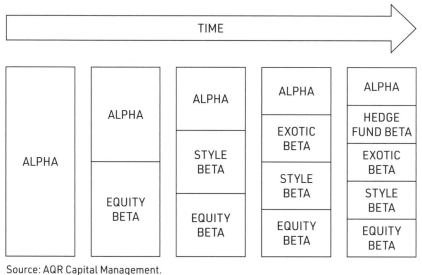

Source: AQR Capital Management.

---

4   "Is Alpha Just Beta Waiting to Be Discovered?" AQR (July 1, 2012).

Perhaps signaling the mainstream arrival of liquid alternative betas is the fact that they now have their own style box, much like that of stocks and bonds. Admittedly simplistic, measuring correlation and volatility relative to global stocks, it at least serves as a foundation to be built upon—much like the original Style Box at its inception in the early 90s (Figure 3.5).

Figure 3.5: Stocks, Bonds and Alternatives Style Boxes

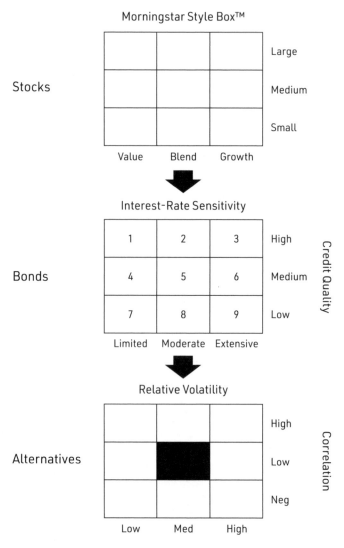

Source: Morningstar.

The Dawn of Evidence-Based Investing

The culmination of all this research around discovering what works and what doesn't in investing has led to a segment of the industry coalescing around a unifying framework for this method of investing: *evidence-based investing.*

A similar movement took hold in the early 1990s, as evidence-based medicine (EBM) attempted to apply the standards of evidence gained from the scientific method to certain aspects of medical practice in a uniform manner. According to the Centre for Evidence-Based Medicine at the University of Oxford, "Evidence-based medicine is the conscientious, explicit, and judicious use of current best evidence in making decisions about the care of individual patients."

While evidence-based investing (EBI) attempts to do the same, it is not as straightforward as it seems. Pinning down exactly what it means to be an evidence-based investor is a daunting task because no two evidence-based investors are cut from the same cloth. As Michael Batnick notes, "Ask ten different investment professionals 'what is evidence-based investing?' and you'll get ten different answers. Not different variations, but completely different responses. One person's evidence is another person's nonsense."

Pinning down exactly what it means to be an evidence-based investor is a futile effort, but more and more allocators seem to be coming around to the idea that EBI and alternatives are not mutually exclusive.

Investment professionals are taking note of the growing importance of alternative investments and are seeking ways to build the foundational skills and knowledge required to confidently evaluate and recommend alternatives on behalf of their clients. Increasingly, allocators are seeking alternative investment skills via the Chartered Alternative Investment Analyst (CAIA) designation. Considering the CAIA association saw a 33% increase in exam registrations in 2020, it seems safe to assume many are viewing it as a necessary complement to other industry designations the CFP® or CFA®.

Technology is Getting Better

History is littered with examples of what venture capitalist Josh Wolfe calls "directional arrows of progress"—technological trend lines that highlight slow and steady improvement over time in speed, convenience, costs, choice, and personalization. These directional arrows of innovation usually point one way and never look back. That has certainly been the case throughout investment history, and it is safe to assume that we can extrapolate the steady march of lower costs, greater convenience, and broader access to the world of alternatives.

Innovation and the Unsung Heroes of Finance

Innovation can be broadly thought of as the ability to do more with less. For example, today's iPhones have 100,000 times more computing power than the computer powering the spacecraft used for the Apollo 11 moon landing. Specific to the realm of investing, innovation has allowed investors to achieve more access, liquidity, and diversification with less time, cost, and risk.

Certain well-known names are instinctively connected to their associated investment innovations. Alfred Winslow Jones is largely credited with the first hedge fund. David Swensen is considered the father of the endowment model of investing. Charles Schwab is synonymous with discount brokerage. Other names are less familiar, but similarly impactful.

Edward Leffler, Paul Cabot, Bill Fouse or Nate Most probably don't ring any bells. But their work was instrumental in shaping the modern investor experience.

- Leffler invented the open-end fund with his launch of the Massachusetts Investors Trust in March of 1924.
- Cabot co-founded State Street Investment Trust just a few months after Mr. Leffler's open-end launch. He also helped influence important securities legislation, most notably the Investment Company Act of 1940.
- Fouse was a leading proponent of bridging the gap between modern portfolio theory concepts and practical investment application. Were it not for Bill's efforts, the original index fund may have never come to fruition.
- Most, an experienced commodities trader, ultimately sparked the idea behind the first Exchange Traded Fund, or ETF.

The groundbreaking work of these unsung heroes has contributed to the democratization of investing and the evolution of modern financial markets. Right now, there are thousands of incredibly bright and hard-working people toiling away, tinkering with the status quo, attempting to discover new methods and build new tools that will alter the alternative investing landscape in exponential ways for future generations. Some will gain widespread notoriety and recognition. Others will fly under the radar and revel in obscurity. One thing is for certain—all of us will benefit.

Democratization and the Birth of the Investor Class

It is awe-inspiring to think about the countless ways in which ordinary people today enjoy the benefits and luxuries that even the wealthiest people of ancient times couldn't dream of. As Laurence Siegel writes, "Until the late 1800s, a king or a president couldn't call his mother unless she was in the next room. Nobody could take penicillin if they got sick; they either died or got better naturally."

According to Matt Ridley, innovation in and of itself—i.e. specific inventions or discoveries—is not what drives economic growth. Instead, it is only when the benefits of those innovations are unlocked that profound impact abounds. The democratization of access is what holds the power to improve the lives of many.

April 24th, 1917 was an important day in investor history. It was on that day that Liberty Bonds were first issued by the U.S. government. It's easy to overlook the significance of these war bonds when today we have literally tens of thousands of investment products to select from. But as research from Brian Portnoy and Magnetar Capital describes, "this innovation marked the invention of the 'investor class.' Prior to then, relatively few households had any access to marketable investments. Now, for the first time, the government invited every household to participate."

The investor class has continued to benefit from democratization through mutual funds, ETFs, indexing, and the availability of low-cost brokerage services. Technology has played an increasing role in shaping our investment behaviors and leveling the playing field. Upstart "fintech" companies have made commission-free trading, fractional shares, and an app-based experience the new status-quo. Generations of digitally native investors have a whole new set of expectations and this type of experience is in the very early innings of making its way into alternative investments.

Few investment concepts have seen such a societal shift in perception as the index fund. Passive index investing has come a long way since being dubbed "Bogle's Folly." Now, they are the default investment option for millions of investors across the globe. In my office hangs a poster from The Leuthold

Group that was created in the 1980s that reads, "Help Stamp Out Index Funds! Index Funds Are Unamerican!" I framed this poster not because I agree with its sentiments, but as a reminder of how some of the most transformative ideas the world has seen were initially met with ridicule and disdain.

Investment Evolution in Action

Using index investing as a case study, we can observe Wolfe's directional arrow of progress in action and then draw parallels between its evolution and that of asset allocation and alternatives.

While indexing took a while to find its footing, once it took off there was no turning back. The initial benefits offered by index mutual funds are now obvious—they provide investors a lower-cost and more transparent way to get market access without the high fees and risk of active management. ETFs improved upon the mutual fund structure from a tax-efficiency standpoint and opened up the floodgates to a barrage of narrow and targeted indices that allowed investors to slice and dice portfolios with absolute precision towards factors, sectors, geographies, duration, credit quality and so forth.

The advent of Direct Indexing allowed for even more granular tax management as the index was owned through individual securities in a separately managed account, rather than in a co-mingled vehicle. That was all well and good, but the high account minimums and transaction costs at the time made Direct Indexing prohibitive for all but the wealthiest investors. That all changed thanks to a little company called Robinhood. Trading commissions had been trending downwards for decades but Robinhood brought them all the way down to zero, leaving incumbents like Charles Schwab and TD Ameritrade with no choice but to follow suit (see Figure 3.6).

Figure 3.6: Trading Commissions Trend, 1989–2019 ($)

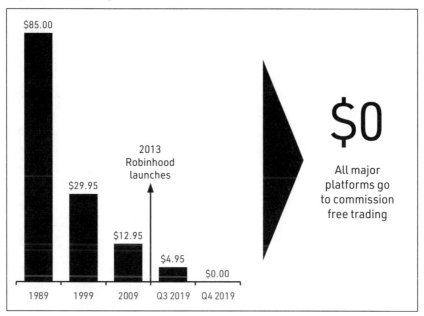

Source: Charles Schwab, Fall Business Update.

It's hard to overstate the ramifications for investors. Strategies like Direct Indexing are no longer solely for the rich and all signs now point to an inevitable future where Custom Indexing reigns supreme for all investors. In addition to providing all the things we know and love about index funds, as shown in Figure 3.7 from O'Shaughnessy Asset Management, Custom Indexing will also allow investors to personalize their own index portfolio across factors, ESG themes, geographies, sectors and at the individual security level.

Figure 3.7: Custom Indexing

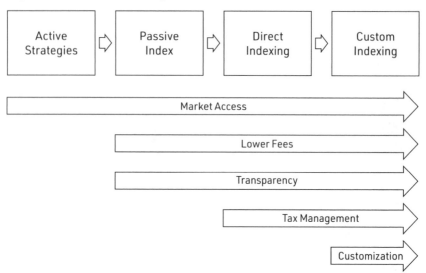

Source: O'Shaughnessy Asset Management.

What does this all have to do with alternatives?

If we follow the same trajectory—starting with 60/40—and examine prior attempts to improve upon it, we can get a glimpse into what the future may look like for asset allocators.

The 60/40 took a great starting premise—a diversified portfolio—and ran with it, riding the secular waves of declining interest rates and generally buoyant equity markets. It served investors well for several decades. More importantly, as time progressed allocators were able to implement it with greater ease and lower cost, which allowed investors to participate in global stock and bond markets in ways that prior generations hadn't. Since we reviewed the headwinds facing 60/40 ad nauseum in chapter 1, we won't revisit them here.

Risk Parity portfolios were pioneered in the 1990s by firms like Bridgewater and AQR, with theoretical underpinnings dating back to the 1950s and 1960s. Designed to be all-weather portfolios, Risk Parity's key differentiators from 60/40 portfolios were its emphasis on risk diversification versus dollar diversification, and the introduction of inflation-sensitive asset classes so that the portfolio as a whole was more resilient to a broader spectrum of economic regimes.

The fly in the ointment of 60/40 portfolios is that they are less diversified than they appear at first glance. Because stocks are magnitudes riskier than bonds, their volatility tends to dominate the risk of the portfolio. Per research from Magnetar Capital, stocks have historically contributed anywhere from 75–100% of the volatility of a 60/40 portfolio.[5] Risk Parity attempted to solve this by levering up lower-risk asset classes so that each bucket—stocks, bonds, commodities, etc.—contributed roughly the same amount to the strategy's risk budget.

While Risk Parity was a step in the right direction, its shortcomings relate to its long-only constraints and the absence of other diversifying asset classes. And because it always seeks to be risk-balanced, the prospect of levering bonds at such an unprecedented time as we are now experiencing may give some pause.

Global Tactical Asset Allocation (GTAA) has some similarities to both 60/40 and Risk Parity portfolios, but its uniqueness lies in its more diverse opportunity set and dynamic risk management approaches. The results of GTAA strategies have been mixed, but one takeaway that today's allocators can adopt from them is an openness to utilize valuation and momentum indicators when making rebalancing and position sizing decisions— particularly at extremes.

Risk Parity and GTAA can be thought of as using many of the same ingredients as 60/40, just with different recipes. The endowment model is a whole other animal altogether. Popularized by Yale's David Swensen, the endowment model sought to capitalize on the indefinite time horizon, tax-exempt status, and distinguished and well-connected alumni base of the institution. This posture oriented the endowment towards broad diversification and a recognition that illiquidity can be a good thing, resulting in heavy allocations to private equity, venture capital, real assets, and absolute return hedge funds.

It goes without saying that the average individual has little in common with an endowment. While many investors have an investing lifecycle that spans several decades, they are not perpetual. And high-net worth families and individuals do not benefit from tax-exempt status. That said, there are valuable lessons to be learned from the endowment model as it relates to the value of non-correlated assets and a rejection of the common assumption that investors should default to 100% liquid portfolios.

Figure 3.8 summarizes how Risk Parity, GTAA, and the Endowment Model have sought to improve upon traditional portfolio construction.

---

5   Litowitz and Portnoy, "The Art And Science Of Knowing What You Own."

Figure 3.8: Alternatives to 60/40 Portfolios

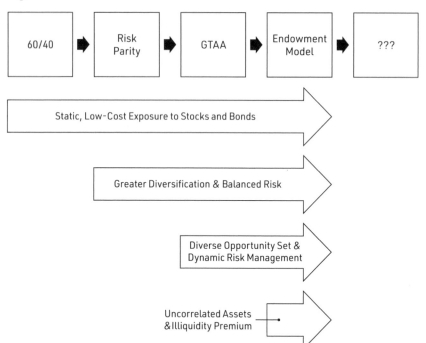

Source: Author.

While none of these alternatives to the 60/40 are without their own flaws, they each bring valuable features to the table that modern allocators can and should consider when building next-generation portfolios on behalf of their clients. And much like the evolution from index funds to custom indexing, these asset allocation adaptations attempt to take a good thing and make it better.

Markets and Portfolios Adapt to Changing Conditions

Our perception of what is considered alternative evolves over time as investment strategies become more widely adopted and institutionalized and subsequently less… alternative. The primary factors that have influenced the *mainstreamification* of alternatives are:

- The natural maturation of nascent asset classes
- The regulatory landscape
- The rise of private markets

What do REITs, high-yield bonds, and emerging markets have in common? They were all once considered alternative.

REITs were established in 1960 by U.S. government regulation aimed at facilitating real estate investment for the average investor. By the end of 2019, there were 179 REITs with over $1 trillion in combined market cap. Nobody on Main Street knew what a junk bond was until they were made infamous by Michael Milken and Drexel Burnham Lambert in the 1980s. Despite the bad press at the time, few investors today would bat an eye at high-yield credit as a strategic component of a fixed income portfolio. The first emerging markets fund appeared in 1987 from Franklin Templeton. Fast forward to today, and other allocators might look at you sideways if you don't have a dedicated EM allocation. And finally, we have Bitcoin. Barely 12 years old and this asset class created out of thin air went from "phony internet money" used for illicit activity to bona fide institutional grade asset class.

The regulatory landscape also plays a critical role in shaping asset management trends. The environment following the GFC made it increasingly uneconomical and onerous for financial institutions to hold certain types of risk on their balance sheets. This meant less supply per unit of demand, leaving a gap to be filled by asset managers. This dynamic has brought forth a handful of rewarded risks, once concentrated on the balance sheets of large financial institutions, towards being distributed more evenly across the balance sheets of millions of individual investors. These risk premiums, previously held captive by financial incumbents via bank lending, trading activities, and insurance underwriting, are now increasingly accessible to investors through innovative fund structures like interval funds.

Another pervasive trend in recent years has been the propagation of private markets and the shrinking universe of publicly traded companies. There are a handful of variables driving this transition. First, young companies are generally in less dire need for capital. In the 1970s, tangible investment was double that of intangible. Fast forward to today, and intangible investment is one and a half times the size of tangible capital investment. The growth of private markets can also be traced to sophisticated institutional investors shifting their allocations in the pursuit of higher returns. Companies weighing the decision to go public or not have to evaluate the benefits relative to the costs, and those costs have gone up since the 1990s. The shrinking of public markets can also be attributed to general market consolidation. The Department of Justice and the Federal Trade Commission have been rather friendly to mergers over the past few decades, leading to greater industry concentration.

The growth of private markets shows little sign of slowing down, with an Information Letter under ERISA being amended in 2020 to allow private equity as an investment option in defined contribution plans. Even Vanguard—the public face of index investing—has announced plans to offer private equity strategies. As we will explore further in chapter 4, it's becoming more difficult for allocators to ignore private markets. Fortunately, several platforms and marketplaces have been launched in recent years by fintech companies seeking to solve the pain points that advisors and high-new worth investors have experienced with private alternatives.

———

As financial innovation flourishes, we continually push new boundaries both in the discovery of novel asset classes and strategies, and the unlocking and democratizing of investments to benefit more people. Technological advancements, academic insights and the tireless efforts of industry practitioners all contribute to a future for investors that allows more opportunities to diversify, removes frictions, lowers costs, and improves access and fairness.

To familiarize ourselves with the bounty of alternatives at our disposal, we will move on to Part II of the book. It is here that we will canvas the landscape of alternatives—past, present, and future—to gain an appreciation for the breadth and depth within this heterogenous universe and to better comprehend which among them best align with investors' portfolio objectives.

THE ALLOCATOR'S CHEAT SHEET

- The investment landscape is constantly evolving as we collectively get smarter, technology gets better, and markets adapt to changing conditions.
- The investable universe is analogous to the progression of the periodic table of elements over time.
- The "directional arrow of progress" points toward a future of alternatives with lower cost, greater convenience, and broader access.
- Several attempts at improving upon traditional asset allocation have brought valuable features to the table that allocators should consider in today's environment.
- If history is a guide, we should expect today's alternatives to become more mainstream over time.

PART II

THE PAST, PRESENT AND FUTURE OF ALTERNATIVE INVESTMENTS

CHAPTER 4
Too Big to Ignore—The Usual
Suspects of Alternative Investing

"When there's an elephant in the room introduce him."
— ***Randy Pausch***

*"I will live in the past, the present, and the future. The
spirits of all three shall strive within me."*
— ***Charles Dickens,*** **A Christmas Carol**

P ART I OF this book presented the **why** behind investing in alternative
assets. Part II delves into the **what** of alternatives. To fully appreciate
the breadth of this universe, we will progress chronologically through this
section of the book by exploring the past, present and future of alternatives.

In this chapter you will be visited by the ghosts of alternatives' past:
private equity, hedge funds, real estate, and natural resources. The coverage of
these categories is not a blanket statement about their place in the present,
nor a prediction about their future. There is simply too much nuance to
declare a stamp of approval or an explicit dismissal of any. Unsatisfying as
it may be, the answer to the question of whether any of these alternatives
warrant consideration from advisors and their clients is "it depends."

These asset categories represent the usual suspects of alternatives in that
they are likely to be among the first mentioned when the topic is brought up.
Each of these unrelated groups boasts trillions of dollars of invested capital.
They are simply too big to be ignored. And while each is well adopted by
the institutional crowd, some have been out of reach to the average investor.

The investment case for each of these areas is mixed, with plenty of devil in the details.

We will begin with private equity (which I combine with venture capital for brevity) before transitioning to hedge funds. Then we will detour to real estate and eventually make our way to natural resources (specifically, gold and commodities). The chapter will close by previewing chapters ahead as we connect the dots between these juggernauts of alternative investing and their modern counterparts.

Private Equity

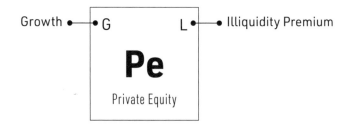

When asked by a reporter why he targeted banks, infamous American bank robber Willie Sutton apocryphally replied, "Because that's where the money is." Institutional investors have stampeded into private equity (PE) and venture capital (VC) in recent years. Why? Well, because that's where the money has been. PE and VC have been the source of some of the investment industry's most impressive and eye-popping returns.

The Growth of Private Markets

More capital was raised through private equity than in public markets for each of the ten years from 2011 to 2020. Let that sink in for a minute.

The number of listed public companies in the U.S. peaked at about 8,000 in 1996 and has seen a steady decline since, with there being about 4,500 publicly traded U.S. companies in 2020. While the big have gotten bigger through mergers and industry consolidation, there has been a fall in entrepreneurship. As Sparkline Capital's Kai Wu notes, "While the whales are busy gobbling up their smaller rivals, nobody has been restocking the pond."

For companies that do decide to go public, they are staying private much longer before taking the plunge. For example, Amazon was only three years old and raised $50m when it went public in 1997. By contrast, Twitter had already raised $800m privately by the time it went public in 2013. More recently, Airbnb raised nearly $6bn in private markets before going public in late 2020 and Uber raised over $24bn before its IPO in 2019. In the 1990s, the average age of a company listing its initial public offering (IPO) was eight years old. Today, that number is eleven years old.

There are several dynamics at play informing the decline in public listings. The institutionalization of fundraising in private markets, the short-termism of public shareholders, and the onerous regulatory disclosure and reporting requirements are chief among them. To wit, the median number of words in annual filings of U.S. companies has more than doubled from ~23,000 in 1996 to ~50,000 in 2014.[6]

Against the backdrop of increased supply of private companies has been a near insatiable appetite for the asset class from institutional investors. According to a McKinsey study, assets in private markets have increased by $4 trillion over the past decade. Stuck between a rock and a hard place of lowering their return assumptions in the face of lower interest rates or taking on more risk to meet their targets, most have opted for the latter. The demand from these institutions, seduced by the allure of historically high returns without the daily mark-to-market volatility of the public markets, has added gasoline to the fire.

Private Markets vs. Public Markets

There are several distinguishing traits that separate private and public equity. Limited regulation, asymmetric information, and a greater degree of hands-on, control-oriented investing are all defining features of PE. But PE is perhaps most known for its inherent illiquidity, with most PE funds having a lifespan of over a decade.

Whether the illiquidity of private markets should be considered a feature, or a bug, is debatable. While there is some evidence of an illiquidity premium, it is time-varying—with higher premiums likely to arise during economic downturns when liquidity is scarce rather than in good times when it is

---

6   "What is the point of the equity market?" Schroders (November 2019).

plentiful. The truth is that most investors do not truly need 100% liquidity in their portfolio, even if they might prefer it.

It's no secret that the lack of frequent marks on private equity portfolios has the effect of smoothing the actual volatility of the investments and creating the appearance of lower risk. While correct, you could argue that there is a positive behavioral benefit that investors in private markets might accrue by not being able to trade frequently or monitor the daily gyrations of their holdings. Private markets naturally force investors to think long term, which is a good thing.

In theory, both public and private equity should tap into the equity risk premium as both represent the pursuit of maximizing long-term shareholder value through their ownership stakes in enterprises. While PE does share some common risk and return characteristics with listed equities, PE also has a history of enhanced returns compared to public counterparts. These excess returns can be attributed to both the compensation for the illiquidity risk involved and the value-creation efforts that PE managers claim to offer. The market compositions between the private and public side also have notable differences related to geography, size, valuation, leverage, and industry weights.

The Nuts and Bolts of PE

There are several strategies employed within PE, most prominently:

- **Buyout** is the quintessential PE style that applies leverage to gain control of mature companies, with the goal of restructuring their finances, improving operations, or cutting costs to eventually improve profitability and monetize value through an exit via public IPO or sale to a strategic buyer. The use of leverage in buyouts can be significant and has the potential to amplify both returns and risk.
- **Venture capital** invests in startups and early-stage companies with the hopes of outsized returns as portfolio companies mature. There are many rounds and stages of VC funding, ranging from angel and seed investing to late-stage growth, with risk being higher the earlier the investment. In 2020 alone, a record $165 billion was invested into venture-backed companies—an 18% increase from 2019 levels.[7]

---

7 "PitchBook Analyst Note: Crossing Over Into Venture," PitchBook (April 20, 2021).

- **Growth equity** can be thought of as the middle ground that sits between VC and traditional PE buyout strategies. This style has become more popular in recent years, as private companies have resisted the urge to go public for longer and technology has become a more prevalent sector in private markets. Unlike early-stage and venture investments, growth equity deals don't require wildly speculative assumptions about product market fit or total addressable market.

Exposure to PE can also be obtained in a variety of ways:

- **Primary funds**: This is the most common way for allocators to access PE. In this format, a general partner (GP) sets up and actively manages a fund that pools funds from limited partners (LPs) and deploys capital into a portfolio of private companies over a multi-year investment period. These funds are typically closed-end in nature, with total fund lifespans typically between 10–12 years.

- **Fund-of-funds**: Investors in fund-of-funds (FoF) are aiming to achieve a level of diversification across managers, strategy types, and vintages that they otherwise could not achieve on their own. While a second layer of fees is involved, investors in FoF are hoping that the manager they choose has privileged access to top-tier primary funds. A FoF may help mitigate the well-documented J-Curve effect in PE that sees negative returns in early years followed by increasing returns in the later years of a fund's life. They may also provide potential liquidity that might not be available through a primary fund.

- **Secondaries**: This growing category within PE refers to the purchase of private equity fund interests from an existing investor prior to fund maturity. Potential advantages of secondaries include diversification, a shallower J-curve, and reduced "blind pool" risk. Secondary fund transactions can also be purchased at a discount or premium to NAV, which can have significant impact on investment performance.

- **Co-investments**: These are non-controlling, minority investments made alongside a private equity firm into a specific portfolio company. Co-investors typically have a pre-existing financial relationship with the PE firm. Naturally, there is a great deal of idiosyncratic risk in co-investments. One benefit, however, is they are often free of management fees and/or carried interest.

- **Direct investment**: While directly purchasing an ownership in a company might have some appeal for the more fee-conscious, most investors lack the requisite expertise to source, negotiate and conduct due diligence on individual deals. Direct investment in private companies is probably outside the scope of all but the most astute and experienced investors. With both direct investments and co-investments, there is the potential benefit of a shortened time horizon relative to investing in a private equity fund.

Private Equity Performance

The idea of PE being uncorrelated to public equities was always largely a myth. But there is some truth to the historical performance benefits. According to research from The Burgiss Group, the median private equity fund has failed to deliver a public market equivalent (PME) score of at least 1.0 in only four calendar years.

Some investors are concerned that private equity has gotten too big to earn the persistently higher returns over public equity that it has historically enjoyed. As buyout funds morphed into mega-buyout funds, it raises the question whether there is too much money chasing too few deals and recalls the old Buffett adage that "size is the enemy of performance."

Instead of allocating to larger brand-name managers, some allocators focus on smaller funds where competition may be scarcer, or opportunities for alpha more plentiful. The trade-offs between greater consistency in returns that larger funds would be expected to provide relative to the higher potential for outsized returns from smaller funds would need to be weighed when assessing commitments. There are several reasons why smaller funds, which naturally invest in smaller companies, might be able to generate higher returns. These include lower purchase price multiples and greater opportunities for operational enhancements.

Table 4.1 compares the performance of buyout funds above and below aggregate investor commitments of $750m over the vintage years from 2000 through 2015. Using both Internal Rate of Return (IRR) and Total Value to Paid-in Capital (TVPI), the smaller buyout funds have experienced greater median outperformance over the full period.

Table 4.1: Comparing Performance of Smaller and Larger PE Buyout Funds (2000–2015)

New IRR VY 2000–2015				New TVPI VY 2000–2015			
Fund Size	Bottom Quartile (%)	Median Performance (%)	Top Quartile (%)	Fund Size	Bottom Quartile (x)	Median Performance (x)	Top Quartile (x)
≤$750m	10.0	17.5	28.1	≤$750m	1.40	1.79	2.30
>$750m	9.1	14.4	21.0	>$750m	1.45	1.69	2.04

Source: Preqin. Data sourced 6/19/2020; returns are as of 12/31/2019, or last reported date, if earlier.

Criticisms of Private Equity

The private equity asset class is not without its share of critics. Detractors will highlight the industry's growing dependence on financial engineering, greater use of leverage, increased competition, and elevated valuations as potential landmines. With over 7,000 PE firms, the market is more mature and competitive than ever before and worries about too much money chasing too few deals may be warranted. Studies have indicated that PE performance has been inflated through increased leverage and multiple expansion, variables that can cause as much or more damage on the way down as they've helped on the way up. According to McKinsey & Co., the two-year rolling average of purchase price multiples for U.S. buyouts has been steadily creeping higher, reaching a record 12.8x EBITDA in 2020. For comparison, that number was 11.9x in 2019 and 10.2x in 2015.[8]

Performance measurement also poses challenges for allocators. Return measurement in PE is a notoriously imperfect science, with an alphabet soup of performance metrics that novice allocators need to familiarize themselves with, including IRR, TVPI, and PME. Peer groups are also inconsistent for benchmarking purposes. The lack of passive fund options in PE makes active management unavoidable.

The wide manager dispersion inherent in PE/VC creates potential adverse selection problems if only investing in one manager or vintage. Different vintages can perform materially differently than others, subject

---

8   M. Gottfried, "As Blackstone Barrels Toward Trillion-Dollar Asset Goal, Growth Is In, Value Out," *The Wall Street Journal* (March 21, 2021).

to the prevailing economic conditions present during the fundraising and investment periods. Investors weighing an allocation must be sober and honest about their ability to source, diligence, and access top-tier managers.

Individual Investors and PE/VC

The institutional imperative to own private assets shows no sign of slowing down. The better question is whether the average individual investor should attend—or even be invited to—this party. Thus far, PE has proven to be an elusive nut to crack for wealth management allocators.

It seems likely that more and more demand for private equity access will arise from retail investors. With index investing behemoth Vanguard making plans to enter the space, stamping the asset class with their imprimatur, one could argue that the floodgates have officially opened. Given this is uncharted terrain for most investors, allocators must help them establish a framework for evaluating such a decision.

Alternatives to PE

For non-qualified investors, or those that lack the appetite to lock up their money for ten-plus years, there are potential substitutes to consider in place of PE and VC.

Research from Dan Rasmussen of Verdad Capital supports the notion that any "alpha" that comes from PE can be attributed to purchasing small companies using leverage at cheap multiples. The contention is that one could largely replicate the historical return experience of PE—albeit with increased market-to-market volatility—by investing in leveraged small and micro-cap public stocks trading at cheap valuations. While an investor employing such a strategy may miss out on any associated illiquidity premium, the cost savings may make up for it. The jury may still be out as to whether the supposed alpha from PE survives when taking these additional factors into account.

Lines are also becoming increasingly blurred between public and private markets. A greater number of crossover funds have emerged that traffic in both. In 2020, over 70% of IPOs included crossover investment in pre-IPO fundraising rounds.[9] We have also recently seen an explosion of activity in SPACs, or blank-check companies, with some investors viewing the vehicle as a chance for retail investors to partake in private equity. While there is evidence to the contrary, the growth of the vehicle itself seems symptomatic of investor interest in private markets. There were nearly 250 SPAC listings in 2020 alone, which was greater than the total during the entirety of the 2010s.[10]

Verdict

The growth and maturation of private markets has strengthened the case for private equity allocations for HNW investors. There is, however, no one-size-fits-all allocation recommendation for investors. There are too many investor-specific circumstances that must be accounted for to make that ultimate determination. Wealthy investors will have to decide whether they find the juice to be worth the squeeze when you factor in cash flow uncertainty, the inflexibility that accompanies illiquidity, and the hassle of managing the cumbersome tax process. And while many tend to consider private equity an alternative investment, allocators would be wise to view such an allocation as a complementary component of an equity program, rather than to mistakenly treat it as a truly uncorrelated asset class.

Questions remain as to whether adverse selection can be avoided given high dispersion of fund returns, or whether layered fees to bring down access minimums to more reasonable levels will eat away at too much of the return. With regulations and technology democratizing access, we may inch closer towards solving the private markets puzzle for individual investors. Ultimately, it's hard to conclude that broadening participation in private markets for qualified individual investors is a bad thing.

---

9   PitchBook Analyst Note: "Crossing Over Into Venture."

10   N. Veronis and A. Jessani, "Individual Investor Access to the New Economy Comes at a (Hefty) Price," (February 11, 2021).

Hedge Funds

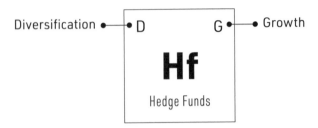

I'm not sure there is a term I dislike more in our industry than "hedge fund." Few comparable examples of investment jargon exist that tell you so little about what an investment actually does. For one to say they are invested in a hedge fund gives little to no information about the underlying strategy.

Despite my disdain for the name, and my failed attempts at coming up with a better one, I do quite admire the hedge fund concept. The treatment of hedge funds as an *asset class*, however, is flawed.

There have been many attempts to aptly describe hedge funds, from the old chestnut that they are "a compensation scheme masquerading as an asset class" to my personal favorite from the refreshingly honest (and often self-deprecating) Cliff Asness of AQR:

> "Hedge funds are investment pools that are relatively unconstrained in what they do. They are relatively unregulated (for now), charge very high fees, will not necessarily give you your money back when you want it, and will generally not tell you what they do. They are supposed to make money all the time, and when they fail at this, their investors redeem and go to someone else who has recently been making money. Every three or four years they deliver a one-in-a-hundred year flood. They are generally run for rich people in Geneva, Switzerland, by rich people in Greenwich, Connecticut."

Jokes aside, it's important to distinguish hedge funds from their conventional money management counterparts. We can distill this down to four key attributes:

1. **Structure**: as limited partnership vehicles reserved for accredited investors and up, they can bypass some of the regulations and restrictions traditional managers face.

2. **Incentives**: the ability to charge performance fees should in theory align incentives with investors, although some would posit that hedge funds are fat and happy enough from the management fees alone.

3. **Flexibility**: the unconstrained nature in which hedge funds can operate, free to roam across asset classes, express directionality both long and short, and utilize leverage and derivatives, is the key to what allows for their differentiated return streams.

4. **Objectives**: instead of being tethered to a benchmark, the absolute return orientation of hedge funds denotes the pursuit—not the promise—of positive returns in all market climates.

From a taxonomy standpoint, there are multiple classification schemes out there that aim to decompose this heterogenous universe of strategies into a cohesive framework. Table 4.2 is an illustrative example from Hedge Fund Research (HFR).

Table 4.2: HFR Hedge Fund Strategy Classifications

Equity Hedge	Event-Driven	Macro	Relative Value
Equity Market Neutral	Activist	Active Trading	Fixed Income–Asset Backed
Fundamental Growth	Credit Arbitrage	Commodity: Agriculture	Fixed Income–Convertible Arbitrage
Fundamental Value	Distressed/ Restructuring	Commodity: Energy	Fixed Income–Corporate
Quantitative Directional	Merger Arbitrage	Commodity: Metals	Fixed Income–Sovereign
Sector: Energy/ Basic Materials	Private Issue/ Regulation D	Commodity: Multi	Volatility
Sector: Healthcare	Special Situations	Currency: Discretionary	Yield Alternatives: Energy Infrastructure
Sector: Technology	Multi-Strategy	Currency: Systematic	Yield Alternatives: Real Estate
Short Bias		Discretionary Thematic	Multi-Strategy
Multi-Strategy		Systematic Diversified	
		Multi-Strategy	

Source: Hedge Fund Research, Inc. (HFR).

The track record of the industry as a whole over the last 20 years has been reasonable, but nothing to write home about considering some of the operational and tax headaches involved when investing in hedge funds. Table 4.3 summarizes the return, risk, and diversification characteristics of several hedge fund indices relative to U.S. equities. Most strategies have generated mid-single digit annualized returns, with decent Sharpe ratios, and mixed correlations and betas to stock and bond markets. The maximum drawdowns have generally been more severe than most would have suspected when they signed up.

Table 4.3: Return, Risk, and Diversification of Hedge Fund Indices (1999–2020)

November 1999– December 2020	Annualized Return	Standard Deviation	Sharpe Ratio	Maximum Drawdown	Equity Risk Premium Beta	Bond Horizon Premium Beta	Bond Default Premium Beta
Russell 1000 TR	7.22	15.47	0.42	-51.13	1.02	-0.41	1.23
S&P 500 TR USD	6.88	15.20	0.40	-50.95	0.94	-0.40	1.07
Credit Suisse Convertible Arbitrage	5.99	6.50	0.68	-32.88	0.19	-0.12	0.50
Credit Suisse ED Distressed	6.52	5.81	0.83	-22.45	0.24	-0.19	0.49
Credit Suisse ED Multi-Strategy	6.29	7.37	0.64	-18.77	0.32	-0.23	0.61
Credit Suisse ED Risk Arbitrage	4.81	4.08	0.77	-8.19	0.15	-0.05	0.27
Credit Suisse Fixed Income Arbitrage	4.57	5.17	0.57	-29.02	0.14	-0.06	0.31
Credit Suisse Global Macro	8.47	5.89	1.15	-14.94	0.12	0.01	0.23
Credit Suisse Long/Short Equity	6.10	8.35	0.55	-22.00	0.37	-0.19	0.58
Credit Suisse Managed Futures	4.12	11.12	0.27	-18.62	-0.03	0.29	-0.10
Credit Suisse Multi-Strategy	6.63	4.85	1.01	-24.72	0.19	-0.12	0.39

Source: Credit Suisse Group AG and/or its Affiliates.

One thing is for sure—the aggregate investor appetite for hedge funds does not appear to be waning. Assets in hedge funds reached $3.8 trillion in the first quarter of 2021, a new record for the industry.[11]

The Hedge Fund Identity Crisis

Dalio. Cohen. Ackman. Soros. Druckenmiller. Simons. Shaw. Tepper. Klarman. Icahn. Loeb. Einhorn. Thorp. Griffin. Paulson. Some of the most legendary investors of all time, whose last names alone garner recognition. All of them are or were hedge fund managers.

The paradox of hedge funds is that these are the exceptions, not the rule. Or as Bridgewater's Ray Dalio exclaimed, "There are about 8,000 planes in the air and 100 really good pilots." All the mystique and intrigue surrounding the hedge fund industry is a by-product of the incredible results generated by these managers (and others) throughout their illustrious careers.

These pioneers deserve their due credit for discovering today's classic hedge fund strategies before they were well known, and for generating alpha in an uber-competitive playground. As investor Bob Seawright recounts, "They are the unicorns that keep the thousands of other funds in business." But the hedge fund world has changed dramatically over the past two decades.

For starters, we found out who was swimming naked when the tide went out during the GFC. The historical betas of hedge funds to equities and high-yield credit have historically been much higher than one would imagine. Research from Magnetar Capital found that since 1993, hedge fund returns had an average beta to equities of about 0.35 and an average beta to high yield credit of 0.61.[12]

Allocators have long understood that most hedge funds had an element of market beta in their returns, but the degree to which many hedge funds suffered major losses at the very time they should have been, well, hedging the rest of their portfolio surprised many. I mean, the word is in the name, after all.

Following the lackluster returns of the GFC, hedge funds began to market themselves differently. The halcyon days of pitching better-than-stock market

11 W. Feuer, "Hedge Fund Assets Hit Record $3.8 Trillion After Strongest Start to the Year Since 2000," *Institutional Investor* (April 21, 2021).

12 Litowitz and Portnoy, "The Art And Science Of Knowing What You Own."

returns with bond-like risk and no market correlation waved bye-bye long ago. The once fertile grounds for harvesting alpha have been largely picked, leaving mainly alternative betas to be grazed upon. As time progressed, expectations continued to ratchet down to a point where things seem to have settled around the perception of offering solid risk-adjusted returns that are somewhat independent of market returns. Not bad, just not what it used to be.

For allocators looking for transparency, consistency, and regulatory protections, hedge funds have been tough sledding. For every master of the universe who knocked the cover off the ball, there have been an equal number of one-hit wonders and high-profile blowups.

To be sure, there are still some amazing hedge funds out there. Even surer, they don't want our money. In fact, many of them have returned all outside capital altogether, converting to family offices and managing assets exclusively for themselves and their staffs. Other renowned managers have wound down their operations completely to spend more time with their money.

The era of the gun slinging, iconoclastic hedge fund manager moving markets with big, bold bets is largely bygone. The present, and perhaps future, of the hedge fund industry seems centered not on the personality-driven epoch of yesteryear, but towards diverse, multi-strategy type vehicles run collaboratively by teams of portfolio managers, traders, data scientists, and risk managers at shops like Citadel, Millennium and D.E. Shaw.

The use case of hedge funds in today's climate is also different than that of 30 years ago. Allocators are more in search of regular singles and doubles instead of home runs and the placement of hedge funds within a portfolio is often as a diversifying, low-volatility bond substitute rather than a vehicle expected to be doing equity-like heavy lifting.

Hedge Funds and Taxes

A review of hedge funds is incomplete without addressing the impact of taxes. Investors in the hedge fund industry are predominantly tax-exempt institutions whose capital need not worry about after-tax returns. For taxable entities and individual investors, the math can change quite a bit when comparing hedge fund results on a pre-tax and after-tax basis. The delta between the two can mean the difference between a sizable allocation and a goose egg when run through an asset allocation optimizer.

Investment manager Aperio Group conducted a study entitled, "What Would Yale Do If It Were Taxable?" in which it calculated pre-tax and after-tax returns of the asset classes in Yale's endowment.[13] Their conclusion was that absolute return-oriented hedge funds should play little, if any, role in the portfolios of taxable investors. This is because the higher turnover of hedge funds makes them more prone to generating short-term gains, which are taxed at ordinary income rates. This raises the return hurdle significantly for high-earning, taxable investors.

Looking Ahead

Fees have always been the number one concern for investors contemplating hedge funds. As Warren Buffett once said, "Performance comes, performance goes. Fees never falter." That said, one positive development in the industry is that fees have been trending lower. According to HFR, the average management fees declined to 1.37% in the third quarter of 2020, while average performance fees fell to 16.36%. These are the lowest numbers on record. Will '1 and 15' become the new '2 and 20'? Time will tell, but we can all agree this is a trend in the right direction.

Hedge funds will always maintain an element of country club allure to certain wealthy investors, as they make for much more entertaining cocktail party chatter than index funds. They offer an air of exclusivity and scratch an itch some of us have to want what we cannot attain. But investors should always ask themselves—why am I seeing this now? And, who passed on this before it ultimately made its way to me? It might be best to take a cue from Graucho Marx and turn down membership to any club that wants you as a member.

Verdict

I would say only allocate to hedge funds if you can access top-tier managers, but since we all grew up in Lake Wobegon, few will readily admit to hiring average (or God forbid *below-average*) talent.

---

13 P. D. McSwain, "Are Hedge Funds Prudent for Taxable Investors?" Fiduciary Wealth Partners (September 2015).

For those insistent on allocating to hedge funds, there are some high-quality liquid alternatives that provide similar exposure to uncorrelated strategies. For qualified investors comfortable with all the risks, there are private alternatives platforms that can help with the due diligence, manager selection, and allocation process. In this vein, a core multi-strategy approach is most sensible for optimal diversification benefits and the potential for greater consistency.

While many are quick to bemoan hedge funds (including yours truly), I would wager if you slipped a little truth serum to even the most staunch "Bogleheads" that ten times out of ten they would jump, if given the opportunity, to invest in the Renaissance Medallion fund. I know I would. So, while there are many reasons to lambast hedge funds, there is still an aura about them.

Despite much of the alpha having been competed away, and with the few great pilots remaining having full flights, what is left over—hedge fund "beta"—can still be quite valuable in a portfolio. It's just not worth 2 and 20.

Real Estate

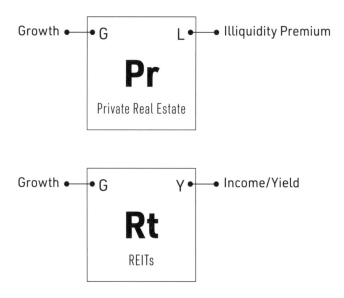

Of all the alternative asset classes out there, real estate might be perhaps the least... alternative. People instinctively "get" real estate in a way that they don't intuit private equity or hedge funds. Mark Anson, author of the *Handbook of Alternative Assets* goes so far as to say, "Real estate was an asset class long before stocks and bonds became the investment of choice... In fact, stocks and bonds became the 'alternatives' to real estate instead of vice versa... it is sometimes forgotten that real estate was the original and primary asset class of society."

Owners of real estate benefit from the perpetual tailwinds of scarcity and priority. Scarcity because the most sought-after locations for businesses or residencies are naturally limited. And priority in the sense that the rent that must be paid by tenants to landlords is among the most senior of financial obligations. These dual traits of high-quality real estate help explain why owners have received attractive returns and income over time.

The Nuts and Bolts of Real Estate

Real estate offers the ability to preserve value over time, net of inflation, through the scarce nature of the land it sits on and the replacement costs of the raw materials in the structure itself. Through leased properties, real estate owners may also benefit from rental income as a significant component of total return on top of that.

Investment in real estate comes in various forms. Passive real estate investors can reap most of the financial benefits while delegating the actual oversight and management to an experienced operator. Direct property ownership is inherently more hands-on, costly, less diversifiable, and management-intensive, but offers further potential for gains.

From an access standpoint, there are opportunities to invest in real estate in both public and private markets, as well as through equity, debt, and hybrid structures. Public equity investments typically come in the form of listed REITs. Private market investments come in both open-end and closed-end flavors. Those seeking more income-producing core/core-plus real estate tend to gravitate towards evergreen vehicles, while capital appreciation-oriented investors prefer finite-life funds.

There is also a spectrum of risk profiles within real estate, with strategies tailored to conservative, income-oriented investors as well as risker approaches geared towards more aggressive investors seeking outsized returns. Those include:

- **Core**: high-quality, stabilized assets in major metros with high barriers to entry, low leverage, and income-heavy returns.
- **Core Plus**: like core properties, but with greater potential upside and modest upgrades required. Leverage is often used to enhance returns.
- **Value-Add**: assets in need of significant improvement or redevelopment to maximize value. This higher risk category sees most of its return come from appreciation.
- **Opportunistic**: greatest risk/reward potential within real estate, typically seeking net returns in the mid-teens. Distressed properties and ground-up development are common here.

Figure 4.1 illustrates the risk and return profiles of these various real estate strategies.

Figure 4.1: Risk and Return of Various Real Estate Strategies

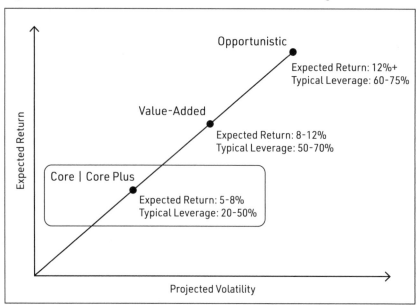

Source: Conway Investment Research (return projections are speculative, subject to change, may not actually come to pass, and are for illustrative purposes).

Types of Real Estate Assets

For a long time, real estate investing was almost exclusively confined to the four major property types: residential, retail, office and industrial. As American society and business has evolved, so have the variety of real estate categories to reflect that change. As such, we are seeing trends towards additional and modernized real estate sectors, as well as greater breadth of opportunities for investors of all sizes to access this essential asset class.

We are currently experiencing monumental shifts in the way we live, work, and consume. While the basic food groups of real estate investing from decades past—retail, apartments, office, industrial—can still serve as a solid foundation, there is a strong case that alternatives *within* real estate will be critical complements to existing portfolios in years ahead. Demographic tailwinds and secular demand trends will only serve to support alternative and niche real estate sectors that are generally more resilient during recessions.

Some of the more alternative, niche, and cycle-resilient sectors include:

- **Medical office**: With the aging populace of America, medical office properties will be one of the most critical real estate sectors for the foreseeable future.
- **Education**: Encompassing everything from student housing to university infrastructure, to early education school buildings, education real estate has historically been countercyclical.
- **Self-storage**: With strong demand in good times and bad, self-storage assets benefit from a barbell distribution of both high- and low-income households as tenants.
- **Workforce housing**: Affordable multi-family housing to middle-income renters, this category sits between luxury rentals on one hand and subsidized low-income housing on the other. This sector has historically been better able to maintain rent rates during economic downturns, while performing quite well during expansions due to inventory constraints.
- **Senior living**: With the baby boomer generation soon reaching their prime years for private-pay, senior living facilities, it is likely that demand will outstrip supply growth in this sector.
- **Data centers**: These highly specialized real estate assets are experiencing secular growth trends from cloud adoption and the outsourcing of

enterprise software in the digital economy. The operational and capital intensity of this subsector create high barriers to entry for operators.

- **Cell towers**: As we enter the next stage of network deployment with 5G, patterns in mobile data consumption should result in steady tailwinds for this subsector.
- **Single-family rentals**: Low supply of new housing, tighter mortgage standards, a growing preference for the flexibility that renting offers, and pent-up demand from delayed household formation by millennials, are all contributing factors to the momentum behind single-family rentals. Despite burgeoning interest among institutional investors over the last decade, only ~2% of SFRs are owned by institutional investors today.

The Building Blocks of Real Estate Returns

The total returns from real estate can be broken down using building blocks. At the foundation you have the yield component, expressed as the capitalization rate, or cap rate, of net operating income (NOI) divided by the property value. Cap rates are influenced heavily by a number of factors—property type, location, building quality, tenant dependability, etc. The riskier the asset, the higher the cap rate will likely be.

Growth in NOI through inflationary rent increases and property improvements can enhance returns. Leverage can also be used in varying degrees to augment returns and there is ultimately the potential for additional gains through asset disposition.

These building blocks are shown in Figure 4.2.

Figure 4.2: Real Estate Total Return Profile Building Blocks

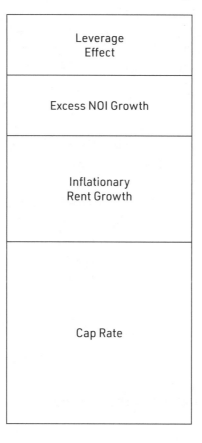

Source: Versus Capital.

Public vs. Private Real Estate

Publicly listed real estate investment trusts, or REITs, are a mechanism for investors of all sizes to participate in the ownership of property in a diversified and tradeable way. Since their arrival, REITs have not only produced returns equivalent to or greater than private real estate (depending on your reference point), they have also outperformed the stock market more broadly—albeit with greater volatility. The U.S. REIT sector today has over 200 stocks and over $1 trillion in market capitalization.

From a diversification standpoint, REITs have maintained a modest correlation to stocks over longer periods of time, with the caveat that those correlations have been steadily rising over time and tend to spike during bouts of volatility. It shouldn't surprise that REITs behave like traditional real estate over longer horizons, as the lease contracts on the underlying assets tend to be many years in length and thus exhibit less sensitivity to other economic variables. Research from LaSalle Investment Management found that the rolling five-year correlation between public and private real estate in the U.S. from 2000–2016 was 0.70. Furthermore, when adjusting for a lag in private market returns those correlations increased to 0.91.[14]

The public vs. private decision in real estate does not have to be an either/or one. The sector dynamics within the two universes are markedly different than one another, allowing diversification from a blended approach. Listed real estate also gives allocators a tool to rebalance and adjust allocations when warranted. Sharp divergences between the valuations of listed and private real estate can occur but tend to converge over time.

In many ways, the public market has evolved much faster than the private world to the prevailing real estate trends, with over 60% of the REIT market today in alternative sectors. In 2020, the largest real estate ETF, Vanguard's VNQ, had over 25% of its exposure in cell towers and data centers alone. Investors who invest exclusively in one side versus the other are potentially missing out on ways to create a more complete allocation to real estate.

Individual Investors and Real Estate

Individual investors today have greater optionality than ever when it comes to how and where they invest in real estate and what they invest in. From mutual funds and ETFs on the public REIT side, to interval funds and non-traded REITs on the private side, there are real estate choices for all types of investors. In addition to pooled vehicles, there are also a growing number of online platforms that allow both accredited and non-accredited investors to invest in direct real estate deals. The fractional ownership and low minimums offered by tech-enabled firms such as Fundrise, PeerStreet, Roofstock, and Cadre are becoming increasingly popular in today's world.

---

14 "Public and Private Real Estate: The Sum Is Greater Than The Parts," LaSalle Investment Management (2017).

Verdict

In many ways, real estate is perceived to be the *safe* alternative. It is probably the easiest alternative for most investors to grasp. There is a tangibility and realness that accompanies it—the homes we reside in, the office buildings we work in, the hotels we stay in and the stores we shop in.

Real estate has historically been—and will likely continue to be—an attractive asset class warranting a strategic spot in a diversified portfolio. The sectors comprising real estate and the vehicles and methods in which we allocate to it will continue to evolve, but its primacy as an asset class and the premise of capturing durable cash flows derived from contractual rents will likely remain intact.

Natural Resources (Gold and Commodities)

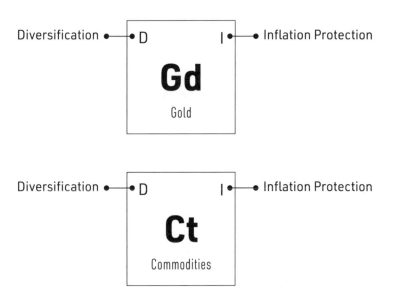

We'll now turn to look at commodities and gold, similar yet different asset classes that both come under the natural resources umbrella.

Commodities

Commodities are one of the few distinct asset classes outside of stocks, bonds, cash, and real estate. At one point, there was a strong and growing case to include a dedicated allocation to commodities as part of a strategic asset allocation. For a lengthy period, commodities had delivered equity-like returns and were relatively uncorrelated to stocks and bonds. The inflationary era of the 1970s demonstrated just how susceptible stocks and bonds were to inflationary shocks. The addition to portfolios of the commodities asset class that could benefit during such regimes made for a compelling story.

What investors often lose sight of when investing in commodities, however, is that they are not investing directly in the underlying resources. Instead, they are buying and selling futures contracts, which introduces an entirely new dynamic to the return stream that at times can overwhelm the actual spot returns of the commodities themselves. Ignoring this impact is not an option.

While commodities have tended to do well when inflation has gone up unexpectedly, some have done better than others. Precious metals have tended to have the strongest inflation-fighting characteristics, whereas energy, industrial metals, and agricultural commodities tend to have greater influence from unique supply and demand factors. And while commodities tend to do well in inflationary environments, the flip side is that they often perform quite poorly in disinflationary environments.

Gold

Gold is perhaps the most polarizing asset in existence. The detractors view it as a non-productive pet rock that produces no income or earnings. On the other hand, you have the gold bugs and *inflationistas*, who view the precious metal as the premier hedge against skyrocketing debt, rising prices, dollar devaluation, and global economic calamity. The answer, of course, lies somewhere in the middle.

While gold is technically a commodity, it can be thought of as distinct from broad-based commodity exposure given its dual purpose as a currency whose value is traded in relation to fiat money. Gold can best be thought of as a monetary store-of-value asset. Like any other monetary asset, it can be argued it is only worth whatever someone else is willing to pay for it.

Unlike some of the other alternatives discussed in this chapter, gold has long been a democratized asset class. Several gold ETFs, backed by bullion, are just a few clicks away for the average investor. And even prior to the availability of gold funds, investors who appreciated its investment characteristics had ways to own and store it in various forms. In many ways, gold has been the everyman's alternative.

The critique of gold lies in its utility and lack of cash flow. You could even argue it's a negative cash flowing asset, given that holding physical bullion can incur storage and insurance costs. The challenge with gold (and commodities generally) is reconciling their expected returns with any sort of risk-based or behavioral explanation as to why investors should expect a positive return premium over time.

Advocates will take the other side, noting its rich history as a reliable store of wealth given its persistence over thousands of years and its scarcity from relatively low supply growth. And the income argument doesn't hold as much water in a world of negative real interest rates. The lower rates go, the lower the opportunity cost hurdle for an asset like gold.

Over extremely long data sets, there is little evidence that gold has generated any sort of meaningful real return. Research from GMO notes that the inflation-adjusted return of gold over centuries has been about zero. In addition, its track record as a portfolio hedge is mixed. It did benefit investors in the GFC, as it gained over 25% relative to the 50%+ decline in equities. Data from BlackRock in Table 4.4 demonstrates gold's mixed track record during other recessionary periods, with correlations all over the place.

Table 4.4: Gold's Mixed Diversification Potential During Recessions

Recessionary Periods	Gold & S&P 500 Return Correlation
Dec 07–Jun 09	−0.01
Mar 01–Nov 01	−0.34
Jul 90–Mar 91	−0.47
Jul 81–Nov 82	+0.59
Jan 80–Jul 80	+0.67
Nov 73–Mar 75	+0.08

Source: BlackRock.

Gold has experienced very lengthy periods where it lost purchasing power, such as August 1993 through December 2005. As Morningstar's Alex Bryan writes, "Investors who bought gold at its record high real price in January 1980 are still waiting to be made whole on an inflation-adjusted basis."

While gold does have some practical application as a commodity asset—namely jewelry—that is not what explains its allure. As investor Sam Lee notes, "The best way to think of gold is as a nonyielding currency with a special trait: The only way to 'print' it is to pull it out of the earth at great cost." While gold tends to move in opposite direction of the U.S. dollar, there is no universal law governing that relationship. Gold's role as a hedge is only as strong as its perception.

An important dynamic to consider for both gold and commodities is how their financialization impacted their behavior on a go-forward basis. Evidence suggests that as asset classes are made more easily investable and more rapidly adopted by investors, the very nature of those asset classes changes. The launch of the GSCI index by Goldman Sachs in the 2000s saw a huge pick-up in the adoption of commodities as an asset class. This passive exposure created spill over effects, as rebalancing of strategic asset allocations meant that equity volatility had implications for commodity flows. Performance and correlations of yesteryear may be less relevant going forward as these asset classes become easier and easier to access. This will be important to keep in mind in later chapters as our discussion turns to areas like alternative risk premia, digital assets, and collectibles.

Verdict

Allocations to commodities and gold can be a hell of a trade at times, but from a buy and hold standpoint they have not provided much benefit above and beyond inflation. While they are each highly diversifying to traditional assets, they offer little to no structural risk premium. Gold can evoke strong emotions, but investors may be better off having it fulfill their material desires rather than their portfolio objectives.

Connecting the Dots

Private equity, hedge funds, real estate and natural resources have long been synonymous with alternative investing. None of these categories are going anywhere, but we are witnessing an evolution in how they are evaluated, used, accessed, and expanded upon. As we progress from the past to the present, some notable themes will emerge as we examine modern alternative investments and their connection to the old guard.

For private equity, technology-enabled platforms are broadening the potential user base and bringing down the exorbitant minimums. And while some may be averse to the ten-plus year commitments common in PE, another private markets asset class—alternative credit (chapter 7)—has matured right alongside PE and may be more palatable to HNW investors.

Some allocators may still balk at the performance fees and hidden beta that can come with hedge funds, whereas others may be interested but sober about their ability to access top-tier managers. Therein may lie an opportunity with alternative risk premia (chapter 5) and insurance-linked securities (chapter 6) to pursue uncorrelated returns the same way hedge funds have for decades, but in a more systematic, lower-cost, and liquid fashion.

Real estate will continue to be a cornerstone diversifier to stock and bond portfolios. But the makeup of the real estate asset class is transforming, with more niche and alternative property types emerging to complement the basic food groups and allow for a more complete real estate allocation that blends public and private assets and is more representative of the modern economy. Furthermore, real estate should be thought of as but one piece of a broader allocation to inflation-sensitive and cash-flowing real assets, with the complementary categories of infrastructure, timberland and farmland rounding things out (chapter 8).

Investors worried about inflation might find merit in gold's digital counterpart, Bitcoin (chapter 9), as a complementary—or substitute— store-of-value asset class. The premier cryptocurrency has several notable advantages to gold that many are coming around to.

THE ALLOCATOR'S CHEAT SHEET

- When most people consider alternative investments, the following asset classes come to mind: private equity, hedge funds, real estate, and natural resources.
- Each category has its pros and cons, and many investor-specific variables will influence their appropriateness.
- These *four horsemen of alternatives* are too big to ignore, and their relevance for individual investors depends on several factors.
- Modern alternatives have their roots in these mainstay asset classes, and in many ways represent an evolutionary shift in how we access diversifying strategies.

CHAPTER 5
When Alpha Met Beta—Systematic Approaches to Alternative Risk Premia

"If I have seen further, it is by standing upon the shoulders of giants"

— **Sir Isaac Newton**

"I'll have what she's having"

— **When Harry Met Sally**

ALTERNATIVE RISK PREMIA (ARP) refers to the systematic application of classic hedge fund strategies in more liquid, transparent, and diversifying structures. The advent of factor models and style investing in equities demystified what was once considered alpha in long-only equity manager performance. Similarly, ARP strategies sought to disrupt hedge funds through the codification and decomposition of their return streams into beta and alpha components.

Throughout this chapter, we will cover the vast landscape of ARP strategies that were once deemed to be alpha, but now are viewed as alternative forms of beta that are much more accessible to a broader range of investors. Specifically, we identify and review the characteristics of:

- Equity Market Neutral
- Style Premia
- Managed Futures
- Global Macro

- Event-Driven
- Variance Risk Premium

Absent from this chapter are a handful of other hedge fund categories that are still alpha-oriented, or which have yet to become widely available in more liquid formats.

Following the evaluation of each ARP strategy, we will review the risks and other considerations that should be evaluated, as well as the role of ARP in the context of a broader portfolio. But first we begin by placing a magnifying glass on the rise and fall of hedge fund alpha and the discovery of new betas.

The Erosion of Hedge Fund Alpha

The early decades for hedge funds were a bit like the Wild West. Some of the early pioneers were handsomely rewarded (and rightfully so) for pushing the frontiers of risk and reward, and for discovering creative and unique ways to make a risk-controlled buck in the market. The sizable and uncorrelated returns generated by the superstar managers of hedge fund lore could only be considered pure alpha given the lack of data and transparency available at the time. But that wasn't for long.

What followed was an onslaught of copycats and also-rans acting on their desire to "have what she's having" by mimicking the behaviors of the early birds. As competition intensified, leaving less alpha to go around, it became clear that the returns of hedge funds were not exclusively the consequence of some unique insight or skill between a manager's ears, but also due to some repeatable, process-driven rewards that could be captured in a more transparent and low-cost manner. As the common knowledge around certain classic hedge fund strategies expanded, the returns to them naturally compressed. They did not, however, disappear.

An increasingly competitive landscape is only one side of the coin. The other side relates to our deepening knowledge and understanding of the drivers of investment returns. Modern finance has largely been an exercise standing on the shoulders of giants who came before us, incrementally learning more about what makes markets tick as each day passes.

The early days of hedge fund investing lacked the data, computing power and academic rigor that permeates today. As research practitioners spent more time poring over hedge fund return data and analyzing the cross section of manager returns, they identified several previously undiscovered hedge fund betas, which we now call alternative risk premia. While we have identified these betas ex-post, we cannot discount the prescience of those who arrived first. Quite frankly, being early to a hedge fund beta is indistinguishable from alpha.

Markets have a way of eroding edges over time as they become more efficient. Most "3 Sharpe" strategies are either ephemeral or lack scalability. Consequently, time has shown that many would-be Market Wizards were merely the man behind the curtain from the Wizard of Oz.

What Exactly is Alternative Risk Premia?

ARP is not an asset class per se. The underlying strategies can and will span across asset classes like equities, bonds, currencies, and commodities. With ARP, how and why it invests the way it does are of greater importance than the what it invests in. As Corey Hoffstein of Newfound Research advocates, "risk cannot be destroyed, only transformed." It is the transformation of traditional risks into non-traditional ones that sits at the foundation of ARP investing.

ARP represents a collection of rules-based, systematic, and market-independent strategies, both macro- and micro-level, that are designed to extract positive excess returns over cash that are uncorrelated with traditional return sources. The strategies themselves are a by-product of the markets they traffic in and the tools and techniques used to target certain risks, while omitting or mitigating others. These tools and techniques include leverage, short selling, and the use of derivatives. See Figure 5.1.

Figure 5.1: The Tools and Techniques of Alternative Risk Premia

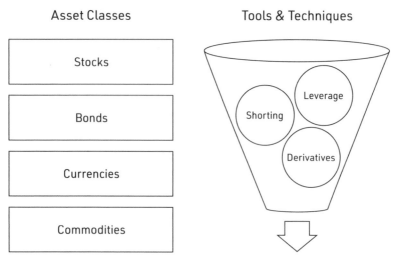

Source: Author.

While the taxonomy of ARP strategies is important for classification and comparison purposes, it is ultimately the resulting themes or bets we are exposed to that matter. These are the atomic units, or elements, that serve as the risk and return drivers of ARP strategies. In allocating to a mix of ARP strategies you are placing a wager that these themes are unique relative to the rest of your portfolio and can be exploited for profit on average and over time. See Figure 5.2.

Figure 5.2: The Themes, or Bets, of Alternative Risk Premia

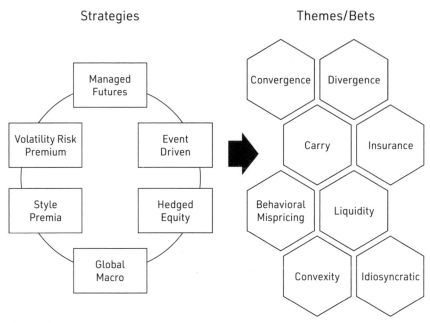

Source: Author.

To gain confidence that a return stream is a true risk premium and not just a passing fad, it should have a strong theoretical basis in one or more of the following explanations:

- **Rewarded risk**: investors should expect reasonable compensation for bearing risks such as liquidity or insurance provision.
- **Behavioral anomaly**: the (at times) irrational behavior of market participants in aggregate can lead to exploitable asset mispricing.
- **Structural impediment**: many market participants face constraints or are non-economic actors, which may lead to opportunity for those without restrictions.

With ARP defined broadly, let's examine the components that fit within it.

Equity Market Neutral: The Long and Short of It

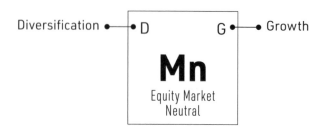

Diversification ● D   G ● Growth

Mn

Equity Market Neutral

Hedged equity is the ubiquitous alternative strategy, dating back to the dawn of hedge funds with Alfred Winslow Jones' pioneering long/short approach. Hedged equity comes in many shapes and sizes, with three broad categories delineated by their dependence on market beta: *long/short equity, equity market neutral*, and *dedicated short bias*.

Given the dynamic presence of sometimes material net market exposure in most long/short equity funds and the explicit negative beta found in dedicated short bias funds, neither category of hedged equity makes for a pure ARP candidate. We must keep in mind that the primary purpose of ARP is to complement traditional market beta with uncorrelated sources of return. The natural independence of equity market neutral (EMN), on the other hand, makes it an ideal fit for ARP to obtain differentiated returns sourced from the spread between the long and short side of a book.

The characteristics that EMN strategies seek in stocks represented in their long books are roughly in line with those of long-only fundamental managers. Painting with a broad brush, EMN funds generally look for:

- Attractive absolute and relative valuations
- Signs of improvement, both fundamental and technical
- Shareholder-friendly management
- High-quality balance sheets
- Sound accounting practices
- Investor sentiment

Conversely, they may look for stocks exhibiting the opposite traits for their short book. By ranking the attractiveness of the universe of stocks based on these (and other) qualities, EMN strategies can initiate long positions in stocks with high scores and short positions in stocks with low scores, netting out all market exposure. Focusing specifically on systematic and quantitative EMN strategies, the idea is to run a highly diversified book on both the long and short side, muting the impact from any individual stock and mitigating much of the idiosyncratic risk.

It's important to remember that market neutral does not mean positive returns in all environments. If your longs underperform your shorts, you can lose money regardless of how favorable you think the trade-offs are between the two sides. The stock market is perfectly capable at times of rewarding expensive stocks with deteriorating fundamentals and junky balance sheets! While not the silver bullet we all crave, EMN has a history of generating meaningful risk-adjusted returns that can work regardless of market direction. Figure 5.3 shows the performance of EMN hedge funds relative to global stocks during notable bull and bear markets of recent decades.

Figure 5.3: Equity Market Neutral During Notable Equity Market Events

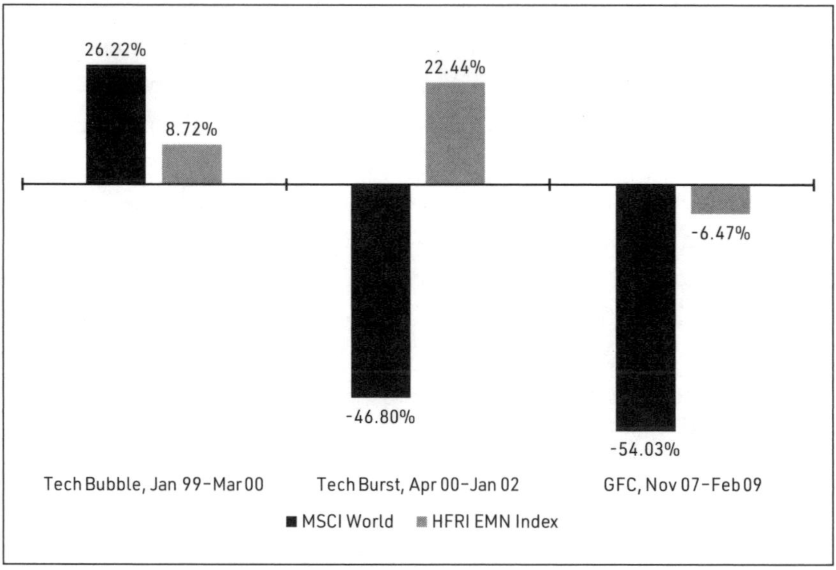

Source: AQR Capital Management, MSCI, HFRI.

Style Premia: Pure Expressions of Classic Investment Styles

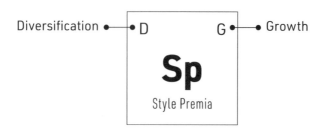

Style premia is the investment industry's fancy way of describing market neutral exposures to classic investment styles like value, momentum, quality, et al. across multiple asset classes. In a way, it is an extension of equity market neutral into other assets outside of stocks where these styles have a history of explaining performance.

A simple example of pure style investing would be investing directly in the value premium by going long relatively cheap assets and short relatively expensive assets. In long-only value equity mandates you end up buying cheap stocks but you also load up on equity market beta and miss out on the other half of the value premium, i.e. the short side. A market neutral expression of the value style isolates the premium itself and removes most or all of the broad market exposure.

Styles are just another flavor of describing factor investing. What often gets forgotten is that factors in an academic sense usually refer to long/short portfolios, yet most investors tend to limit their access to long-only investment vehicles that don't capture the entire premium and come with a healthy dose of market risk.

Value is the most cited example of style investing, but other commonly targeted styles include momentum, carry, quality, and low-risk. Each is described at a high level below:

- **Value** is the tendency of cheap assets to outperform relative to expensive ones. A variety of value metrics exist that aim to draw comparisons between assets based on fundamentals, including price-to-book, price-to-earnings, price-to-cash flow, and price-to-sales. While the value style is most associated with equities, it also extends to bond markets (real yields) and FX markets (purchasing power parity relative to the U.S. dollar). For many value investors today, the bloom is off the rose following more than a decade of disappointment. But just as it's always darkest before the dawn, the best time to maintain or establish a value orientation has often been when everyone else is running away.

- **Momentum** refers to the tendency of assets with strong (weak) relative performance to continue outperforming (underperforming) in the immediate future. High momentum assets tend to bunch together, leaving them prone to simultaneous crashes. In addition to that risk, there are several behavioral biases attributed to the momentum effect.

- **Carry** is expectations of higher returns arising from positions in higher-yielding assets that are financed (through borrowing or shorting) by assets with lower yields. Some common carry trades are FX carry, commodity carry, and bond futures carry.

- **Quality** is the expected return from being long high-quality assets and short low-quality assets. Predominantly an equity phenomenon, some common quality metrics include gross profitability, return on assets, earnings quality, earnings stability, and low leverage. There is also evidence of quality styles working in credit markets.

- **Low risk** is the counterintuitive propensity of lower-risk assets to generate better risk-adjusted (and in some cases absolute) returns than their high-risk peers. This anomaly exists because investors demonstrate an aversion to leverage, which leads them to overpay for assets with lottery-like characteristics. Low risk can be measured by market beta, residual volatility, and other risk-based metrics.

There is a reason just a handful of styles receive a broad stamp of approval. Only those with the following characteristics should warrant attention:

- **Intuitive**: supported by logical economic rationale.
- **Persistent**: long history of in and out-of-sample evidence in explaining asset returns.
- **Pervasive**: broad existence across geographies and asset classes.
- **Liquid**: survives implementation and trading costs in liquid instruments and markets.

There is no questioning the highly diversifying nature of long/short style investing and the mountain of evidence supporting its efficacy. But the free lunch of diversification comes with a subtle, hidden cost of weaker intuition and harder storytelling. When your long-only value manager is underperforming, it's simple to arrive at a narrative explanation for said underperformance. When you invest across multiple styles, across multiple asset classes, in a market neutral manner, the narrative gets lost in translation. This can unfortunately result in weakened conviction from investors when things aren't going their way.

Managed Futures: Befriending the Trend

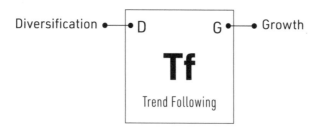

It may seem hypocritical that after encouraging you to think differently throughout this book, I am now advocating that you begin following the crowd. Before you paint me as two-faced, let me explain.

Trend following refers to the expected return from going long assets that have been increasing in price and going short assets that have been decreasing in price (see Figure 5.4). The strategy is grounded in behavioral finance and based on historical patterns of price trend behavior that are unrelated to fundamentals.

Figure 5.4: Trend Following

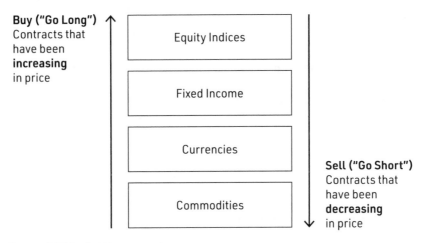

Source: AQR Capital Management.

Managers of such strategies often trade many distinct assets across equities, interest rates, credit, foreign currencies, and commodities. Trend following on just one asset class can work, but it is a risky endeavor. Spreading your bets through asset class diversification has historically led to better risk-adjusted returns for trend followers.

Trend following is often used interchangeably with the term managed futures. The liquidity of futures markets makes them the preferred instrument for executing such a dynamic and high turnover strategy. Managed futures managers are also commonly referred to as CTAs, or commodity trading advisors.

Trend following may sound eerily similar to momentum as described under style premia. It's best to think of the two phenomena as kissing cousins that are closely related with slight differences. Whereas momentum evaluates recent price movement *relative* to other assets, trend following analyzes price movements in *absolute* terms relative to an asset's own history. In technical terms, this is called time-series momentum.

The historical patterns of market trends stem largely from common behavioral biases that investors exhibit in aggregate. Biases such as anchoring and disposition are typically present at the inception of a trend, while herding and overreaction behavior appear as trends begin to accelerate. Central bank actions, passive fund flows, and the risk management activities of other quantitative volatility targeting strategies can also influence market trends. This pattern of market trends is illustrated in Figure 5.5.

Figure 5.5: The Pattern of Market Trends that Trend Following Seeks to Exploit

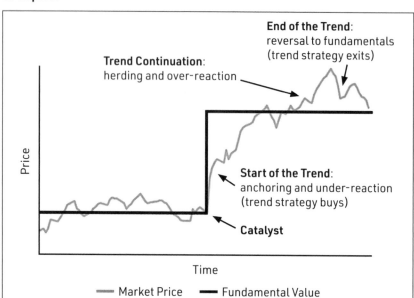

Source: AQR Capital Management.

Managed futures has a rich history as an incredibly powerful diversifier. While correlations to other asset classes fluctuate over shorter time frames, over long periods managed futures has proven to be structurally uncorrelated to just about every major asset class. Table 5.1 highlights the correlations to stocks, bonds, and hedge funds over all periods, as well as during up or down periods. As you can see, the overall correlation of managed futures across all periods is quite low, but perhaps the most notable data is the tendency to become more negatively correlated to stocks when they are down. This is diversification in action exactly when you need it most.

Table 5.1: Correlation of SG Trend Index to Stocks, Bonds, and Other Alternatives

	Overall Correlation	Correlation–Up Periods for Index	Correlation–Down Periods for Index
S&P 500 Index	-0.09	-0.08	-0.32
MSCI World Index	-0.06	-0.08	-0.30
Bbg Barclays US Bond Index	0.24	0.16	0.02
Bbg Barclays Global Bond Index	0.25	0.28	0.05
HFRI Hedge Fund Index	0.09	0.14	-0.19

Source: Graham Capital.

Not all managed futures funds are the same, as there are many ways to skin the cat and a healthy amount of dispersion across managers. In fact, there is a strong argument for implementing a multi-manager approach when allocating to managed futures. Some of the important distinctions across managed futures funds relate to their:

- **Trend speed**: When do the signals kick in? This is an important consideration for managed futures as some managers focus on short-term trends while others gravitate towards longer-term trends. In a given market environment, the difference in look-back periods could mean the difference between success and failure. A blend of timing signals is prudent for diversification purposes.
- **Risk management**: Because managed futures strategies look to achieve a relatively stable risk profile over time, they tend to adjust in reaction to volatility changes rather than letting it run. In practice, this means positions sizes may get smaller as an asset's volatility increases, and vice versa.
- **Beta caps**: Allocators often use managed futures for explicit equity portfolio protection. In response, some managers impose caps on the amount of directional stock market exposure the strategy can have.
- **Market selection**: There are dozens, if not hundreds, of markets that managed futures funds can traffic in. Each market varies in liquidity and strategy capacity, which is an important consideration for managers that allocate to less liquid markets.

The Return Profile of Managed Futures

It is often said that managed futures works best when things go from good-to-great or from bad-to-worse. Given its convex return profile, managed futures can similarly be thought of as disaster insurance with a positive expected long-term return. This non-linear payoff profile is illustrated in Figure 5.6 with the quarterly returns of global stocks (MSCI World) exhibited on the x-axis and that of managed futures (SG Trend Index) on the y-axis. The strong performance during many stocks' worst quarters is referred to as crisis alpha and the curved best-fit line is known as the managed futures smile, or smirk.

Figure 5.6: The Non-Linear Payoff Profile of Managed Futures

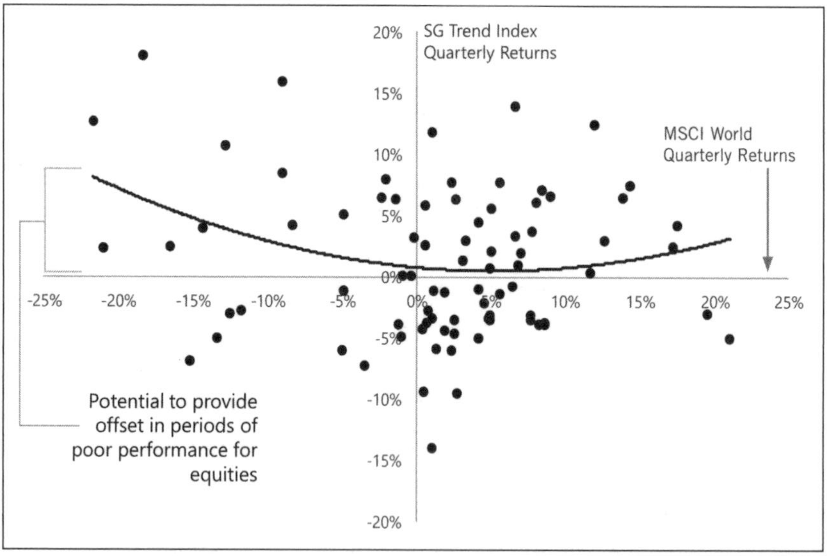

Source: Graham Capital.

The convexity of managed futures lies in the fact that equity bear markets do not take place in a vacuum. As equities suffer, trends can develop in interest rates, commodities, and currencies—all within the domain of trend followers. A wider breadth of strong trend signals can amplify the ability of a managed futures strategy to capture price trends in both directions across asset classes.

This behavior can also be seen in Table 5.2, which examines the performance of the SG Trend Index during the worst ten quarters for the S&P 500 since 2000. In seven of the ten periods, SG Trend was positive in absolute terms and in all ten periods it outperformed in relative terms.

Table 5.2: Managed Futures Performance During the Worst Ten Quarters of Equity Performance

Period	Event	S&P 500 Total Return Index	SG Trend Index	Difference
Q4 2008	Bear Market in U.S. Equities led by Financials	-21.9%	+12.7%	34.6%
Q1 2020	COVID-19 Pandemic	-19.6%	+2.3%	21.9%
Q3 2002	WorldCom Scandal	-17.3%	+18.0%	35.3%
Q3 2001	Terrorist Attacks on World Trade Center and Pentagon	-14.7%	+3.9%	18.6%
Q3 2011	European Sovereign Debt Crisis	-13.9%	+2.4%	16.3%
Q4 2018	Equity Market Upsets and Increasing Volatility	-13.5%	-5.1%	8.4%
Q2 2002	Continuing Aftermath of Technology Bubble Bursting	-13.4%	+15.8%	29.2%
Q1 2001	Bear Market in U.S. Equities led by Technology	-11.9%	+10.6%	22.5%
Q2 2010	European Sovereign Debt Crisis, "Flash Crash"	-11.4%	-3.1%	8.3%
Q1 2009	Credit Crisis Continues	-11.0%	-2.7%	8.3%

Source: AlphaSimplex Group.

While managed futures tends to do best in severe and prolonged drawdowns like the financial crisis of 2008–09, it is not immune to performance struggles. Markets that experience frequent whipsaws and few strong trends can be damaging to managed futures performance.

Both stocks and trend following have undergone drawn-out periods of negative excess returns. However, both have demonstrated strong positive excess returns—they simply accrue at different times!

The returns of managed futures on down days/months for stocks is basically a coin flip. Trend followers don't change their positioning based on daily signals, as fluctuations over such a short period would not meet the definition of a trend. All trend-based systems need some amount of time to adjust and change direction, from several weeks to up to a year depending on the nature of the underlying strategy. If a managed futures fund is positioned long equities in the beginning of a drawdown, it should not be surprising if it is not profitable at that stage.

Uncertain backdrops, such as those experienced amid the COVID-19 crisis, raise questions about the validity of inherently backward-looking fundamental data. To the contrary, strategies that rely upon real-time market data such as prices and trading volumes dispassionately avoid the need to make fundamental-based forecasts. Trend following, the quintessential price-based investment strategy, has a demonstrated history of profitability and low correlation to traditional assets since managers began adopting it in earnest during the 1970s and 1980s. Like any trading strategy, trend following tries to capture behavioral tendencies rather than absolute ironclad laws, making systematic and highly diversified approaches paramount to success. Trend following simply aims to profit from trends—positive or negative—wherever and whenever they occur, without any regard for analyst forecasts, macroeconomic data, or market narratives.

Global Macro: A World of Opportunity

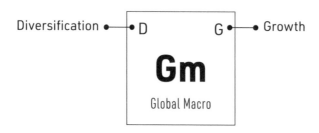

Global macro investors can be roughly divided into two camps:

1. **Discretionary global macro**: The swashbuckling, gunslinging discretionary traders like George Soros and John Paulson that are often associated with the "greatest trades ever."
2. **Systematic global macro**: The systematic, computer-driven trading programs run by nameless, faceless algorithms.

This section is about the latter.

What these two camps share is a focus on top-down trading of a diverse mix of asset class instruments, the ability to take long or short positioning, and the use of macroeconomic data such as inflation, exchange rates, debt levels and supply-demand dynamics. The practitioners of discretionary macro, the subject of outsized financial media attention, are willing to take concentrated bets. Their systematic cousins, by contrast, extoll the virtues of broad diversification and a cold, emotionless investment process.

The return drivers for systematic global macro are the capital flows triggered in global asset classes because of large, macroeconomic events. Global supply and demand, monetary and fiscal policy, economic growth differentials and the gyrations of short- and long-term interest rates all impact the volatility and directionality of stock, bond, credit, commodity, and currency markets around the world. The hallmarks of systematic macro strategies are their diversification and adaptability. As volatile conditions produce price trends and relative value among similar assets, these managers seek to capture profits through long and short expressions, position sizing, and risk management. Agnostic to the direction of markets, systematic macro offers the potential for profits in rising and falling environments—as evidenced by the performance of this category through the GFC.

Much like managed futures, systematic macro strategies behave as diversifying investments to traditional assets like stocks and bonds, with a return profile that tends to offer its best returns in challenged markets. This form of crisis alpha can be quite valuable in the context of a diversified portfolio. The shared characteristics with managed futures of wide breadth, adaptability to changing market conditions, and bidirectionality (long or short) give systematic macro an uncorrelated return stream that can offer a potent combination of portfolio protection and growth.

Event-Driven Investing: The Science of the Deal

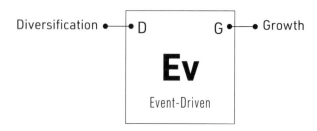

Wall Street is a perpetual deal-making machine: mergers, acquisitions, IPOs, secondary offerings, spin-offs. The list goes on and on. An entire ecosystem—the investment banking industry—exists for the sole purpose of financing, structuring, and selling these deals. And while some might lead you to believe that deal-making is an art form, systematic approaches to investing in and around these deals can be more science than art.

A variety of trading strategies in and around corporate events aim to take advantage of market dislocations driven by supply and demand imbalances. These imbalances can arise when market participants demand liquidity during capital raising events such as equity, convertible bond, and debt issuance, as well as control events such as mergers or bankruptcies. Arbitrageurs, in effect, are betting on the convergence of related securities at the completion of the event and expect to be compensated by bearing the risk of deal failure or other unfavorable market conditions. These strategies are present throughout the corporate life cycle—from expansions and slowdowns to recessions and recoveries.

Figure 5.7: Trading Strategies and the Corporate Life Cycle

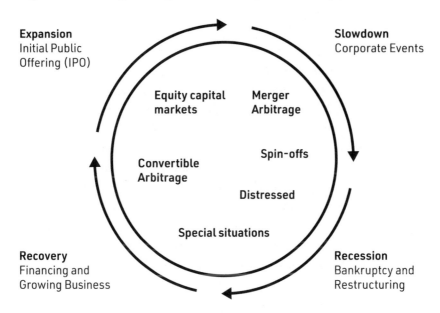

Source: AQR Capital Management.

The potential benefits of event-driven investments include:

- Expected returns in the mid-single digit range across different market environments.
- A unique source of return.
- Shallower drawdowns than equities.
- Modest correlation and beta to stocks and bonds.
- Minimal impact from rising interest rates.

The goal of any event-driven, or arbitrage, strategy is to generate positive risk-adjusted returns by capturing a liquidity risk premium caused by event-induced capital flows. This liquidity risk premium has historically been differentiated from traditional equity and bond risk premia and can be thought of as a reward for bearing the risk of a collection of *mini fire sales* that arise from corporate activities. With the appropriate hedges, it can produce returns that are generally uncorrelated with stock and bond markets. The various sub-strategies under the broader event-driven banner all have modest correlations with each other as well, allowing for additional diversification.

Merger Arbitrage

The most oft-cited example of event-driven investing is a strategy known as merger arbitrage. Pioneered in the 1980s, this strategy—also referred to as risk arbitrage—seeks to profit by investing in companies involved in publicly announced corporate events such as mergers and acquisitions (M&A), buyouts, tender offers, and takeovers. The opportunity to profit from these deals comes from the presence of what is known as the deal spread, or the differential between what the acquiring company has agreed to pay to complete the deal and the price the target company currently trades at.

As existing shareholders of the target company seek an immediate exit to lock in their profits, rather than wait around for the deal to consummate, arbitrageurs will step in to provide them liquidity while bearing any potential risk of deal failure. Merger deals can be all cash, all stock, or part cash and part stock. In the case of stock deals, arbitrageurs will also typically sell short the shares of the acquiring company to hedge out any market risk and lock in the deal spread. Once transactions are announced, shares of companies involved in M&A deals often trade in line with the fundamentals of the deal, rather than broader market movements.

Provided the deal goes through as intended—at its announced takeout price and in line with its expected timeline—the position will have a defined upside (the deal spread) and a defined duration (the completion date). Investors can mitigate the idiosyncratic risk of failure at the individual deal level through broad diversification. You are still bearing the uncertainty of deal failure—and thus the potential for earning the associated return premium—but meaningful diversification means that no one deal will make or break you.

Not all deal spreads are the same—some are narrow, while others are wide. And they can change in an instant depending on a variety of risk factors. The largest driver of deal spreads is the deal risk itself, which can be heavily influenced by regulatory, financing, and shareholder approval issues. The timing until deal close, along with prevailing risk-free rates, will also have an impact on the size of deal spreads. These drivers of the deal spread are illustrated in Figure 5.8.

Figure 5.8: Drivers of the Merger Arbitrage Deal Spread

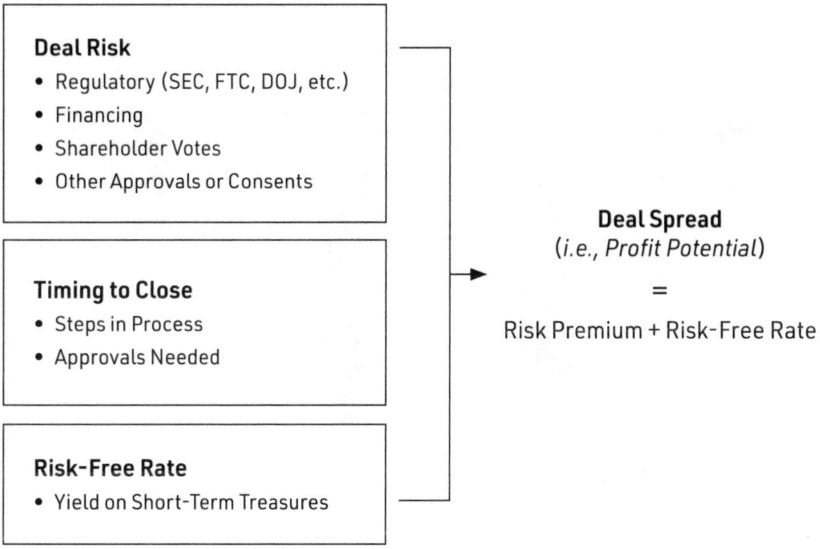

Deal Risk
- Regulatory (SEC, FTC, DOJ, etc.)
- Financing
- Shareholder Votes
- Other Approvals or Consents

Timing to Close
- Steps in Process
- Approvals Needed

Risk-Free Rate
- Yield on Short-Term Treasuries

Deal Spread
(*i.e., Profit Potential*)

=

Risk Premium + Risk-Free Rate

Source: Water Island Capital.

In the context of a broader portfolio, merger arbitrage strategies can offer some attractive characteristics. In addition to having low betas and low correlations to equity and credit markets, merger arbitrage often exhibits relatively low volatility and the ability to preserve capital over time. In addition, because of the impact that risk-free rates have on deal spreads, rising interest rates have the potential to act as a tailwind to merger arbitrage, which can help offset some of the duration risk inherent in bonds. Therefore, many allocators often source merger arbitrage from the fixed income sleeve of a portfolio. From a return standpoint, Figure 5.9 highlights the strategy's ability to perform in both positive and negative stock market environments, while providing less downside risk in true market crises.

Figure 5.9: Merger Arbitrage in Positive and Negative Stock Environments

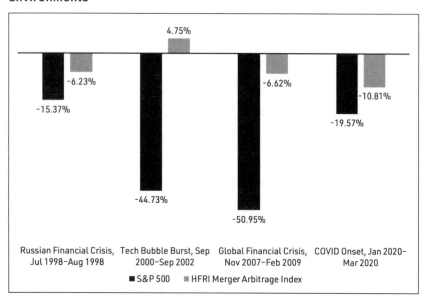

Source: AQR, HFRI Merger Arbitrage Index, S&P 500 Index.

Convertible Arbitrage

Convertible arbitrage seeks to capitalize on dislocations in the prices of convertible bonds away from their theoretical value. Sometimes referred to as "equities with training wheels," convertible bonds are a bit of an afterthought to most asset allocators.

The appeal of issuing convertible bonds stems from their lower financing costs: corporations typically pay a lower coupon on convertibles than on traditional fixed income securities due to the value of the underlying equity option. The lower interest costs, and path to equity issuance at a premium to today's stock price, make them desirable sources of liquidity for cash-strapped businesses. Convertible bond issuance usually takes place during the recovery and expansion phases of the business cycle when companies are financing and growing their businesses.

Convertibles are usually issued at par value (i.e., 100) with a stated fixed coupon rate. Unlike other bonds, that fixed coupon rate comes attached with a call option on the issuer's stock. The difference between the embedded option's strike price and the current price of the stock is known as the *conversion premium*.

Convertibles can be roughly bucketed into three categories—busted, balanced, and equity-like—depending on the stock price. The sensitivity of convertible bond prices, known as their *delta*, increases and decreases with the stock price. Busted convertibles, due to their low stock prices, contain little value from the deep out-of-the-money call options and are much more impacted by changes in interest rates and credit spreads. Balanced convertibles have an asymmetric return profile, sitting right in the sweet spot of having higher upside potential than downside risk. Lastly, equity-like convertibles often trade in tandem with the underlying stock with a higher degree of downside given their distance from the bond floors. Typically, you see a fair amount of profit-taking when a convertible bond's delta reaches 100%.

So wherein lies the arbitrage, you might ask? Given convertible bonds can be synthetically recreated by combining their underlying components—a traditional corporate bond and a call option on the stock of the company—we have a mechanism by which to compare and analyze their actual prices relative to their theoretical values. Discrepancies between the two can be attributed to the relative illiquidity of convertible bonds and the periodic dislocations that take place in the asset class due to supply/demand imbalances.

Because convertible bonds can at times trade cheap or expensive relative to their theoretical value, arbitrageurs can step in, taking long or short positions based on the convertible bond's attractiveness, and hedge out most of the unwanted equity, credit and interest rate risk. This results in an uncorrelated exposure that can pay off, if and when the bond converges towards its theoretical value.

Other Event-Driven Strategies

In addition to merger arb and convertible arb, there are a cornucopia of other event-driven strategies that invest opportunistically around corporate activity, special situations, and other market events. Arbitrage strategies focused on SPACs maintain an asymmetric payoff structure with a well-defined downside and low correlation to other corporate arbitrage strategies. Closed-end fund (CEF) arbitrage is a mean-reversion strategy that seeks to capture market inefficiencies driven by retail investor flows that impact CEF premiums and discounts. Other examples include:

- Spin-offs
- Equity index arbitrage
- Stub arbitrage
- Dual share class
- Activism
- Distressed/bankruptcy

The opportunity set is constantly evolving within event-driven, reflecting changes in universe size, corporate issuance trends, deal activity and the regulatory environment, among other variables. A diversified event-driven strategy may be able to adapt to these changing opportunities, while improving the risk-adjusted returns of a traditional portfolio.

Variance Risk Premium: Selling Market Insurance

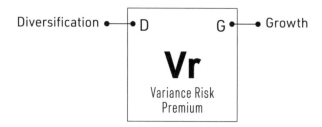

Just as individuals buy insurance on their lives and homes, there are natural buyers with a need to purchase market insurance in the form of options contracts. Corporations and other entities need to protect themselves from adverse price moves in myriad different asset classes.

Sellers of market insurance aim to earn a profit as compensation for taking on price risks that businesses and other entities willingly pay to avoid. The academic term for this type of strategy is the variance risk premium (VRP) and it is harvested through the systematic selling of options tied to an array of financial instruments. Almost any tradable instrument where there is a demand and a premium for price hedging—lean hog futures, interest rate swaps, VIX futures, etc.—can act as a source for harvesting the VRP.

From a technical standpoint, the VRP is the spread between implied volatility and realized volatility in option prices. Implied volatility represents the expected volatility of an asset over the life of an option contract. As expectations for future volatility change, option premiums react accordingly. Implied volatility is directly influenced by the supply and demand of the underlying options and by the market's expectation of an asset's price movement, up or down. Implied volatility has been persistently higher on average than ex-post realized volatility. This insurance risk premium embedded in options reflects investors' risk aversion and their propensity to miscalculate the probability of significant losses.

Magnitude > Direction

Harvesting the VRP is less intuitive than traditional investments in asset classes like equities. When buying stocks, investors are making a directional bet on the asset. If an investor is wagering the asset's value will go up, they take a long position. If they anticipate a security will go down, they either avoid altogether or take a short position.

Conversely, when selling options to capture the VRP it is the magnitude of price moves, not the direction, which ultimately matters. Instead of playing the fruitless game of trying to guess whether markets will go up or down, diversified hedge sellers can earn a differentiated source of returns by systematically providing market insurance against severe price shocks in either direction. Any entity that holds risks on its balance sheet that it needs to hedge is likely to act as a price-insensitive structural buyer of options. Let's look at some real-world examples.

The largest line item expenses for Southwest Airlines, or any airline for that matter, are typically fuel costs. Without proper hedging in place, a massive spike in fuel costs could wipe out a significant portion of their profits. The government of Mexico has the opposite problem to that of the airlines. With energy exports as its largest revenue source, it is much more concerned about a sharp decrease in the price of oil.

These contrasting examples demonstrate why the magnitude, not the direction, of asset prices drives the VRP. There are plenty of other instances where two different entities care about the opposite type of volatility on the same asset. Japanese importers are concerned about a weaker yen, whereas Japanese exporters worry about a stronger yen. Rising livestock prices could wreak havoc for fast food chains, while farmers could be hurt by a sharp decline in livestock prices.

Periods of heightened volatility—to the upside and the downside—lead to elevated options prices. Being a consistent seller of options in good times and bad ensures that you will be placed to take advantage and collect the VRP when it is most valuable.

Protection Comes with a Cost

The flip side of the VRP are systematic buyers of option protection. If systematic sellers of market insurance have earned a positive return premium, on average and over time, we can intuit that systematic purchasers of market insurance would have earned a negative premium.

Research from AQR compared the returns of the S&P 500 to those of the S&P 500 with a protective put overlay on top from 1996 through 2016. The annualized return of the S&P over that time was 5.1%. While the protective put strategy reduced volatility, it came with the expense of sacrificing nearly all the returns, with an annualized rate of a measly 1.8%. The resulting Sharpe ratio of the protective put strategy was a mere 0.14, much lower than the 0.32 of the S&P 500.

The Challenge with VRP

As described, there are two camps of volatility investors: those who are long volatility and purchase protection, and those who are short volatility and sell protection.

From an intuition and historical data standpoint, the obvious choice seems to be to side with short volatility. Where that can fall short, however, is when there are failures in risk management and implementations. Volatility is a fickle thing, with 100-year floods showing up more frequently than once a century. The potential for significant downside is ever present in short vol strategies and that downside tends to coincide with downturns in other risk assets—muting its diversification potential when it's needed most.

Long volatility, or tail risk strategies, on the other hand, are negatively correlated with stocks and provide tremendous diversification benefits exactly when you would want them. The catch-22 with long vol is that it is a negative expected returning strategy long term, due to its high cost of carry.

In other words, unless you get the timing right, your odds of losing money are almost certain.

Sitting between long and short vol strategies are relative value strategies that seek to identify mispriced volatility and are neither structurally long nor short. While intriguing, these types of strategies may introduce a healthy amount of manager-specific risk and at the present time few such strategies are readily available to non-institutional investors.

If there is anything to be learned from some of the volatility shocks in recent years, it's that selling options is a tough business. Any time you are dealing with derivatives with convex payoffs, being caught on the wrong side of a big move can be the difference between making money and going bankrupt. Absent proper risk management, the potential for harvesting the VRP can evaporate.

We must also recognize the impacts that certain secular forces are having on market microstructure and by extension volatility and options markets. This has led some to believe that the stock market is now a derivative of the options market and not the other way around.

Too Much of a Good Thing?

Markets are complex adaptive systems and one must wonder whether Goodhart's Law applies to ARP.[15] As products focused on factors and alternative risk premia have ballooned in recent years, some have begun to worry whether the strategies are becoming too popular. Or as Yogi Berra might say, "nobody invests there anymore. It's too crowded."

Overcrowding refers to environments in which the magnitude of flows into or out of a strategy can distort the properties of the investment itself. It's a worthy concern as factor overcrowding can lead to an ugly unwinding if many asset managers pursuing similar strategies need to de-lever or head for the exit at the same time.

Another consideration related to that of crowding is that of general popularity. In other words, the more people that know about and trade on a certain risk premium, the more likely that same premium will experience some level of degradation or erosion over time. There is a kernel of truth

---

15   Goodhart's Law: When a measure becomes a target, it ceases to be a good measure.

to this as we should not expect to earn the same returns as those earned by the first movers in these strategies. As investment manager ReSolve Asset Management notes, "the market finds a new equilibrium premium that is just large enough to keep the most disciplined investors engaged, but much smaller than the original pre-publication premium."[16]

While premiums may erode over time and are unlikely to repeat at levels seen before their discovery and broader adoption, those that are grounded in risk or behavioral biases stand more than a fighting chance of persisting long term. They will certainly fluctuate in performance, but a bad stretch is not necessarily indicative of total obsolescence. Just ask the value factor, which by now has more lives than a cat.

Investors should also be leery of backtests that look *too good* as new index funds are launched aiming to replicate the success of certain ARP strategies. We should always look at any backtest with skeptical scrutiny. As Michael Batnick jokes, "the worst ten-year period of any backtest is the next ten years."

While it may appear that ARP strategies are experiencing rapid growth, we must recognize that many of these dollars are merely shifting from funds that have been pursuing the same factors indirectly or in a more discretionary manner towards funds that employ more rules-based and systematic approaches. Tangentially, some ARP managers themselves have evolved their approaches to take advantages of alternative datasets and machine learning to analyze unstructured and textual data, rather than numerical. Quantitative investing continues to embrace cutting edge research and techniques.

Abnormal, or unpleasant, performance over short-term periods is simply a reflection of the fact that these premia, while pervasive and persistent over long periods of time, are not a free lunch. Despite the poor performance of ARP strategies in recent years, it seems likelier that they have merely stalled, as opposed to completely running out of gas. All successful investment strategies experience ebbs and flows, some tougher to withstand than others. A focus on strategies that have an intuitive risk-based, behavioral and structural reason for existing in the first place can help maintain conviction during inevitable periods of challenging performance.

---

16   "Are we living in a post factor world?" ReSolve Asset Management.

ARP in a Portfolio

To observe the impact of ARP in a portfolio, I have constructed a blend of ARP strategies. For simplicity, I have limited it to three of the strategies discussed in the chapter: managed futures, style premia, and event-driven. The ARP blend is allocated as follows:

- **50% Managed futures**: represented by the SG Trend Index.
- **25% Equity market neutral**: represented by the HFRI Equity Market Neutral Index
- **25% Event-driven**: represented by 1/3 HFRI Merger Arbitrage Index, 1/3 HFRI Convertible Arbitrage Index, and 1/3 HFRI Event-Driven Index.

Managed futures has received a larger allocation due to its lower correlation to traditional assets than the other ARP categories. It should also be noted that the HFRI indices are not pure representations of ARP, as they include both systematic and fundamentally driven strategies within the respective categories. They do, however, provide us with the longest data set to analyze.

The standalone results of the blend going back to the beginning of 2000 are shown in Table 5.3.

Table 5.3: Asset Class Characteristics of ARP Blend

1/1/2000–12/31/2020	ARP Blend
Annualized Return	4.99%
Volatility	7.23%
Maximum Drawdown	-10.94%
Correlation to Global Stocks	0.13
Correlation to U.S. Bonds	0.25

Source: Author.

When a 20% allocation to the above blend was incorporated into a 60/40 portfolio on a pro-rata basis, returns were roughly the same, volatility was materially lower, and the maximum drawdown was over 20% shallower (Table 5.4).

Table 5.4: Addition of ARP Blend to 60/40 Portfolio

1/1/2000–12/31/2020	60/40	60/40 + 20% ARP Blend
Annualized Return	5.84%	5.78%
Volatility	9.44%	7.89%
Maximum Drawdown	-36.48%	-29.07%

Source: Author.

An Alternative to Hedge Funds

Hedge funds have long played a pivotal role in institutional portfolios, acting as a source of diversification and uncorrelated returns. But they have been far from perfect. As competition intensified, many funds no longer justified the excessive fees being levied. Concurrently, alpha became more scarce and other sources of hedge fund returns—alternative risk premia—became more widespread in their availability and adoption.

Many individual investors have long avoided hedge funds because of illiquidity, opaqueness, fee sensitivity, and tax reporting, among other reasons. ARP represents an opportunity to introduce diversifying return streams into a portfolio with lower expenses, greater transparency, and regulatory oversight. Today, there are several high-quality options within each of the categories described in this chapter in liquid, '40 Act vehicles. Generally speaking, it would be wise to house ARP funds inside of non-taxable accounts, as they face similar tax headwinds as their hedge fund cousins due to their higher turnover and propensity to distribute capital gains.

ARP strategies *work* in the sense that they experience positive results more often than not. To paraphrase Cliff Asness, "if your car worked like this, you'd fire your mechanic." But just because something doesn't work all the time, doesn't mean that it isn't valuable.

THE ALLOCATOR'S CHEAT SHEET

- Most forms of historical alpha end up simply being undiscovered beta.
- Much how factor models and the emergence of style investing disrupted long-only equity investing, the decomposition of risk and return within hedge funds has created the category of alternative risk premia, or ARP.
- ARP strategies like trend following, style premia, and event-driven can serve as valuable diversifiers with explainable sources of return.
- Potential risks of ARP include data mining, crowded strategies, non-static correlations, and potential tax inefficiencies.
- In the context of a portfolio, ARP strategies can introduce structurally uncorrelated returns that are diversifying to stocks and bonds, resulting in greater portfolio efficiency.
- ARP can play a similar role in a portfolio as hedge funds historically have, but with lower fees, less dependence on market beta, and more access points for investors.

CHAPTER 6

The Investor as Underwriter— Natural Diversification from Catastrophe Reinsurance and Insurance-Linked Securities

"If it keeps on rainin', levee's goin' to break
When the levee breaks, I'll have no place to stay."
Kansas Joe McCoy and Memphis Minnie (1929),
popularized by Led Zeppelin.[17]

I N THIS CHAPTER, we look at how investors can broaden their portfolio horizons by acting like insurance underwriters. There are meaningful risk premiums that investors can access that exist as compensation for bearing insurance-related uncertainty. Specifically, we will focus on the reinsurance risk premium related to natural catastrophe risk.

Before we dive in to look at this asset class, it's worth taking a moment to define the insurance risk premium and how it arises.

---

17 This song is about the Great Mississippi Flood of 1927, 78 years before the levees broke during Hurricane Katrina, causing the greatest single-event insured losses in history.

Insurance as Risk Transfer

Insurance policies exist because human beings are risk-averse creatures. Each and every year, people spend billions of dollars transferring the risk of undesired outcomes to insurance companies via premium payments. The buyer of an insurance policy pays to eliminate the financial impact of an extreme, rare downside event. The seller of that policy happily collects that premium, along with the premiums of many others, to take advantage of risk pooling and the law of large numbers. These insurers are, in effect, a provider of risk transfer services to the marketplace and are compensated as such.

Risk transfer services can be broken down into two components to determine the price a seller must charge for providing such a service:

1. An expected payout.
2. A risk premium to compensate the seller for assuming the uncertainty associated with the nature of these payouts, which can be abrupt and dramatic.

The term "risk transfer service" sounds a lot more complicated than it is. Just about every trade can be viewed through the lens of risk transfer. One party buys or sells an asset to offload a risk. The party on the other side of that trade provides a service by assuming the risk of that trade paying off for their counterparty.

Insurance throughout History

The well-documented history of human beings using insurance goes back several millennia. The Code of Hammurabi, the Babylonian Code of Law dating back to ~1750 B.C., contained 282 laws inscribed on stone stele that dealt with all aspects of public life, citizen's rights, and the kingdom's justice system. Some of those laws covered risk related to maritime insurance, in which a merchant would pay a lender some money in exchange for the lender providing a guarantee that he would cancel the loan if the shipment sank or was stolen.

Fast forward to the 17th century, where Lloyd's of London began as underwriters conducting business with one another at a coffee house known as Mr. Lloyd's. In the centuries to follow, the role of insurance became integral to the functioning of our economies and societies. Today, the dollars collected from global insurance premiums are in the trillions.

Despite its ubiquity and necessity, insurance from a buyer's perspective is a bad trade. Not a bad trade in the literal sense that it doesn't provide value. Quite the contrary—insurance is actually quite valuable for the role it plays in managing large risks. After all, the debt on your mortgage isn't forgiven if your house burns down. Purchasing insurance is 100% prudent and benefits both sides of the trade. But the protection obtained from insurance is not without cost. In investor parlance, it has a negative expected return. You don't buy insurance to make money. You willingly pay your premium and hope that you (or your loved ones) never have to collect on a claim.

Every trade has two sides, though. So if buying insurance is a bad trade, then it is fair to assume that the opposite end of that trade—the seller of insurance—is engaging in a good trade, or one with a positive expected return. The reason insurance sellers experience a return premium over time is because investments that entail insurance-selling characteristics have negative skew, or what many might recognize as the *bad* type of tail risk.

Figure 6.1: Negative Skew

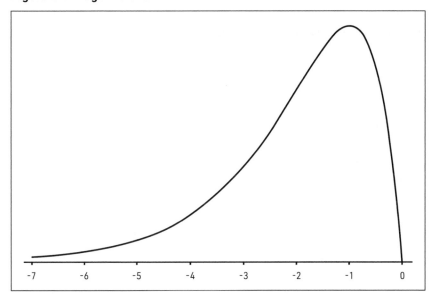

Traditional assets like equities are also exposed to negative skew, or left-tail risk. What distinguishes insurance-linked investments from equities is that the tails in question are of a different nature altogether. These distinct sources of risk and their associated returns streams make insurance-linked investments incredibly powerful as diversifiers to traditional assets.

And now with that defined, let's move on to look at catastrophe reinsurance.

Catastrophe Reinsurance

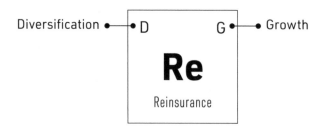

As mentioned, buying insurance is a bad trade from a profit-seeking perspective. Yet we all do it, with our cars, our homes, our lives and more. We willingly and gladly pay a premium to financially protect our families against unforeseen and disastrous events.

Insurance companies are happy to take the other side of this trade by selling us policies. Insurance companies are not altruistic; they do not sell these policies at cost. They sell them at cost plus an expected risk premium. They seek to earn a profit by pooling a diversified set of risks so that on average and over time they will take in more in premiums than they pay out in claims.

Figure 6.2: Insurance Risk Transfer in Action

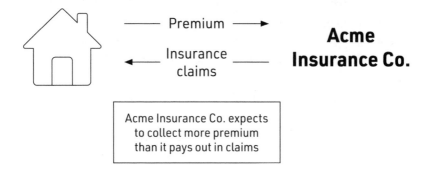

Insurance companies also need insurance of their own at times, known as reinsurance. The reinsurance industry operates around the globe, pricing and holding remote risks that insurance companies for a variety of reasons cannot afford to hold on their balance sheets. Much like insurers, reinsurers offer a risk transfer service to the market by putting their capital at risk to earn a long-term risk premium.

We can use the analogy of options markets to provide framing around an investment in reinsurance. Fundamentally, it is very similar to selling out-of-the-money (OTM) put options on catastrophic events. Figure 6.3 is an illustration of what is known as the "waterfall of reinsurance risk."

Figure 6.3: Waterfall of Reinsurance Risk

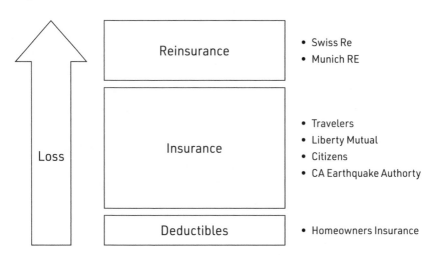

The reinsurance business has existed for centuries. The first reinsurance contract was written way back in 1370 and well-known reinsurer Swiss Re has been around for over 150 years. Reinsurers have generally been profitable throughout history by selling insurance above fair value, building up retained earnings in low-loss years and holding a portfolio of largely unrelated risks in their books.

While the reinsurance risk premium is far from novel, the ability for most investors to access it is still in its infancy. Hedge funds have been dabbling in reinsurance for decades, in both dedicated reinsurance vehicles as well as sleeves within multi-strategy mandates. The availability of such funds has until recently been the exclusive domain of institutional investors. The emergence of the catastrophe bond market and the growth of alternative capital sources in the reinsurance industry has allowed innovative firms such as Stone Ridge Asset Management and Amundi Pioneer Asset Management to create 1940-Act registered investment funds that financial advisors can utilize in client portfolios. Non-accredited investors now have a relatively new way to invest in a very old way of making money.

Insurance-Linked Securities

In the aftermath of Hurricane Andrew in 1992, the reinsurance industry began to turn to third-party capital. The unexpectedly large losses from this hurricane led to increased demand for catastrophe protection. While Hannover Re developed the first catastrophe bond in 1994, many recognize 1997 as the beginning of the catastrophe bond market in earnest, with five such transactions that year.

The tumultuous hurricane season of 2005, which saw the devastating impacts of Hurricanes Katrina, Rita, and Wilma, led to over $120bn in insured losses. As one would expect, the demand for reinsurance capital skyrocketed. In the two years following Katrina, reinsurance premiums increased by a magnitude of 62%. The increase in the price of insurance following major events is what's referred to as a "hard market." It is imperative that reinsurance investors stick around to benefit from the higher premiums. Therefore, it is critical not only to stay in the trade after a bad stretch, but also to potentially rebalance to your strategic target or even lean into it by increasing your allocation.

Investors participate in catastrophe risk through transactions in insurance-linked securities (ILS). ILS differs from traditional reinsurance, which is maintained on the balance sheet of reinsurance companies. There are many different types of ILS, described in more detail in Table 6.1.

Table 6.1: Types of Insurance-Linked Securities

Format	Key Characteristics
Catastrophe (Cat) Bonds	• Precise level protection above certain trigger • Secondary market • Low frequency, high severity events • Multi-year terms
Quota Shares	• Investor shares in P&L of portion of a reinsurer's book • Highly diversified • Illiquid • Usually one-year term • More gradual loss curve
Collateralized Reinsurance	• Customizable across regions, perils, and risk layers • Usually one-year term • No secondary market • Exposure to insurer underwriting risk
Industry-Loss Warranties (ILWs)	• Customizable across regions, perils, and risk layers • Loss calculated by industry wide loss (not insurer specific) • Binary payout • Typically one-year or shorter-term

Source: Amundi Pioneer Asset Management.

We can witness the strong growth of the ILS market in Figure 6.4 from Cliffwater that divides the market between traditional reinsurance capital and ILS. The size of the ILS market has almost quadrupled over the past decade, reaching $92bn through the third quarter of 2020.

Figure 6.4: Growth of the ILS Market

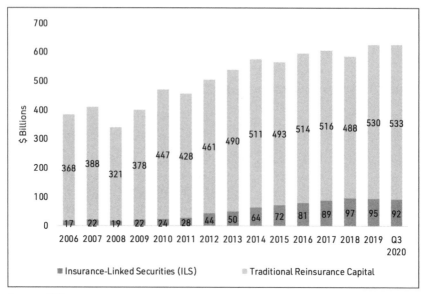

Source: Cliffwater.

For the remainder of this chapter, I will focus specifically on catastrophe bonds and quota shares.

Catastrophe Bonds

The most liquid types of insurance-linked securities are catastrophe bonds (Cat bonds). The market for Cat bonds has grown significantly over the last two decades and shows no signs of slowing down any time soon.

The Swiss Re Global Cat Bond Index is the reinsurance equivalent to the S&P 500 or Barclays Aggregate Bond Index in that it represents a market cap weighted index of all natural catastrophe bonds. The historical returns of Cat bonds, as measured by the Swiss Re Index, have rivaled those of equities and high-yield corporate bonds. Cat Bonds typically pay a fixed spread above a floating short-term rate, thus providing limited interest rate sensitivity. In addition, collateral is held separately in a trust and invested in short-dated Treasury paper, leaving Cat bonds with virtually no credit risk.

Figure 6.5 shows the calendar year returns of the Swiss Re Global Cat Bond Index going back to its inception in 2002.

Figure 6.5: Calendar Year Returns of Swiss Re Global Cat Bond Index (2002–2020)

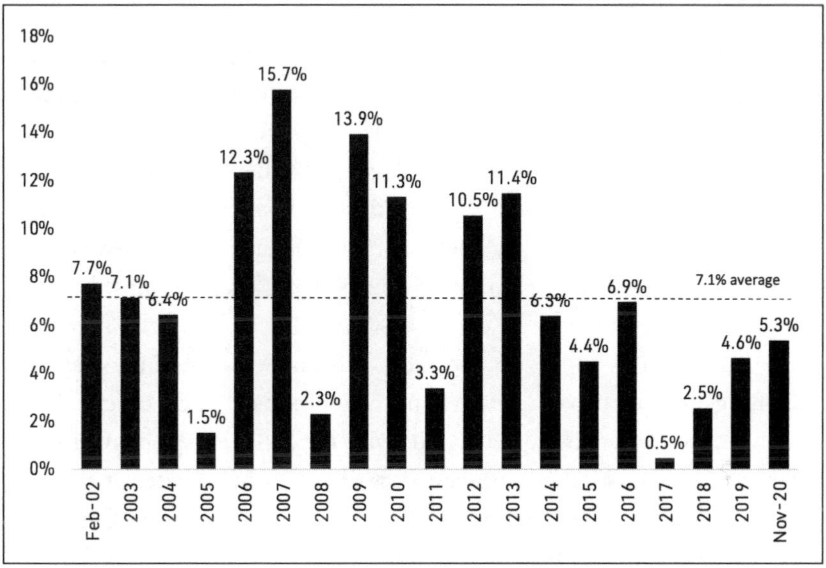

Source: Swiss Re.

Some investors might give pause to Cat bonds because they typically carry a non-investment grade rating from the major rating agencies, such as Moody's and S&P. Further, high-yield corporate bonds have become increasingly correlated with equities during periods of market stress. However, Cat Bonds, despite carrying an average credit rating of BB, have historically shown minimal correlation to equities, even during severe market declines. The non-investment grade ratings of Cat bonds have less to do with the creditworthiness of the issuer and more to do with the fact that these are risky securities and should be treated as such when it comes to the potential downside risks involved.

Quota Shares

Quota shares can be thought of as partnership transactions, in which the investor shares in the economics of the policies written by reinsurance companies. With quota share transactions, reinsurers typically retain the majority of the risks they underwrite, which aligns their interests with those of their capital partners.

Investors in diversified reinsurance funds that are invested heavily in quota shares are effectively taking a slice of the book of risks underwritten by many of the world's largest reinsurers, such as Swiss Re, Munich Re and TransRe. These contracts, generally one year in term, allow for pro-rata participation in the profits and losses of pools of reinsurance contracts. Expected returns from quota shares are generally higher than those of Cat bonds, since Cat bonds are further out of the money than quota shares. Quota shares also offer the potential for a more diversified set of risk exposures. Cat bonds tend to be concentrated in peak perils such as US hurricanes, whereas quota shares can provide greater exposure to non-peak perils and regions, as well as non-natural catastrophe risks.

While interval funds focused on reinsurance contain substantial weightings to quota shares, there is no commonly accepted index for this type of ILS like there is for Cat bonds with the Swiss Re Global Cat Bond Index. For that reason, any subsequent analysis in this chapter of the long-term risk and return characteristics of reinsurance will focus on Cat bonds, given the availability of meaningful index data.

Internal and External Diversification

Aside from the historically high returns of the asset class, one of the most attractive features of reinsurance is that it is one of the most naturally uncorrelated asset classes that exist. No one would argue that interest rate spikes or weakening economic conditions would trigger a hurricane or a wildfire. Conversely, even the most severe storms and disasters in history have not caused any meaningful financial market cataclysms. Table 6.2 shows a correlation matrix that demonstrates the very low correlations that Cat Bonds have had with traditional asset classes.

Table 6.2: Correlation Matrix of Catastrophe Bonds to Other Asset Classes (2002–2020)

	CAT Bonds	U.S. Equities	Commodities	U.S. IG Bonds	U.S. High Yield Bonds
Cat Bonds	**1.00**	0.00	0.02	0.01	0.02
U.S. Stocks	0.00	**1.00**	0.30	-0.28	0.34
Commodities	0.02	0.30	**1.00**	-0.11	0.27
U.S. IG Bonds	0.01	-0.28	-0.11	**1.00**	0.06
U.S. High Yield Bonds	0.02	0.34	0.27	0.06	**1.00**

Source: Morningstar Direct. Cat Bonds = Swiss Re Global Cat Bond Total Return index; US Stocks = S&P 500 Index; Commodities = Bloomberg Commodity Total Return Index; US IG Bonds = Bloomberg Barclays US Aggregate Bond Index; US High Yield Bonds = ICE BofA High Yield Index.

One of the other defining characteristics of ILS are the diversification benefits offered *within* the asset class in addition to those offered in contrast to other asset classes. While a global recession would likely cause stocks of all types to correct, different types of perils and those in different geographies have little to do with each other. In other words, a typhoon in Japan is not likely to cause an earthquake in California.

While past is not prologue, Cat bonds have performed as one would expect during the most severe equity contractions of the past 15 years. In Figure 6.6, we can see the disparity of returns between global stocks and reinsurance. In addition to the Swiss Re Global Cat Bond Index, we can see performance results for the EurekaHedge ILS advisors index, which is an equal-weighted index of 33 constituent ILS funds. Despite the chaos that ensued in equity markets during those periods, reinsurance returns were either up, flat or down slightly.

Figure 6.6: ILS Performance During Periods of Market Stress

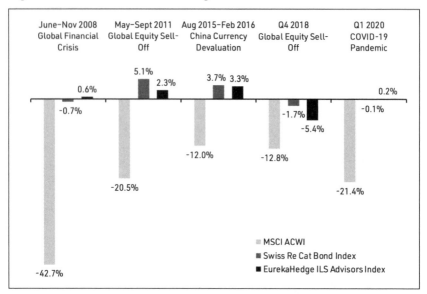

Source: Cliffwater.

Importantly, the drawdown of reinsurance during Q4 of 2018 was not because of stock market stress, but rather coincident timing of natural catastrophes—Japanese Typhoons, California Wildfires, and Hurricane Michael, the largest storm to hit Florida since 1992. For that reason, we must remember that reinsurance is a diversifier, not a hedge.

The uncorrelated nature of returns can work in reverse as well. The reinsurance industry experienced the three of the worst consecutive years for insured losses on record from 2017–2019. In conjunction, many ILS strategies suffered losses when stocks were posting positive returns.

Peril Regions

A prudent allocation to reinsurance involves broad diversification across geographies as well as peril types. Perils can be divided into natural catastrophe and non-natural catastrophe risks. Natural catastrophes can be further sub-divided into peak perils and non-peak perils.

Table 6.3: Sample List of Peril Region Exposures

Australia/ NZ	Europe	Asia/ Africa	Americas	Non-Natural Catastrophe	
AU Bushfire	EU Windstorm	Japan Windstorm	US Windstorm	Marine	
AU Windstorm	EU EQ	Japan EQ	US EQ	Aviation	
AU Hail	EU Flood	Turkey EQ	US Tornado	Political Risk	
AU EQ	UK Flood	Middle East EQ	Canada Windstorm	North Sea Energy	
NZ EQ	Germany Hail	SE Asia Windstorm	Canada EQ	Downstream Energy	Agriculture
NZ Windstorm		China EQ	Mexico Windstorm	Fine Art	Cyber
		South Africa EQ	Mexico EQ	Event Cancellation	Nuclear
		South Africa Hail	LatAm EQ	Excess Mortality	
		Algeria EQ	Caribbean EQ	Industrial Facilities	
			Caribbean Windstorm		

Source: Stone Ridge Asset Management.

Peak perils are considered to be US hurricane, US earthquake, European windstorm, Japan earthquake, Japan typhoon, and, after 2018, U.S. wildfire. Examples of non-peak perils are Caribbean hurricane and European flood. Cat bonds tend to be concentrated in peak perils, whereas quota share transactions can provide additional sources of diversification in risks such as agriculture, aviation, marine, cyber, event cancellation and terrorism.

Seasonality of Reinsurance

Relative to other asset classes, reinsurance exhibits a higher degree of seasonality. Wind-based catastrophes, such as U.S. hurricanes, European windstorms, and Japanese typhoons, are most frequent from June to

November. And while hurricane season technically begins in June, things tend to pick up in August.

Figure 6.7: Property Catastrophe Insurance Industry, Percentage of Annual Accrual

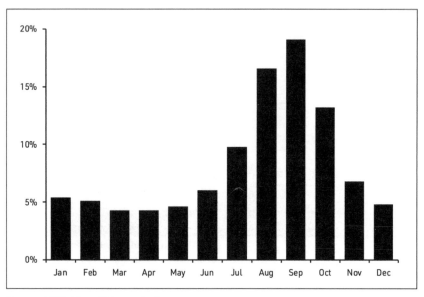

Source: RMS, Stone Ridge analysis.

Due to this dynamic, and the fact that wind-based perils represent the largest component of global catastrophe risk, more premiums tend to accrue during periods when risk is greater. History has shown that most of the returns for the Swiss Re Global Cat Bond index have come in the second half of the year. Understanding this is important in setting expectations around asset class performance.

A Stealth ESG Asset Class?

Reinsurance can bring tremendous benefits to a portfolio purely from a risk, return and diversification standpoint. But there is also a potential ancillary benefit that might be appealing to the more socially conscious investors. When there are losses to a diversified reinsurance portfolio, that capital goes towards supporting the rebuilding efforts that follow natural disasters.

While it's never fun to see your investment balance go down, the truth is that all asset classes with any risk involved are sure to experience periodic loss. If there's any solace to be had when reinsurance is experiencing an inevitable rough patch, it can come from knowing the value of pooled risk in helping people get back on their feet in the aftermath of perhaps the most devastating moment of their lives. Insurance—and by extension reinsurance—is the best defense we have against the types of risk that would wipe us out completely if not properly managed.

Climate Change and Reinsurance

It is a virtual certainty that the most common question allocators will receive from clients when introducing reinsurance will be, "but what about climate change?" The media does a questionable job in their coverage when linking catastrophes to climate change. Here are some important considerations to keep in mind when the subject comes up:

- **Investing in reinsurance is NOT the same as betting against climate change**. The anticipated effects of climate change are incorporated into reinsurance underwriting. Reinsurers have been adapting to changes and trends for hundreds of years.
- **The uncertainty of climate volatility and weather patterns are what drives premiums**. Climate change takes place over decades, while reinsurance premiums are updated annually. As more uncertainty is introduced, pricing should reflect it.
- **Reinsurers have as much incentive as anyone to understand climate change**. Hundreds of risk professionals and climate scientists are employed by reinsurers and catastrophe modeling firms. Catastrophe modelers use cutting edge science to build physical simulation models of natural catastrophes. The industry recently adapted to the rising risk of wildfires and now treat them as a peak peril, with correspondingly higher premiums.
- **Incentives drive better behavior**. Policyholders in high-risk areas can pay lower premiums by building more resilient structures. An example is homeowners in wildfire-prone sections of northern California constructing homes out of concrete instead of wood.

- **Recency bias is real**. The experience of the last few years may make it seem like a higher degree of large-scale disasters are a permanent fixture of society. The data shows no obvious long-term trend in the frequency or destructiveness of hurricanes and typhoons. The fear-mongering headlines we see today were present following Hurricanes Katrina, Dennis, Rita, and Wilma from 2005. A headline from *The Wall Street Journal* in 2006 read "Are Hurricanes Uninsurable?" The following eleven years didn't see a single major hurricane, leading to one of the most profitable decades on record for reinsurers.

Reinsurance in a Portfolio

Now that I have reviewed the history of reinsurance and the emergence of insurance-linked securities, it is time to examine the impact on a hypothetical allocation within the context of a diversified portfolio. First, let's review the asset class characteristics in isolation, using the Swiss Re Global Cat Bond Index as our proxy for reinsurance. This is shown in Table 6.4.

Table 6.4: Asset Class Characteristics of Reinsurance

2/1/2002–12/31/2020	Swiss Re Global Catastrophe Bond Index
Annualized Return	6.95%
Volatility	2.95%
Maximum Drawdown	-15.30%
Correlation to Global Stocks	0.37
Correlation to U.S. Bonds	0.12

Source: Author.

From the index inception in February 2002 through the end of 2020, reinsurance returned just under 7% annualized, with volatility of roughly 3%. The maximum drawdown for the index was just north of 15%. This happened in 2017 when Hurricane Irma was aimed at Miami-Dade County as a category 5 hurricane, before swerving 50 miles to the west and hitting the Everglades.

It should be noted that the low standard deviation masks the underlying risk of reinsurance. To be clear, underwriting reinsurance is not low risk—hence the historically large premium associated with it. The left-tail nature of the risk in reinsurance means that most of the time it will feel like a low-risk investment, punctuated by relatively rare periods where the true downside risk manifests itself. The last two years of unusually high insured damage from natural catastrophes highlight this important feature. That said, for over 15 years, neither stocks nor bonds came anywhere close to matching the risk-adjusted returns of reinsurance.

Now, we will look at the impact of adding a 20% allocation to reinsurance to a 60/40 portfolio, with the allocation coming pro-rata from the stock and bond slices, as shown in Table 6.5.

Table 6.5: Addition of Reinsurance to 60/40 Portfolio

2/1/2002–12/31/2020	60/40	60/40 + 20% ILS
Annualized Return	7.19%	7.22%
Volatility	9.36%	7.57%
Maximum Drawdown	-36.48%	-29.03%

Source: Author.

What we see is almost identical total returns, but with significantly lower risk for the portfolio including ILS. Both the volatility and maximum drawdown are materially less in the more diversified portfolio.

The case for reinsurance as a standalone investment is warranted, given its risk and return traits juxtaposed against traditional asset classes. It also helps that the story of the historical risk premium is highly intuitive. The validation for an allocation to reinsurance only grows stronger when considered within the context of a diversified portfolio.

An Allocation, Not a Trade

The diversification benefits that reinsurance can bring to a portfolio are about as compelling as they come. There are very few truly structurally uncorrelated asset classes in existence, and this unique risk premium is accessible to financial advisors and non-accredited investors via mutual funds and interval funds that vary in risk profiles.

Despite the last few years being challenging for reinsurance returns, many of the weak hands have folded and the elevated premiums that have resulted from sequential loss years are a net positive for future expected returns. While catastrophic risk can be modeled, it cannot be predicted. As such, this is an asset class designed to be a long-term strategic allocation and not one to market time.

THE ALLOCATOR'S CHEAT SHEET

- Despite its ubiquity and necessity, insurance from a buyer's perspective is a bad trade.
- Providers of risk transfer services have historically earned meaningfully positive return premiums that are also diversifying in relation to traditional investments.
- Insurance companies need insurance of their own at times, known as reinsurance. While the reinsurance risk premium is far from novel, the ability for most investors to access it is still in its infancy.
- One of the most attractive features of reinsurance is that it is one of the most naturally uncorrelated asset classes that exist.
- While there is a seasonality to reinsurance returns, it is not an asset class to try and market time.
- While climate change should not be ignored, it's important to remember that reinsurance investors are not betting against climate change.

CHAPTER 7
Keeping It Real—Cash Flow and
Inflation Protection from Essential Assets

"Buy land, they're not making it anymore."
— Mark Twain

"Infrastructure is much more important than architecture."
— Rem Koolhaas

G LOBAL EQUITY AND fixed income investors have been conditioned to expect high single digit returns for traditional balanced portfolios. As discussed in prior chapters, one variable that could knock those asset classes off their pedestal is the rising tide of inflation. By shifting some exposure into a diversified mix of real assets, allocators can address this risk.

We'll begin this chapter with an overview of the relationship between inflation and asset prices. Then, we will explore what investment consultant Callan Associates calls the "triple play" of real asset categories—infrastructure, farmland and timberland. These asset classes, once the exclusive domain of institutional investors, are now more accessible to individual investors. These asset classes can round out and complement an existing real estate allocation to create a more comprehensive real assets program. After reviewing each category, we will look at their risk and return traits, along with those of real estate, and how they compare to traditional assets.

Inflation and Asset Prices: It's Complicated

Predicting inflation surprises is tough sledding. There's a reason they call it unexpected inflation. Expected inflation is baked into market prices and is easily monitored. Research from FED confirms that inflation expectations are strongly correlated with prior inflation but have an almost nonexistent relationship with actual realized inflation. Specifically, they found that going back to 1981, there was a 0.69 R-squared between trailing inflation and inflation forecasts, but only a 0.13 R-squared between expected inflation and actual inflation. See Figure 7.1.

Figure 7.1: Predicting the Timing of Inflation

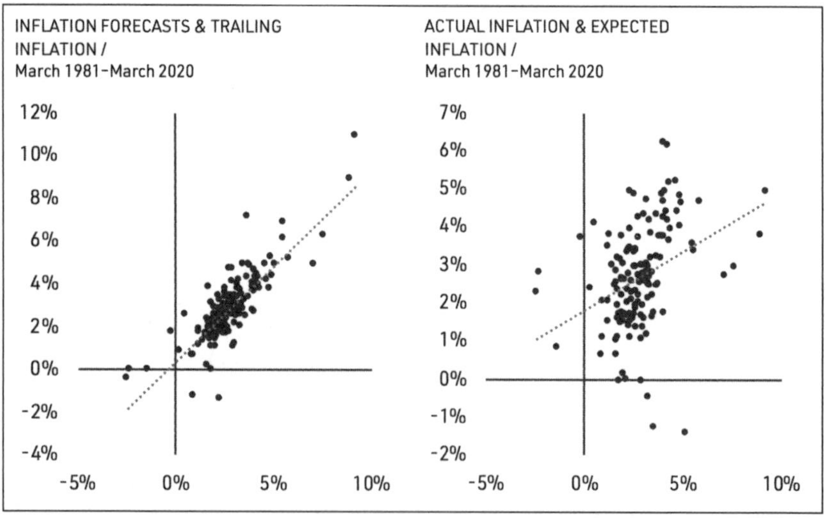

Source: Fund Evaluation Group, LLC.

Knowing the havoc that high or rising inflation can wreak on stocks and bonds, it is wise to consider ways to add inflation-sensitive components to a portfolio. The trouble is that there is no single asset class that perfectly hedges unexpected inflation (the only kind we should care about) while also delivering meaningful returns. Trade-offs must be made.

From examining the behavior of a variety of inflation-linked or related asset classes, we arrive at several observations. First, the relationship between asset classes and inflation is tenuous. Some assets work well in certain inflationary environments, but not so well in others. The starting level of inflation, and whether it is accelerating or decelerating, matters for results. See Figure 7.2.

Figure 7.2: How Asset Classes Behave in Different Inflationary Environments

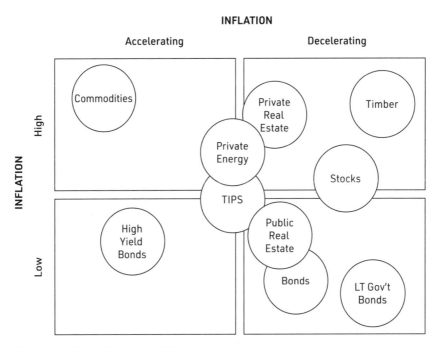

Source: Fund Evaluation Group, LLC.

While assets like TIPS, commodity futures and gold may have higher sensitivity to changes in inflation than other real asset classes, that protection comes at a cost in the form of lower expected returns. For example, both gold and commodity futures underperformed inflation over five-year periods roughly 40% of the time from 1973–2019. In the case of natural resource stocks, their higher sensitivity to inflation might be overwhelmed by their equity beta. It's also worth noting that market-duration TIPS can be as sensitive to changes in interest rates as they are to changes in inflation expectations. A solid rule of thumb is that the better the hedge, the greater the opportunity cost.

A well-rounded real assets allocation should do more than simply attempt to hedge against inflation—it should also bring multidimensional benefits to a long-term portfolio, such as low correlation, income generation and capital appreciation. A balance should also be struck between protection against short-term volatility in inflation and the ability to generate positive real returns over a long horizon.

Why Real Assets?

Real assets represent a broad universe of physical assets that have some tangible, intrinsic value that is not derived from a contractual claim on a stream of future cash flows. Individually, and collectively, they can provide several benefits when added to a traditional portfolio. According to some, the "real" in real assets stems from the Latin root *res*, or things. Others believe it's derived from the Latin word *rex*, meaning royal, as it was common for kings to own all the land in their kingdom.

Every day, our lives are dependent upon real assets and the essential roles they play in our economies and societies. By the time you arrive at work each morning, it is likely you have had several direct or indirect interactions with real assets. Let's look at the average Joe's morning routine:

- He wakes up in his home (timberland—hardwood).
- He puts on his clothes for the day (farmland—cotton).
- He has some eggs and fruit for breakfast (farmland—permanent crops).
- He gets in his car and takes the tollway to work (infrastructure—transport).
- He arrives at work. Before starting his day, he scrolls Twitter on his smartphone, which connects to a local wireless tower (infrastructure—communications).
- Finally, Joe sits down at his desk, and reviews a stack of papers (timberland—pulpwood).

I could go on and on, but you probably get the picture—real assets are of immeasurable value in modern society and impact our lives all day, every day. They have been a primary source of wealth and investment for ~5,000 years. Yet despite their ubiquity and tremendous size, most retail investors have little to no exposure to real assets in their portfolios.

The case for a strategic real assets allocation is strong, with several benefits on both a standalone basis and as complements to traditional assets. Among them:

- A source of portfolio diversification
- Durable income streams
- Capital appreciation potential
- Attractive risk-adjusted returns
- Inflation protection

While real estate has historically provided many of these attributes, those who were overly exposed in the GFC learned a valuable lesson in diversification. The real assets triple play of *infrastructure*, *farmland* and *timberland* is a means to build a complete allocation to income-producing, tangible assets with built-in inflation sensitivity and meaningful risk-reward characteristics. We will now review each of these three asset classes in detail.

Infrastructure

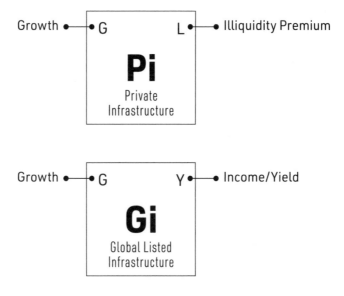

Infrastructure, according to Cliffwater, represents "the basic physical systems required to allow a business, community, or nation to function." The inflation-linked revenues, low operating costs, and high margins of infrastructure investments have drawn the attention of allocators.

The need for higher levels of infrastructure spending in developed and emerging markets alike is front and center. A study from McKinsey ("Bridging Global Infrastructure Gaps," June 2016) estimates that $3.3 trillion will need to be invested in infrastructure by 2030 to support the rate of economic growth. This spending may provide an attractive opportunity for patient investors.

The wake of the Global Financial Crisis brought a handful of key developments that shaped the trajectory of infrastructure investment. Many governments reduced infrastructure spending as a percent of GDP due to persistent fiscal pressures. Regulatory requirements forced banks to shore up their balance sheets and, as a result, curtail much of their financing activities in this space. Lastly, the low interest rate environment that defined the decade after the GFC spurred the search by many investors for alternative sources of yield.

With projects dependent upon the private sector for funding, infrastructure has emerged as a full-fledged, distinct asset class deemed worthy of investor attention. Once considered niche, infrastructure is now one of the leading areas in real assets from the perspective of fundraising and investor demand. That said, it is still early innings for individual investors as they continue to familiarize themselves with the attractive risk-adjusted return potential and diversification properties of infrastructure.

Defining the Infrastructure Universe

The universe of infrastructure investing is broad and deep. Far from a homogenous asset class, it offers a wide array of asset types across a spectrum of risk profiles. These long-lived and capital-intensive assets provide essential products and services to society. Table 7.1 summarizes the many categories and sectors within infrastructure, ranging from toll roads and airports, to wireless towers and wind farms.

Table 7.1: Types of Infrastructure Assets

Transport	Utilities	Communications	Renewable Power
Toll Roads	Electricity Transmission	Broadcast Towers	Hydroelectric Power
Airports	Gas Distribution	Wireless Towers	Wind
Seaports	Water Distribution	Satellite Networks	Solar
Railways	Wastewater Collection	Fiber/Wireline Networks	Geothermal

Source: Versus Capital.

Regardless of sector, the common shared attributes of most infrastructure investments are:

- High barriers to entry
- Relatively inelastic demand
- Resilience to economic cycles
- Long duration
- Relatively stable and predictable cash flows
- Positive correlation to inflation

Like the real estate risk spectrum, infrastructure investment styles can be bucketed as core, core plus, value-added, and opportunistic. There are some investments focused on equity, while others are focused on debt. Greenfield infrastructure refers to assets that still have some level of embedded development or construction risk. Brownfield, on the other hand, indicates established assets in need of operational improvements.

Table 7.2: The Risk/Return Scale for Infrastructure Assets

	Debt	Core	Core Plus	Value-Added	Opportunistic
Net return estimate	Typical 3–5% over a fixed frate such as LIBOR	5–7%	8–10%	10–12%	13%+
Asset	Asset-level loan Corporate-level debt	Stable asset	Existing asset	Enhancement of existing asset	Development of a new asset
Cash flow to investors	Interest payments	Regular distributions from operating cash flow	Semi-regular distributions from operating cash flow	Cash flow may be reinvested into the assets and not paid to investors until the enhancement is complete.	No cash flow during the development of the asset, which may take 3-10 years depending on the type of asset and complexity to develop.
Investment stage	Debt	Brownfield	Brownfield	Brownfield	Greenfield

Source: Callan.

The Building Blocks of Infrastructure Returns

The primary return driver of infrastructure investments is the free cash flow (FCF) yield generated by the underlying assets. Inflation escalators built onto long-term contracts are additive to returns as well, as are other organic growth and structural drivers. Lastly, the high quality and stable nature of most infrastructure assets allows for modest application of leverage to augment returns. Figure 7.3 shows the building blocks of infrastructure total returns.

Figure 7.3: Potential Infrastructure Total Return Profile Building Blocks

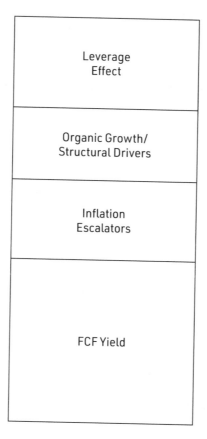

Source: Versus Capital.

Portfolio Benefits of Infrastructure

There are several characteristics that make infrastructure an attractive investment proposition and a valuable addition to a portfolio. Some of those factors are:

- Natural monopolies with high barriers to entry.
- Royalty streams tied to economic growth and inflation.
- Substantial income with predictable and stable cash flows.
- A lack of public funding and the emergence of privatization.

From a return standpoint, infrastructure has historically offered meaningful total returns, with low volatility relative to equities and a higher dividend yield. Analysis from Brookfield suggests that infrastructure can improve the risk-adjusted returns of a portfolio.

Figure 7.4: Historical Risk and Reward of Infrastructure

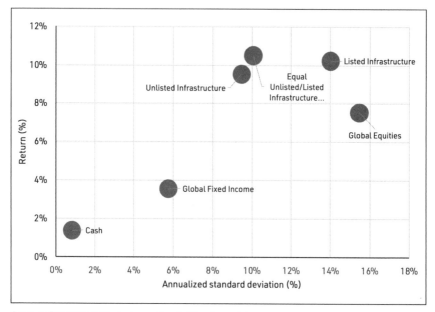

Source: Brookfield, Bloomberg, Cambridge Associates.

Performance results in public and private infrastructure have been remarkably similar over time. While the volatility of private infrastructure is naturally lower, the difference is negligible once it is unsmoothed to account for the lack of mark-to-market.

How to Access Infrastructure

The infancy of third-party capital investing in infrastructure can be traced back to the mid-1990s when the Australian government directed that the country's superannuation funds, or pension funds, allocate a portion of their assets to certain infrastructure assets of the country.

Today, infrastructure investment opportunities exist across the liquidity spectrum via public and private markets. Direct investment in infrastructure is inaccessible to most individual investors. Private fund structures, with long lock-up periods and high minimum investments, are geared towards large-scale institutional investors such as endowments or pension plans. That said, investors of all stripes have options when it comes to investing in infrastructure.

A variety of liquid mutual funds and ETFs are available to access the listed shares of infrastructure companies. They come in active and passive flavors, with the option to choose funds with either a global focus or a U.S./North America focused approach. While private infrastructure fundraising gets all the attention, investors shouldn't completely ignore public, listed infrastructure companies. Much like how public REITs can complement a private real estate allocation, global listed infrastructure (GLI) can do the same. Despite the higher equity market beta, GLI can offer cheaper access and better liquidity.

There are a handful of options for individual investors to access private infrastructure, directly or indirectly. For non-accredited investors, certain interval funds have a portion of their portfolio dedicated to private infrastructure equity and debt. Accredited investors and qualified purchasers may also be able to access dedicated private infrastructure funds via feeder funds available on alternative investment platforms like iCapital and CAIS. These private funds can be structured as either open-end or closed-end, although closed-end is more common.

Table 7.3 further compares the attributes of unlisted (private) and listed (public) infrastructure markets.

Table 7.3: Comparing Private and Public Infrastructure

	Unlisted (private markets)	Listed (public markets)
Investments	Typically asset-level investments, some corporate-level investments possible.	Publicly traded stocks of companies engaged in infrastructure-related activities.
Return type	Income and/or appreciation depending on the particular strategy.	Emphasis on appreciation.
Portfolio construction	Portfolios consist of large assets; can take months to source and structure deals and multiple years to deploy capital.	Portfolio can be constructed in relatively short time period via the public markets.
Vehicles	Commingled products are used by most investors; some very large investors (e.g., sovereign wealth funds) can invest directly into single assets.	Offered through commingled products or created for a single investor via separate account.
Volatility	Appraisal-based valuations dampen volatility.	Publicly traded securities are subject to equity volatility.
Weakness	Diversification can be challenging due to large asset sizes.	Shares volatility with equity markets.
Liquidity	Low; limited secondary market.	High; public markets provide liquidity.

Source: Callan.

A blend of private and public can result in a more balanced sector composition, with private leaning more heavily towards energy and renewables, and public having more exposure to transportation and utilities. The same can be said for geographic exposure.

Interest Rate Risk

The long duration nature of infrastructure projects might lead some investors to believe that the asset class would perform poorly during a period of rising interest rates. That may be true in some cases, but the evidence is mixed. The interest rate sensitivity of specific projects will ultimately depend on whether they were financed with fixed or floating rate debt and whether or not interest rate hedging programs were used to manage the risk.

Interest rate fluctuations affect both the discount rate applied and the cash flows generated from the assets. Certain infrastructure investment might benefit from rising rates, to the extent that higher rates are being driven by increasing inflation. The cash flows of many projects are linked to inflation escalators, allowing for higher costs to be passed through.

Farmland

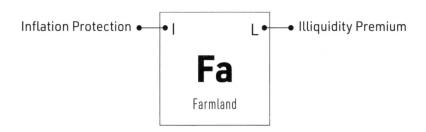

In thinking about farmland, we often envision a small, family-owned operation. And for good reason—most farmland in the United States is owned that way, often passed down or inherited over multiple generations. But we may be in the early innings of a paradigm shift in the ownership of farmland, which is increasingly gaining mainstream acceptance as an institutional asset class.

At about $3 trillion in aggregate value as of 2020, according to the USDA, farmland is a much larger asset class than most realize. It has been historically difficult to access directly, as markets are thin and the costs of acquisition, management, and disposition are high. The market for farmland is highly fragmented since institutional penetration has been slow-moving. As of 2021, the US Department of Agriculture estimated that institutional ownership represented just over 2% of the market.[18] Farmland is also an incredibly low turnover asset class, with less than 1% of U.S. farmland trading hands annually.

However, things may be changing. Thousands of farmers have been leaving the industry every year. Between 2008 and 2018, roughly 13,000 farmers left the industry due to a dearth of growth opportunities, a lack of

---

18 J. Evans, "Bill Gates' farmland buying spree highlights investment appeal," *Financial Times* (March 29, 2021).

profitability, and the absence of clear succession plans, among other reasons. The consolidation in the sector as of late has been driven by reduced farm income from the trend of disappointing commodity prices. Farmers with little to no profit margins to ride things out have been liquidating assets and selling/leasing their farmland to institutional investors. Today, a mere 13% of farming enterprises control 75% of farmed cropland in the U.S.[19]

Farmland can be broken down broadly into three categories: row crops, permanent crops, and livestock farming. For this chapter, we are focused on row and permanent crops. Row crops, such as wheat, are typically planted and harvested on an annual basis. Permanent crops, as the name implies, refers to assets like perennial trees, vines and shrubs that produce things like fruits and nuts, which are grown and harvested over a multi-year horizon. Permanent crops represented nearly 40% of the NCREIF Farmland Index as of 9/30/2020. Table 7.4 summarizes these types of farmland assets.

Table 7.4: Types of Farmland Assets

Row Crops		Permanent Crops	
Corn	Vegetables	Almonds	Wine Grapes
Soybeans	Wheat	Walnuts	Cranberries
Cotton	Potatoes	Pistachios	Macadamia Nuts
Rice		Apples	

Source: Versus Capital.

Farmland in a Portfolio

From an investment perspective, there's a lot to like about farmland. In addition to being resilient throughout the economic cycle, farmland has provided attractive long-term returns that have been diversifying to traditional assets like stocks and bonds. The pervasiveness of low interest rates on government bonds across the globe makes the yield on U.S. farmland attractive by comparison. According to NCREIF data, the yield on U.S. farmland in Q2 2019 was 4.39%.

---

19   J. Newman, "U.S. Farmers Vie for Land as a Grain Rally Sparks Shopping Spree," *The Wall Street Journal* (March 28, 2021).

Despite the significant yield advantage to bonds, farmland has experienced a similar level of volatility to that of 10-year U.S. Treasuries. The low return volatility historically experienced by farmland has been particularly advantageous during periods of financial and economic uncertainty. The durability and consistency of farmland returns throughout economic cycles reflects global population growth and the need for sustenance from a limited land resource base.

Relative to stocks, farmland (as measured by the NCREIF Farmland Index) outperformed the S&P 500 from 1995 through 2019. And it did so with lower volatility. See Table 7.5.

Table 7.5: Risk-Adjusted Performance of U.S. Farmland Relative to U.S. Equities (1995–2019)

	S&P 500	NCREIF Farmland Index
Average Annualized Returns	10.14%	11.51%
Standard Deviation	18.40%	7.08%
Sharpe Ratio	0.42	1.30

Source: S&P, NCREIF.

Farmland has also been quite resilient when equities have struggled, posting positive returns in 2000–2002, 2008, and 2018—all periods where equities declined. The NCREIF Farmland Index, which represents about $12 billion of professionally managed farmland assets, has had only one quarter of negative returns since 1999. The annual rental income from farmland is a fairly smooth contributor to total returns.

The Building Blocks of Farmland Returns

Income is the largest return component for farmland investors. This income can be variable, given the price volatility of the underlying commodities and their perishable nature. The appreciation of land value is the next largest contributor to asset returns. In short, there is less of it to go around—since 1950, U.S. farmland has dwindled by 25%.[20] Improvements

---

20 Newman, "U.S. Farmers Vie for Land," *The Wall Street Journal.*

in productivity can also be accretive to total returns. Figure 7.5 shows the return building blocks for farmland.

Figure 7.5: Potential Total Return Profile Building Blocks

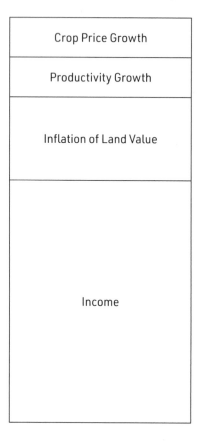

Source: Versus Capital.

Much of the investment thesis around farmland is related to supply and demand factors. The scarcity of arable land, coupled with population growth, an emerging middle class and the need for food security and animal protein, all give farmland unique properties as an investable asset class. In short, people need to eat.

Timberland

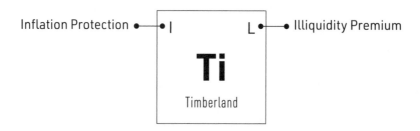

Timberland shares some common ground with farmland. Both are biological asset classes that involve the growing of living organisms. And both require a large amount of land. Some would even go so far as to say that timberland is just tree farming. While at the surface these two asset classes seem cut from the same cloth, closer examination will highlight the distinctiveness of timberland.

Without overstating the obvious, the output from timberland harvesting is wood. But the different tree types and end use cases for each of them is quite varied. Timberland can be broadly sorted into hardwoods and softwoods. Hardwoods are typically used for things like furniture and flooring. Softwoods are usually the source of lumber in construction. A more granular look at the various types of wood and their corresponding outputs is displayed in Table 7.6.

Table 7.6: Types of Timberland Assets

Pulpwood	Softwood	Commodity Hardwood	Precious Hardwood
Paper	Building Materials	Building Materials	Furniture
Packaging Materials			Remodeling

Source: Versus Capital.

As an investor in timberland, you are effectively purchasing commercial timberland plantations of various tree species. Managers operating timberland assets are usually structured as timberland investment management organizations (TIMOs). Outside of TIMOs, there are also a handful of Timber REITs that trade on public markets.

From a geographic standpoint, the U.S. is the most developed of global timberland markets. There are also considerable amounts of timberland activity in Australia, New Zealand, and South America.

The Building Blocks of Timberland Returns

Relative to farmland, income is a much smaller component of returns. Because trees don't have to be harvested at any given time, timberland managers have the optionality of being able to wait, factoring market conditions into their decisions while allowing volume growth to be stored *on the stump*. The biological growth of the trees over time is the largest single return source for the asset class, between 5–7% annually. And this tree growth has been uncorrelated to traditional assets. Typical rotation cycles range from 25–35 years, depending on the type of wood. The appreciation of land value and the income generated from tree harvesting round out the potential return drivers from timberland assets. Figure 7.6 shows the return building blocks for timberland.

Figure 7.6: Potential Total Return Profile Building Blocks

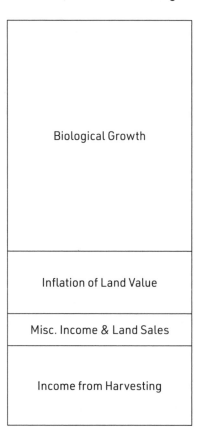

Source: Versus Capital.

One important note as it relates to biological tree growth is that the value of the tree per unit expands as they grow and move from pulp to soft to hardwood. A metric ton of pulp is worth less than a metric ton of hardwood. Because of this, the value of a tree grows geometrically over time.

Lastly, a growing source of revenue for timberland owners is the market for carbon offsets. In essence, large corporations seeking to reduce their carbon footprint will pay timberland owners not to cut down their trees. The longer the trees stand, the more carbon they remove from the atmosphere.

Timberland in a Portfolio

The recent returns of timberland haven't been anything to write home about, but the longer-term returns have nearly matched those of stocks, with significantly lower volatility. Timberland has outperformed U.S. bonds, and has demonstrated close to zero correlation with stocks and bonds. Table 7.7 shows the five-year, ten-year and 20-year returns, risk, and correlation of timberland with U.S. Stocks and Bonds.

Table 7.7: Historical Returns, Risk, and Correlation of Timberland with U.S. Stocks and Bonds

	NCREIF Timberland	S&P 500	Barclays U.S. Aggregate Bond Index
5-Year			
Annualized Return	3.1%	11.7%	3.0%
Standard Deviation	0.5%	5.5%	1.6%
Correlation to Timberland	-	-0.04	-0.31
10-Year			
Annualized Return	4.4%	13.6%	3.7%
Standard Deviation	1.5%	6.3%	1.5%
Correlation to Timberland	-	0.04	-0.14
20-Year			
Annualized Return	5.9%	6.1%	5.0%
Standard Deviation	2.4%	7.8%	1.7%
Correlation to Timberland	-	-0.06	0.03

Source: Meketa, NCREIF, and Bloomberg. Data as of 12/31/2019.

The recent decline in Timberland returns can be somewhat attributed to the influx of institutional demand for the asset class against a backdrop of fixed supply. Time will tell as to whether the reduced yields are a cyclical phenomenon or something more structural. Regardless, even with modestly lower returns the Timberland asset class may provide great diversification properties to traditional portfolios.

Implementation Challenges and Risks for Farmland and Timberland

While farmland and timberland are large asset classes in absolute terms, the underlying assets turn over so infrequently that it limits the amount of capital that can be invested into the asset class at certain times. This can potentially create delays for investors in achieving allocation targets. The universe of funds and managers in both asset classes is somewhat limited, but there is plenty of room to grow as these spaces become more institutionalized.

Both farmland and timberland are subject to changing climate and weather conditions. Fires, storms, droughts, flood, and extreme temperatures can lead to lower crop yields, crop failure and tree damage. Pests, weeds, and disease can also cause biological damage to farm and timber assets. Other common risk factors for both farmland and timberland are the underlying commodity prices, supply chain issues, and regulatory concerns such as tariffs, subsidies, and restrictions on exports and/or foreign ownership. Some risks can be mitigated at the asset level with insurance and investment in property improvements. At the portfolio level, geographic and crop/tree species diversification can go a long way.

Private Real Assets in a Portfolio

We can see from Table 7.8 that each real asset class has provided solid diversification benefits relative to stocks and bonds. Within real assets there are correlation benefits also, although real estate tends to be modestly correlated to infrastructure, while timberland and farmland tend to be somewhat correlated as well.

Table 7.8: Low Correlations Among Real Assets

	Real Estate	Infrastructure	Timberland	Farmland	Stocks	Bonds
Real Estate	**1.00**	0.55	0.23	0.12	0.19	-0.10
Infrastructure	0.55	**1.00**	0.17	0.08	0.64	0.37
Timberland	0.23	0.17	**1.00**	0.64	-0.11	0.07
Farmland	0.12	0.08	0.64	**1.00**	0.09	-0.15
Stocks	0.19	0.64	-0.11	0.09	**1.00**	0.23
Bonds	-0.10	0.37	0.07	-0.15	0.23	**1.00**

Source: Brookfield, NCREIF, Cambridge Associates, and Bloomberg as of 6/30/2016.

Figure 7.7 breaks down the historical total returns of each real asset class into capital appreciation and income components from 2006 through 2016. We can see that for each real asset, income has represented a substantial portion of total return, although it has been higher for real estate and farmland.

Figure 7.7: Ten-Year Capital Appreciation and Income Returns of Real Assets (2006–2016)

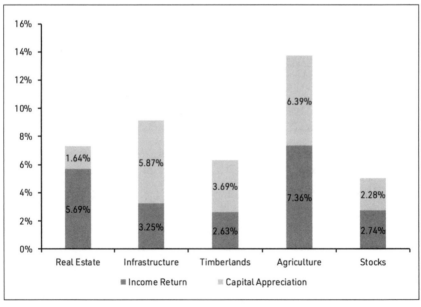

Source: Brookfield.

The total returns of real assets have been attractive on both an absolute and risk-adjusted basis, as depicted in Table 7.9. Private infrastructure and private farmland outperformed U.S. stocks over the period measured, while private real estate and private timberland lagged slightly behind U.S. stocks but outperformed U.S. bonds. It should be noted that all of the private real asset categories had higher Sharpe ratios than U.S. stocks and bonds, and significantly shallower max drawdowns than stocks.

Table 7.9: Performance Statistics of Real Assets (1/1/1992–9/30-2020)

	Annualized Return	Standard Deviation	Sharpe Ratio	Beta to 60/40	Max Drawdown
Private Real Estate Index	8.7%	4.1%	1.5	0.1	-24.1%
Private Infrastructure Index	12.5%	7.1%	1.4	0.0	-12.4%
Private Farmland Index	11.1%	6.1%	1.3	0.1	-0.1%
Private Timberland Index	7.7%	5.7%	0.9	0.0	-6.5%
U.S. Stocks	9.8%	16.2%	0.5	1.7	-45.8%
U.S. Bonds	5.5%	3.7%	0.8	0.0	-3.9%
Private Real Assets Index Blend	9.5%	3.1%	2.3	0.0	-9.9%
U.S. 60/40 Portfolio	8.3%	9.4%	0.6	1.0	-26.9%

Source: Versus Capital. Private real assets index blend represented by a 50% allocation to private real estate, and a 16.66% allocation each to private infrastructure, private timberland, and private farmland; private real estate represented by the NCREIF Property Index (NPI); private infrastructure represented by the JP Morgan OECD Core/Core+ Infrastructure; private timberland represented by the NCREIF Timberland Index; private farmland represented by the NCREIF Farmland Index.

While not perfect hedges for inflation, real assets have generally provided benefits during inflationary periods. All four categories of private real assets have seen strong 12-month returns when inflation has been greater than 2%. Private real estate and private timberland showed the most notable upticks in returns during higher inflationary periods, whereas private infrastructure and private farmland provided relatively high returns irrespective of the inflation rate over the 30-year period measured. In addition, farmland data from the 1970s shows that private farmland outperformed inflation by 11% annually during that inflationary decade, according to research from the TIAA Center for Farmland Research. The returns of various real assets in different inflationary environments are illustrated in Figure 7.8.

Figure 7.8: Average 12-Month Return when Inflation has been Above and Below 2%

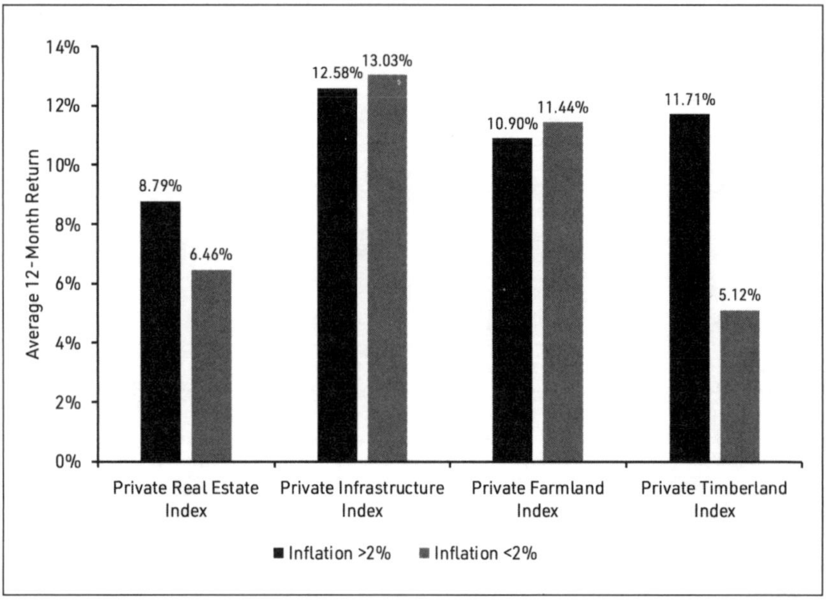

Source: Versus Capital.

Private real assets have also performed admirably during periods of rising interest rates, which is an acute concern today given the low yields across the globe, with only one direction to go. In the nine non-recessionary periods since 1990 where the 10-year Treasury yield has increased by 1% or more, private real assets have outperformed U.S. bonds anywhere from 10–166%, on average. This is illustrated in Figure 7.9.

Figure 7.9: Private Real Assets Return Premium over US Core Bonds during Rising 10-Year Treasury Yield Periods (1990–2020)

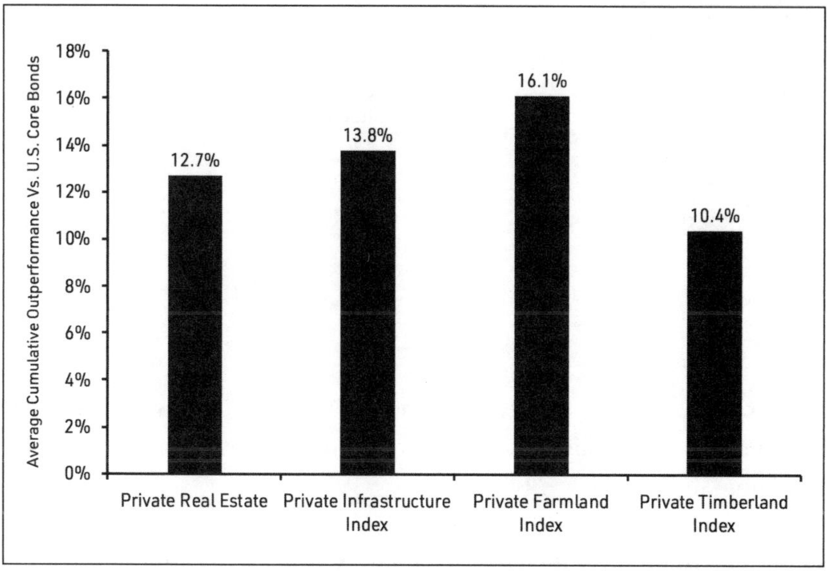

Source: Versus Capital.

We can also examine the impact of a 20% allocation to a diversified real assets mix when added to a 60/40 portfolio. To do so, I have constructed a backtested real asset mix that is divided into the following:

- 20% NCREIF Property Index
- 20% S&P Global REIT TR Index
- 20% DJ Brookfield Global Infrastructure Index
- 20% NCREIF Farmland Index
- 20% NCREIF Timberland Index

The results of the blend are shown in Table 7.10. Correlations are quarterly given the NCREIF reporting frequency.

Table 7.10: Asset Class Characteristics of Real Assets Blend

3/1/2003–12/31/2020	Real Assets Blend
Annualized Return	10.45%
Volatility	7.64%
Maximum Drawdown	-23.36%
Quarterly Correlation to Global Stocks	0.03
Quarterly Correlation to U.S. Bonds	0.12

Source: Author.

A 20% allocation to this real assets blend when added pro-rata to a 60/40 portfolio resulted in higher returns, roughly equal volatility, and a smaller maximum drawdown. See Table 7.11.

Table 7.11: Addition of Real Assets Blend to 60/40 Portfolio

3/1/2003–12/31/2020	60/40	60/40 + 20% Real Assets Blend
Annualized Return	8.09%	8.63%
Volatility	9.35%	9.30%
Maximum Drawdown	-36.48%	-33.55%

Source: Author.

Direct access to private infrastructure, farmland, and timberland funds is off limits for most individual investors due to hefty minimums and significant illiquidity. However, asset managers like Versus Capital and Principal have created interval funds that offer diversified, multi-manager access to these asset classes with greater liquidity, 1099 tax reporting, lower minimums, and no investor accreditation requirements. More information on the interval fund structure will be found in Chapter 10.

A Valuable Toolkit

With the benefit of hindsight, it is tempting to assume that high levels of inflation are a phenomenon of yesteryear. This would be a mistake. Inflation dynamics are inherently fickle and there will always be competing inflationary and deflationary trends. A failure to account for the risk of an extended period of accelerating inflation is something that most allocators to traditional stock-bond portfolios are guilty of today.

The case for a strategic allocation to a diversified mix of real assets is as strong as ever and the available toolkit is now better than ever. A critical function of an effective real asset allocation is that it cannot be contingent upon an inflation shock to make money. After all, if the negative effects to the portfolio during periods of low or falling inflation outweigh the potential benefits during times of high and/or rising inflation, it may all be for naught. Investors should therefore seek a mix of asset classes that have positive expected returns across *all* environments, but with an asymmetry that tilts the outcomes in their favor during the rare—but not necessarily unlikely—inflationary regimes.

Even if the inflation bogeyman remains subdued for the foreseeable future, there are still strong justifications to consider a material real asset allocation:

- Modest to low correlations to traditional asset classes.
- High and stable income as a source of return.
- An expanding opportunity set.
- Structural demand-drivers for essential assets across the globe, particularly in emerging markets.

Shocks to the system like the COVID-19 crisis are reminders of how diversified, long-lived assets such as farmland, timberland and infrastructure can provide resilience and low return variance to an investor's portfolio. Real assets can serve as a valuable tool to insulate a portion of a portfolio from exogenous economic and financial shocks, bringing more consistency to overall results.

THE ALLOCATOR'S CHEAT SHEET

- Stocks and bonds are vulnerable to high and rising inflation environments. Real assets represent an opportunity for diversification and inflation protection under such conditions.
- There are many trade-offs to consider when evaluating the inflation sensitivity of any asset class.
- Total return, income, and diversification properties should all be considered when designing a real assets allocation.
- Most real asset programs are concentrated in core real estate, TIPS, gold and/or commodities.
- While core real estate remains a valuable diversifier and strategic allocation, it can be improved upon through supplementary allocations to infrastructure, farmland, and timberland.
- Allocators have greater breadth in how they can access these asset classes across vehicle types, for both accredited and non-accredited investors.

CHAPTER 8

Extra Credit—Filling the Income Void with Non-Traditional Lending Strategies

> *"I'll gladly pay you Tuesday for a hamburger today."*
> — *J. Wellington Wimpy*

> *"More money has been lost reaching for yield than at the point of a gun."*
> — *Raymond DeVoe Jr.*

I N THIS CHAPTER, we uncover non-traditional credit and lending strategies as a means to supplement core bond portfolios that are at risk of falling short of aggregate investor demand for sustainable income.

With the regulatory environment causing banks to scale back in their lending activity, non-bank lenders and asset managers have largely stepped in to fill the gaps. Many of them, through technological and financial innovation, are expanding the credit opportunity set across a host of new borrower types and verticals. These forms of extra, or alternative, credit are in some cases less tethered to the overall economic and market cycle and are more diversifying than traditional credit sectors. We will navigate this growing opportunity set, and its implications for allocators, throughout this chapter.

The Trouble with Traditional Credit

When most people think of investing in credit, they think of publicly traded fixed income sectors like high-yield bonds (corporate credit), non-agency mortgage-backed securities (securitized credit), or emerging market debt (sovereign credit). These forms of credit can still play a role in a portfolio, but given the low-yield environment they do not presently offer the greatest risk-reward trade-off.

The seemingly never-ending decline in interest rates has driven the compensation for bearing traditional credit risk down to razor-thin levels that leave investors in the unenvious position of minimal upside against asymmetric downside. As *The Wall Street Journal's* Jason Zweig writes, "investing for income in today's markets is like slogging across the Sahara looking for a cold drink." The dearth of yield globally is problematic for income-oriented investors looking for relatively safe assets producing steady cash flow. To put things in perspective, as of July 2020:

- 85% of global fixed income assets yielded less than 2%.
- 25% had negative yields.
- Only 1% yielded over 4%.

This represents a significant problem when you consider what fixed income investors have grown accustomed to over time. Just ten years ago, when the first baby boomers retired, investors could obtain 3–5% yields across Treasuries and AAA corporate bonds.

Figure 8.1: Yields When the First Boomer Retired in 2010 vs. Yields in 2020

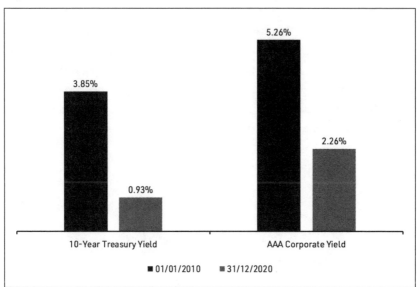

Source: FRED.

Making matters worse, the interest rate dynamics present globally have incentivized corporate CFOs to (rationally) engorge themselves in a borrowing binge to lock in lower rates for longer periods of time. This has deteriorated the credit quality within the investment grade market, with BBB bonds now representing the largest segment.

Corporate credit in public markets—both investment-grade (IG) and high-yield (HY)—is priced at levels that do not seem to compensate for the underlying risks. For investors seeking durable income, traditional allocations to public corporate debt are likely not the best answer in this low-yield environment. In addition to lower yields, correlations to equities of both IG and HY credit have risen in recent years. Allocators must begin to think differently in their approach to filling the income void, while simultaneously keeping an eye on risk and obtaining meaningful diversification.

What is Alternative Credit?

The universe of credit investments extends well beyond that of investment-grade and high-yield corporate bonds, and publicly traded securitized credit. A rich opportunity set exists across a spectrum of different categories with varying risk/reward profiles, spanning both public and private markets. The non-exhaustive spectrum from PIMCO in Figure 8.2 provides a sense of just how broad the scope of credit is.

Figure 8.2: Spectrum of Public and Private Credit

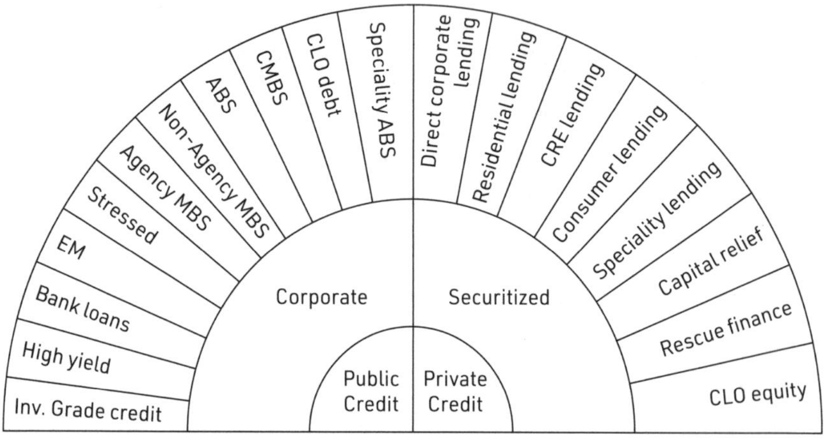

Source: Used with permission from Pacific Investment Management Company, LLC. For illustrative purposes only

Alternative credit can be broadly defined as either less-trafficked areas of traded credit markets or private credit strategies where debt is financed by non-bank lenders targeting high yielding corporate, asset-based, or other financial assets. For allocators with the flexibility to step outside of traditional credit markets, alternative credit can offer investors several portfolio benefits. These include:

- **Higher return potential**: illiquidity, complexity and uncertainty are more pronounced in private markets and investors should require a higher hurdle as compensation for those variables.

- **Durable cash flows**: high yields supported by cash flows and/or assets with strong underlying fundamentals.
- **Stable performance**: Less vulnerable to panic selling—lack of daily mark-to-market helps protect against sentiment-related flows during periods of stress.
- **Diversification**: less correlation to equity markets and macro factors than publicly traded credit.
- **Low duration**: minimal exposure to interest-rate risk due to the floating rate nature of most private credit deals.

Despite its potential benefits, alternative credit is not without risks. The primary risks with this asset class are:

- **Liquidity risk**: investors seeking to sell or redeem may receive an adverse price or not be able to liquidate their position in a timely manner.
- **Default/credit risk**: possibility of loss arising from borrower's failure to meet their principal and/or interest payment obligations.
- **Idiosyncratic risk**: diversification can be a double-edged sword. While some alternative credit sectors may be less correlated to traditional markets, they do come with their own unique risk factors.

Sacrificing liquidity might be challenging or new to some investors, but with a long enough time horizon there can be real benefits. As alluded to earlier, an attractive feature of alternative credit is the return premium it can exhibit compared to traditional credit. Research from Cliffwater supports the expectation of an additional 2–4% from private credit relative to liquid credit. This excess return can be decomposed into three underlying return drivers:

- **Illiquidity**: lack of trading and longer lockup of capital.
- **Complexity**: additional negotiating, structuring, and underwriting relative to public deals.
- **Uncertainty**: more opaque markets; information not as widely available.

Figure 8.3: Deconstructing the Private Credit Premium Over Traditional Credit

Source: BlackRock.

The Growth of Alternative Credit

The past two decades gave witness to a transformation in the composition of credit markets. Banks and other financial institutions curtailed their lending activities in the face of more onerous regulations designed to rein in risk and shore up balance sheets. Meanwhile, private credit grew by leaps and bounds. According to Preqin, the amount of assets managed by private debt funds has grown more than 2.5x since 2010. It's estimated that private credit represents roughly 17% of outstanding credit as of 2021 and that it has grown roughly twice the rate of public credit since 2000, according to Bank of America Merrill Lynch.[21] Figure 8.4 shows the growth in private debt assets under management.

21 C. Beard, "How the Pandemic Affected Private Credit, and What's Next," Callan (February 24, 2021).

Figure 8.4: Private Debt Assets Under Management (2000–2020)

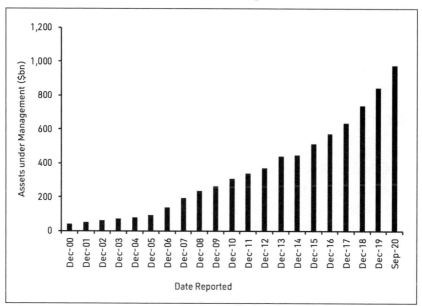

Source: Preqin.

When one door closes, another often opens. In this case, non-bank lenders and asset managers kicked the door open and stepped in to fill the void left by banks. Over the last 25 years, banks' share of U.S. middle-market lending has declined from 70% to 10%. While private credit assets have ballooned, there is still substantial room to run still given the continued supply-demand imbalance in credit markets.

While the emergence of private credit has its roots in corporate lending, it has migrated to other areas of the credit markets as well. Today's non-bank lenders are highly sophisticated with impressive underwriting capabilities. Many of them have expanded their creative financing solutions to other specialized lending activities outside the corporate realm. This has included areas like consumer lending, real estate/real asset lending, structured finance, receivables and equipment leasing, and others. Ares Capital describes the evolution of alternative credit in terms of *gaps* and *boxes*: filling gaps where overlooked or misunderstood sectors are experiencing a supply/demand mismatch; and working outside the box that traditional Wall Street likes to place borrowers neatly into for scale and efficiency.

The democratization of alternative credit markets taking place today benefits allocators as it unlocks previously difficult to access asset classes. Advisors who can source and diligence managers with deep experience and domain expertise in these specialized lending verticals have an opportunity to address the income conundrum that so many investors are wrestling with.

The Universe of Alternative Credit

This should come as no surprise, but there is no universally agreed upon taxonomy of the sub-categories and constituents within alternative credit. I have given it my best shot in Figure 8.5, but given the degree of overlap across certain strategies and the evolving and complex nature of this growing asset class, it remains a work in progress.

Figure 8.5: Taxonomy of Alternative Credit

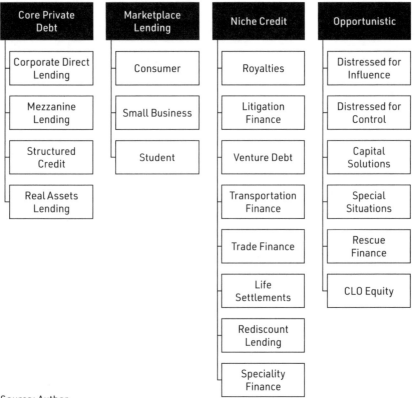

Source: Author.

It should be noted that this chapter won't cover much related to opportunistic/distressed credit. The reasons are twofold. First, there aren't many ways to access this category outside of private, drawdown fund structures which limits the potential audience. Second, these strategies are often found inside the private equity bucket of institutional allocations given their high expected upside and the significant portion of returns expected to come from price appreciation rather than income.

Where allocators land within this broad spectrum of alternative credit strategies will largely depend upon their objectives as each segment varies significantly in its ability to preserve capital, generate yield, offer diversification and benefit from price appreciation.

While there are many avenues to peruse within alternative credit, this chapter will focus on three areas that are accessible by financial advisors today and deemed worthy of more immediate consideration: *corporate direct lending, marketplace lending,* and *niche credit.*

Corporate Direct Lending

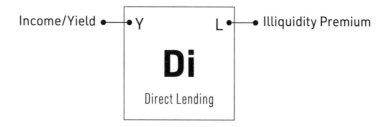

Corporate direct lending is generally considered to be loans made by non-bank lenders to privately-owned, middle-market ($10–$100m of EBITDA) companies with an established market presence, customer base and cash flows. It's estimated that there are roughly 200,000 middle-market companies in the U.S. These corporations represent about one-third of private sector GDP, generate approximately $6 trillion in revenue, and employ nearly 50m people. While not exclusively, these firms are often backed by private equity sponsors. Middle-market companies often lack the access to traditional sources of debt financing like bank loans and syndicated debt due to their size or lack of coverage by ratings agencies.

Relative to broadly syndicated loans, middle market loans tend to be structured more conservatively—with stronger covenants, lower leverage multiples and higher interest coverage. Some additional characteristics of these types of loans are:

- Typically held to maturity instead of being traded. All else equal, you tend to do better when you intentionally hold to maturity.
- Often floating rate in nature, with average effective lives ranging from three to five years, interest rate sensitivity is removed from the equation, resulting in a pure play on credit.
- While there are varying levels of seniority in the underlying loans, most managers focus on senior secured debt.
- Loan-to-value (LTV) ratios are usually in the 45–70% range.
- Presence of covenant-light terms less prevalent than in broadly syndicated loan markets.

The growth and maturation of corporate direct lending over the last two decades has been remarkable as institutional investors embraced the asset class as an alternative to bank financing. And with risk-taking by banks unlikely to reach pre-GFC levels, middle-market borrowers seem comfortable with the speed, flexibility, reliability and alignment of interests offered by non-bank lenders.

In terms of historical performance tracking, risk measurement, and benchmarking, the Cliffwater Direct Lending Index (CDLI) has emerged as the dominant index for this asset class. Since its inception, the CDLI has generated returns of over 9% with volatility of 3.6%. Meanwhile, its beta to stocks has been negligible and it has exhibited no meaningful correlation to interest rates. The maximum drawdowns during the GFC and the COVID-19 crises were roughly 8% and 5%, respectively. The max drawdown and recovery time for various asset classes, including the CDLI Index for comparison, are shown in Table 8.1.

Table 8.1: Max Drawdown and Recovery for Various Asset Classes (September–March 2011)

Asset Class	Maximum Drawdown (%)	# Quarters to Full Recovery
Bloomberg Barclays U.S. Aggregate Bond Index	N/A	N/A
Swiss Re Global Cat Bond Index	N/A	N/A
Cliffwater Direct Lending Index	-8	4
HFRI Fund Weighted Index	-19	7
NCREIF Property Index (Real Estate)	-24	12
Cambridge Private Equity Universe	-25	9
Bloomberg Barclays High Yield Bond Index	-27	8
S&P/LSTA U.S. Leveraged Loan	-30	8
Russell 3000 Index	-46	18

Source: Cliffwater, "US Direct Lending: Comparative Performance Through the Financial Crisis" (July 30, 2019).

Corporate direct lending has also experienced lower realized losses than publicly traded high yield bonds and senior bank loans. This is illustrated in Figure 8.6.

Figure 8.6: Average Realized Loss Rates (2005–2020)

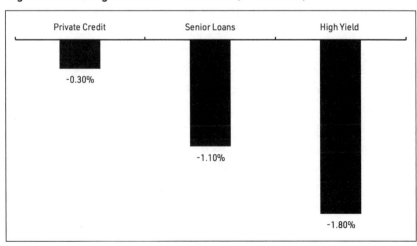

Source: Cliffwater, JPM Default Monitor. As of 6/30/2020.

While corporate direct lending is by no means without risk, allocators can manage risk through:

- **Focus on seniority**: while these loans have lower yields, they also carry lower risk of loss, lower volatility, and lower market beta.
- **Diversification**: the risk of loss can be reduced with broad diversification across borrowers, sectors, size, and style.
- **Fee conscious**: certain multi-manager vehicles can negotiate low-cost SMAs, while also participating in co-investments and secondaries as appropriate.

Marketplace Lending

Formerly known as peer-to-peer lending, marketplace lending refers to the financing of consumer, small business and student loans originated by technology-enabled online lenders. The peer-to-peer term is a nod to the original premise of these marketplace platforms—serving as matchmakers between individuals seeking a loan and others looking to fund them and earn a decent return on their investment. As the sector has grown, larger pools of investor capital followed and today institutions, hedge funds, and other opportunistic investors dominate the funding of loans.

The widening gap between the interest received in a bank savings account and the interest rate charged by credit card companies is what prompted finance and technology entrepreneurs to address this issue by creating a better experience for borrowers and lenders. Marketplace lenders have become a significant presence in the market for small business owners and consumers, with prominent names like LendingClub, SoFi and Square gaining traction. These platforms use technology to underwrite more efficiently and lend to borrowers that were underserved by banks.

With gross yields of about 12–15%, it's important for investors to recognize and account for the inevitable credit losses and platform fees that are part and parcel of this asset class. This should allow for more reasonable expectations around net performance, likely in the mid-to-high single digit range. Expected returns from Cliffwater are for 6% net, as shown in Table 8.2.

Table 8.2: Expected Returns for Marketplace Lending

	Returns (%)
Gross Unlevered Yield (including OID)	13.00
minus Servicing Costs	(1.00)
Unlevered Yield	12.00
minus Unrealized & Realized Losses	(5.00)
Unlevered Yield net of Credit Losses	7.00
plus Yield from Leverage minus Interest Expense	1.00
Net Yield before Fees	8.00
minus investment Fees (on Net Assets)	(1.50)
minus Fund Administrative Expenses	(0.50)
Net NAV Yield (after all fees, credit losses, leverage)	6.00

Source: Cliffwater.

While there is no widely used commercial index to track marketplace lending, there are a handful of private funds and closed-end interval funds that allocate exclusively to the category. The largest player by far is the Stone Ridge Alternative Lending Risk Premium Fund (LENDX) that has been around since June of 2016. From inception through 11/30/2020, the fund—which purchases loans across 15 platforms spanning consumer, small business, and student loans—has delivered:

- **Attractive returns**: annualized inception-to-date returns of 7.6%.[22]
- **Low volatility**: a standard deviation of 3.9% and only two down months in over four years.

---

22 As a result of economic incentives received from platforms that may not be repeated, early LENDX performance was unusually strong for the period shown, and should not be extrapolated to future periods. Q4 2020 LENDX performance was unusually strong as a result of equity returns relating to platform IPOs and should not be extrapolated to future periods.

- **Low correlation**: near-zero correlation to stocks and bonds since inception.
- **Low duration**: an average duration of 1.1 years for loans in the portfolio.

Due to the economic sensitivity of consumer and small business credit, risk management and an emphasis on quality are paramount. Firms like Stone Ridge focus only on prime and super prime borrowers and have a high bar of due diligence to approve a platform's loans for purchase in their funds. Deep relationships with the various lending platforms is critical to execute with best-in-class terms and fees. Online lenders value the long-term capital that strategic investors in the asset class bring to the table.

The disruption of traditional banking by marketplace lending platforms has enabled more access and lower rates for consumers relative to credit cards, while also providing meaningful risk-adjusted returns to investors. While the spillover effects from the COVID-19 crisis are still unfolding, the resilience shown by the top-tier segments of borrowers on the highest-quality platforms should provide confidence that the asset class is here to stay. What started as peer-to-peer has matured into an institutional grade asset class. In a slight twist of irony, LendingClub went so far as to sunset the ability for retail investors to fund loans on their platform in late 2020.

Niche Credit

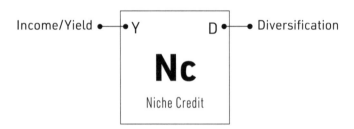

Whereas corporate direct lending and marketplace lending have become more mainstream, there are a wide array of specialized and niche credit strategies that exist outside the purview of most allocators. For those wishing to push the frontiers of credit and income-oriented investing, there are private funds and interval funds that invest in these areas.

What exactly makes an investment niche? According to alternative asset manager Variant Investments, which operates a credit interval fund dedicated to unique and uncorrelated income opportunities, common attributes of niche asset classes include:

- **Hard-work investments**: assets that are difficult to source, with a heavy amount of due diligence, complex structures, and challenging execution.
- **Unique beta**: Low correlation to traditional markets with a structural and explainable source of return that is idiosyncratic in nature.
- **Uncrowded markets**: Areas with high barriers to entry and limited public access that are underserved by banks and too early to have gained broad institutional acceptance. The limited Total Addressable Market (TAM) of many niche credit categories means that fewer people are willing to spend the time underwriting their complexity.
- **Bond-like**: Contractually obligated cash flows that accrue over time and deliver a high batting average of positive returns.
- **Mitigated risk**: Senior secured assets with short durations and limited downside.

Another way to think about niche credit relative to something like corporate direct lending is its focus on asset-based lending, i.e. private lending secured by assets (or a stream of cash flows) that do not require taking a point-of-view on the solvency of a business.

While there are plentiful nooks and crannies to explore within niche credit, I will highlight two specifically: *litigation finance* and *intellectual property royalties*.

Litigation Finance

Litigation finance is an emerging segment of lending that provides working capital to entities involved in costly litigation activities. The investment returns on these generally non-recourse loans are predicated on the outcomes of specific legal cases (or portfolios of cases). Firms that specialize in litigation finance provide capital to borrowers—usually law firms or corporate plaintiffs/defendants—that helps cover attorney's fees (in the case of corporate borrowers) and business expenses (in the case of law firm borrowers.)

Borrowers typically tap litigation finance specialists for the following needs:

- Funding to pursue litigation that they can't get from banks.
- Working capital to pursue other projects.
- To share the risk connected to uncertain legal outcomes.

Legal cases can be incredibly costly and lengthy before they are resolved, which creates potential cash flow challenges for law firms. By bearing some of the operational risk tied to contingencies or settlements and providing a service that can reduce cash flow sensitivity for borrowers, litigation finance managers expect to earn a meaningful return on their capital.

Today, commercial litigation is more common than personal litigation, as commercial cases are larger and easier to invest the time in underwriting. Personal litigation is still underwritten on a more binary, one-size-fits-all basis.

Currently, there are maybe a few dozen firms that manage private funds dedicated to the asset class. The barriers to entry are high given the dual expertise required on both the legal and debt structuring sides. Funds in the category are usually structured like typical private equity/credit funds, with a two- to three-year investment period and a four- to six-year fund term after that. These funds will typically diversify across counterparty, industry, claim type, and geography to mitigate risk.

Intellectual Property Royalties

As the name implies, royalty investing involves financing future royalty streams that are generated by intellectual property (IP). Owners of IP rightfully seek to capture the economic rents associated with the value created by their ideas, inventions, or processes. Patents are a way to monetize IP through royalty payments as companies license related products and services. IP owners may then choose to sell those royalty streams should they decide they want or need capital to develop new products and services, fund growth expenditures, or pay expenses.

Most royalty strategies are focused in one of these two areas:

1. Healthcare and pharmaceuticals.
2. Media and entertainment.

Regardless of their sector, royalties are attractive through their minimal exposure to the movements of public markets, relative resilience to the ebbs and flows of the economic cycle, and their ability to provide high current income.

Healthcare and pharmaceutical royalties capture the cash flows from the sales of pharmaceutical drugs, medical devices, and other healthcare products. With an aging U.S. population and an accelerating pace of innovation in healthcare creating a growing need for capital from pharmaceutical firms, the opportunity set is large. Marathon Asset Management estimates there to be roughly $25bn of potential deal flow in the asset class per year.

Whereas sellers of healthcare royalties are universities, hospitals, and life science companies, *media and entertainment royalties* are typically acquired from talent agencies, production companies, and artists and their estates. In 1997, legendary musician David Bowie became the first artist to securitize his song royalties, packaging them into so-called Bowie Bonds. Fast forward to 2020, and multi-platinum producer, artist and DJ Calvin Harris was rumored to sell his song catalog to Vine Alternative Investments for upwards of $100m. The current boom in media streaming services through the likes Spotify, Netflix and YouTube has led to a surge in demand for content and created more opportunities for royalty streams.

Royalty monetization strategies require both legal expertise in deal structuring as well as domain expertise within the respective verticals. There is limited competition and high barriers to entry in these asset classes, leaving plenty of runway for additional opportunity. Royalty investments can provide idiosyncratic return streams with compelling risk-reward characteristics, making them an excellent diversifier.

Other types of niche credit

Additional niche credit sectors include:

- **Transportation finance**: Equity and debt investments in aviation, shipping, rail, containers, and other transportation sectors.
- **Trade finance**: Financing the acquisition and transportation of goods from buyer to end seller.
- **Life settlements**: Secondary market purchases of existing life insurance contracts at a discount to the face value of the policy.

- **Venture debt**: Non-dilutive financing provided to VC-backed companies to fund working capital and other expenses.

Clearly, there is no shortage of interesting ideas within these esoteric and growing areas of private credit markets. Though a bit further out on the risk spectrum than corporate direct lending, there is the potential for higher returns as well as lower correlation to financial markets. A varied portfolio of niche credit strategies can serve as a valuable diversifier with a high degree of cash flow.

Allocating to Alternative Credit

The ubiquity of credit is obvious. Governments borrow to finance spending. Corporations borrow to invest and grow their businesses. And individuals tap credit markets to buy homes, start new ventures, purchase goods and services, and improve their skills. Despite credit's familiarity and intuitiveness, few treat it as a distinct allocation within a portfolio. Some describe credit as equities in bond's clothing. And while equity correlations of credit are higher than those of government bonds, that alone is not enough to dismiss it entirely.

Despite being one of the oldest ways to make a buck known to man, credit has also been the source of error for many investors. This often stems from a blind eye to risk management in the pursuit of attractive yields. What separates credit from equities is that credit investors are rewarded for avoiding risk, not taking it. Not avoiding all risk in the literal sense, but by steering clear of unrewarded risks and demanding sufficient returns and protections to compensate for the risks chosen.

Amid the increasingly varied range of opportunities (and opinions) within credit, Cliffwater conducted a study on the credit premium to determine whether it warranted treatment as a distinct asset class in a portfolio. They found that "credit risk provides investors a significant positive excess return over time that has a low correlation to interest rate and equity excess returns, and therefore should be treated as a separate asset class for asset allocation purposes."

With many ways to access credit markets, today's allocators must first discern what they are attempting to accomplish with this sleeve of a portfolio. What is clear is that alternative credit is not a one-for-one trade-off with core bonds. The higher expected returns, additional diversification potential, and reduced liquidity are not without cost and any allocation should at least be partially sourced from the *risky* portion of the portfolio.

Higher yields and total returns would not exist if trade-offs and risks were not involved. And while investors can get in trouble blindly chasing what Verdad Capital calls "fool's yield," they can also augment existing portfolios through the addition of an alternative credit allocation if they are mindful of the risks and can take measures to manage the downside.

There is no one-size-fits-all allocation appropriate for all investors in alternative credit. Given the breadth of strategies offered within alternative credit, they can reside in different parts of investor portfolios. Strategies like corporate direct lending, with more of a capital preservation focus, might easily act as a replacement for traditional corporate credit within the fixed income allocation. Niche credit, on the other hand, might slot better as an uncorrelated alternative given its orientation towards corners of the credit markets with less economic and market sensitivity. Marketplace lending might fit somewhere in between.

Alternative Credit in a Portfolio

While we lack appropriate benchmark index data representative of marketplace lending and niche credit, we can use the CDLI Index to look back at the impact an allocation to middle market direct lending would have had on a 60/40 portfolio. Table 8.3 provides the characteristics of the index on a standalone basis.

Table 8.3: Asset Class Characteristics of CDLI Index

10/1/2004–12/31/2020	Cliffwater Direct Lending Index (CDLI)
Annualized Return	9.29%
Volatility	5.23%
Maximum Drawdown	-7.73%
Correlation to Global Stocks	0.65
Correlation to U.S. Bonds	-0.07

Source: Author.

If we were to allocate 20% of a 60/40 portfolio to CDLI, taking pro-rata from the stock and bond allocation, it would have resulted in higher returns, lower volatility, and a smaller maximum drawdown over the full period. See Table 8.4.

Table 8.4: Addition of CDLI Index to 60/40 Portfolio

10/1/2004–12/31/2020	60/40	60/40 + 20% CDLI
Annualized Return	7.18%	7.66%
Volatility	9.53%	7.96%
Maximum Drawdown	-36.48%	-30.64%

Source: Author.

With dispersion of fund returns wider than those in traditional markets, manager selection is a critical component of the allocation process in alternative credit. Allocators may consider multi-manager offerings where applicable to lower their manager-specific risk.

Investing in alternative credit requires dipping into illiquid holdings and as such, requires stepping outside of daily liquid mutual fund and ETF vehicles to gain exposure. Interval funds, which are registered under the Investment Company Act of 1940 like mutual funds but have limited liquidity provisions, are an increasingly popular method for allocators to access private credit. Similarly, alternatives platforms for wealth managers are expanding access to private funds for Accredited Investor and Qualified Purchaser clients through direct and feeder funds that allow for allocations at smaller bite sizes than going direct. These fund structures will be covered in detail throughout Chapter 10.

While recent returns have been favorable for the various sub-sectors of alternative credit, they are not immune to downturns or performance struggles. When those inevitably arise, allocators should exercise patience and treat alternative credit as a strategic component of a diversified portfolio. With the cyclicality inherent in credit, a focus on well-structured and prudent lending at or near the top of the capital stack will likely make the experience easier to stick with over time.

Opportunities in credit, both public and private, tend to be more robust following challenging economic times. Allocators should view downturns as opportunities to rebalance, or even increase allocations, to take advantage of higher spreads and elevated risk premiums.

The Future for Alternative Credit

The rise in alternative credit has been propelled forward by two tailwinds: the low interest-rate environment and the pullback in lending from banks in the aftermath of the Global Financial Crisis. The resulting financing gap and thirst for yield has enabled non-bank lenders to step in.

Concurrently, an explosion of new data sources and business models have emerged that never used to exist before. This requires novel forms of financing from innovative lenders.

This maturation of alternative credit markets has led to the significant growth and increased breadth at our disposal today. Now, more than ever, there is a strong case for credit as a standalone allocation. While the risk/reward trade-offs in traditional credit are facing major headwinds, alternative credit sub-asset classes offer diversification characteristics and return potential not found in public markets.

While alternative credit has gained widespread adoption as an integral component of institutional portfolios, wealth managers continue to grapple with the vexing issue of how to responsibly generate income from a portfolio for their clients. As they continue to educate themselves about the potential benefits of alternative credit, it stands to reason that the various strategies within this broad category will start to feature more prominently in advisor-guided portfolios.

As is the case with all private assets, investors must reconcile their own comfort level with the inherently less transparent and more complex nature of these assets. The burgeoning menu of compelling options available in the alternative credit arena has given allocators another portfolio building block worth exploring.

THE ALLOCATOR'S CHEAT SHEET

- Credit is one of the oldest asset classes in existence but has also been a bane for investors who turn a blind eye to risk or get caught chasing yield.
- While most investors are familiar with publicly traded corporate and securitized credit, there is an alternative universe of sub-asset classes within credit, primarily in private markets, that may allow for better diversification, higher expected returns, and the potential for an illiquidity premium.
- Three categories of alternative credit that have diversification and return potential that today are more broadly available to retail investors and their advisors are: corporate direct lending, marketplace lending, and niche credit.
- An allocation to alternative credit should be examined and designed through the lens of what trade-offs an investor is looking to balance—total return, income, diversification, and/or liquidity.
- While the risk-reward trade-off in traditional credit is not attractive in today's low-rate world, alternative credit is still priced to deliver expected returns commensurate with the risk taken.

CHAPTER 9

The Future Investable Universe— Novel Asset Classes at the Intersection of Finance and Technology

"Software is eating the world."
— Marc Andreessen

"The story of finance is the story of a technology: a way of doing things. Like other technologies, it developed through innovations that improved efficiency."
— William Goetzmann, Money Changes Everything

"Any sufficiently advanced technology is indistinguishable from magic."
— Arthur C. Clarke

THOSE WORDS FROM venture capital luminary Marc Andreesen, written in 2011, could not have been more prescient for the decade that followed. Software indeed ate the world in more ways than we could have imagined. This phenomenon was captured in the excess profits and gains reaped by both the tech industry's giants and its most disruptive upstarts. What's clear is that software's appetite has yet to be sated, and its next meal may be our portfolios.

The impact that technology and innovation are having, and will continue to have, on our investments—both in the way we invest and the things we invest in—has not been fully realized. The stock market was a natural starting point for fintech, and we are now seeing megatrends like custom indexing being offered at lower minimums than ever thought possible, thanks to commission-free trades, fractional shares, and beautifully designed front-end interfaces that foster an experience of collaboration and customization between advisors and their clients.

More recently, we are seeing breakthroughs in the ways that non-traditional investments are being democratized and offered to broader audiences. In other instances, we are seeing the birth and emergence of new asset classes altogether, as new (or previously inaccessible) return streams are made possible through technological prowess, creative thinking, and innovations in structuring and packaging. Some of these novel assets will continue to be accessed through traditional fund structures. Others will seek to bypass the fund industry altogether in going directly to the end consumer.

A major theme we are witnessing across the fintech landscape today is what John Street Capital refers to as the "Financialization of Everything." Software, like Pac-Man, is gobbling up asset class after asset class and empowering consumers along the way. Some of these asset classes still reside exclusively with the innovators and early adopters, while others are on the cusp of "crossing the chasm" into the mainstream.

The focus of this chapter is on the future of alternatives for asset allocators. While we have covered the past and present at great length, it is imperative we keep an eye on tomorrow even if it doesn't affect our choices today. It is expected that some (or all) of these investment categories will sit alongside the other alternative components discussed in prior chapters as elements of future diversified portfolios. Return streams tethered to human capital, home price appreciation, recurring revenue streams, shared affinity, and digital scarcity—among others—are being unlocked in front of our eyes.

Specifically, this chapter will explore:

- Digital assets, such as Bitcoin and Ethereum
- Collectibles
- Fine art
- Shared home equity contracts
- Income share agreements
- Recurring revenue streams

Due to their novelty and the breadth of asset classes covered, we will merely scratch the surface of each, leaving a deep dive into these categories in the hands of the reader.

Digital Assets

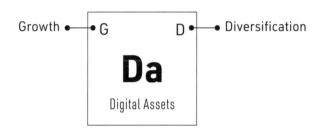

It's quite rare for a new asset class to appear out of thin air. But that's exactly what happened just over 12 years ago.

We didn't know it at the time, but the online posting of a pseudonymous white paper on Halloween of 2008 would go on to change the world of finance. The paper ("Bitcoin: A Peer-to-Peer Electronic Cash System") and its still unknown author(s) (Satoshi Nakamoto) laid the foundation for a revolution in blockchain technology, cryptocurrencies (crypto) and digital assets that would capture the imaginations of software developers, economists, investors, policymakers and central bankers in the decade-plus that followed.

While the future for digital assets remains uncertain, one thing is becoming increasingly clear: this is no passing fad and crypto, blockchains and the idea of borderless, decentralized assets are not going away. With a combined market capitalization of over $1 trillion in January 2021, digital assets have undergone a remarkable transformation from a hobbyist asset for the libertarian-minded, to a potentially valuable diversifier and legitimate asset class in the minds of financial institutions (Fidelity, Stone Ridge, CME Group), large endowments (Yale, Harvard, Stanford), leading corporations (PayPal, Square, Tesla), life insurers (MassMutual, New York Life), and legendary investors (Paul Tudor Jones, Bill Miller).

While there are literally thousands of cryptocurrencies in existence, most attention is paid to the two with the largest and strongest networks, Bitcoin and Ethereum.[23]

Bitcoin

At its core, Bitcoin is a decentralized network of value storage. The technology underlying Bitcoin's blockchain was novel in the sense that it allowed for the transfer of value between network users without the need for a centralized authority. Prior to Bitcoin, the notion that we could have a distributed database that maintains a verifiable record of the truth without the control of a third-party was not possible.

What attracts many to Bitcoin's architecture relative to that of other monetary systems are the rules programmed into the protocol that govern its supply. The total supply of all Bitcoins that will ever exist is predetermined and capped at 21m. Stone Ridge CEO Ross Stevens argues that Bitcoin is the best technology for money the world has ever seen, with a supply that is non-responsive to changes in demand.

The primary use case for Bitcoin seems to be as a monetary asset or long-term store of wealth. Research from Paradigm notes that any monetary asset must possess the following traits to be considered useful: *scarcity*, *portability*, *fungibility*, *divisibility*, *durability*, and *broad acceptability*. It could be argued that Bitcoin possesses an advantage relative to gold in all qualities besides the last (as yet). Hence Bitcoin's nickname—*digital gold*.

If we are to believe that it is competing with gold for the privilege of being the store-of-value asset of choice, then we can look to the size of the gold market to approximate the total addressable market of Bitcoin. Vitalik Buterin, the co-founder of Ethereum, has even said, "one of the more underrated bull cases for cryptocurrency that I have always believed is simply the fact that gold is lame, the younger generations realize that it's lame, and that $9 trillion has to go somewhere."

One constant with Bitcoin is the presence of "bubble" proclamations. By most conventional measures of a bubble, Bitcoin's bubble has burst many times in its mere 12 years of existence, experiencing peak-to-trough declines of over 70% on four different occasions. That very frequency of bubble-like

---

23   Over 6,700 as of January 2021, per Vanguard.

behavior makes it atypical from bubbles we have witnessed in other assets. History's greatest financial bubbles have either proved to be one-hit wonders (hello tulips and Beanie Babies) or have laid dormant for many years after popping (Japanese stocks). The counterargument to the notion that Bitcoin is in a bubble is that its wild volatility is merely a function of the price discovery process taking place in a relatively nascent asset class, with each passing "bubble" only adding stability and legitimacy over time.

Because of Bitcoin's open-source nature, the activity on the network is observable and the code can be copied. The ecosystem, however, cannot. This creates a large moat around the digital asset that would be challenging to replicate. As investor holding periods increase and the amount of new supply diminishes, the network will continue to grow stronger. According to research from NYDIG, as of November 2020, over 88% of all Bitcoins ever to exist have already been mined, there are now over 25m addresses that hold bitcoin, and over 60% of current supply has been held for at least one year.

As NYU professor Aswath Damodaran states, "Not everything can be valued, but almost everything can be priced." Without cash flows to discount, bitcoin—like gold—becomes a challenging asset to value, fitting somewhere between currencies and commodities (with a sprinkle of venture capital) in how it's priced.

Bitcoin is best modeled as a network. After all, that's what money is. Metcalfe's Law states that the value of a network is proportional to the square of the size of its user base. Analysis from NYDIG reveals that the number of Bitcoin addresses squared explains over 90% of the growth in Bitcoin's market cap.

Ethereum

Microsoft and Salesforce both sell software, but their software is designed to do different things. Digital assets are the same in that they're all tied to blockchain technology but are each optimized for different use cases. Ethereum, while the second largest digital asset by market cap, holds the distinction of being the most actively used blockchain in the world.

Ethereum was born in 2015 with the idea that the narrow list of functions that Bitcoin supported could be expanded upon. With the ability to be programmed to do anything a general computer can do, Ethereum's use of *smart contracts* brought to life a platform of *programmable money* that inserts if/then logic into value exchange.

The rise of Ethereum can't be mentioned without also mentioning the emergence of decentralized finance (DeFi). Alternatives to traditional financial services like savings, loans, insurance, and trading are all being pursued by DeFi applications and are made possible by the general programmability of Ethereum. As of April 2021, eleven DeFi apps worth more than $1bn were hosted on the Ethereum blockchain.

An investment in Ethereum is akin to a wager on early-stage, high-growth technology companies. If we are entering a new internet paradigm— one of decentralization—it stands to reason that Ethereum may serve as the foundation upon which many other valuable applications can and will be built.

Digital Assets in a Portfolio

There are several potential benefits of digital assets in a portfolio, including:

- **Asymmetric upside**: A bet on future appreciation related to a large runway left for network growth.
- **Potential inflation hedge**: One of the biggest challenges society faces is the unprecedented rate of global money printing and potentially harmful effects it may cause long term.
- **Diversification**: While its history may be limited, Bitcoin has exhibited a near zero correlation with just about every traditional asset class, giving it valuable diversification properties. And while correlations are not static over time, even at extremes the correlations between Bitcoin and other assets have been modest. That said, time will tell if the financialization of digital assets brings to bear spillover effects similar to those experienced by gold and commodities.
- **High volatility**: This can be a good thing, as it makes even a small allocation go a long way if regularly rebalanced. That said, its volatility has been trending downward over time.

A study from Bitwise Investments, using only Bitcoin due to its longer history than other digital assets, found significant positive impacts. When added to a traditional 60/40 portfolio, returns improved on both an absolute and risk-adjusted basis.

From January 2014 through September 2020, a 2.5% allocation to bitcoin, rebalanced quarterly, improved portfolio returns by over 23% while keeping volatility roughly the same. Using rolling-period analysis, the portfolio with the 2.5% allocation to bitcoin outperformed the 60/40 allocation in 74% of one-year periods, 97% of two-year periods, and 100% of three-year periods. Table 9.1 summarizes the impacts of various allocations to bitcoin when added to a 60/40 portfolio.

Table 9.1: The Impact of Adding Bitcoin to a Portfolio (January 2014–September 2020)

Portfolio	Cumulative Return	Annualized Return	Volatility (Annualized Std. Dev.)	Sharpe Ratio	Maximum Drawdown
Traditional portfolio, quarterly rebalanced	50.61%	6.26%	10.32%	0.54	-21.07%
Traditional portfolio + 1.0% bitcoin	59.89%	7.21%	10.33%	0.63	-21.32%
Traditional portfolio + 2.5% bitcoin	74.47%	8.61%	10.53%	0.75	-21.80%
Traditional portfolio + 5.0% bitcoin	100.51%	10.87%	11.26%	0.90	-22.76%

Source: Bitwise Investments.

Because a little can go a long way, in all instances the positive impact from return attribution outweighed any negative impact from risk contribution. The average boost to Sharpe ratios was 41%. Due to the non-linearity of risk contribution from Bitcoin, a ceiling of 5% of a total portfolio would be prudent, with 1–2% being reasonable given the volatility.

Allocators should exercise caution in extrapolating the numbers above far out into the future. Bitcoin and other crypto are still quite nascent in the grand scheme of things and we know with the benefit of hindsight we are analyzing a period of abnormally positive returns. Any predictions about the future returns to digital assets made with extreme hubris and certitude should be taken with a grain of salt.

Investing in Bitcoin and Digital Assets

Digital assets are now top of mind for many allocators and financial advisors, who are on the receiving end of growing client inquiries as mainstream awareness and interest in the space grows. While the history of the asset class is limited in its data, there is an increasing perception that certain characteristics of Bitcoin and other digital assets may hold diversification value in a portfolio, despite their inherent volatility. The narrative, particularly around Bitcoin, seemed to change in 2020. Advisors who maybe owned some personally, but felt it was too risky to include in client portfolios, are singing a slightly different tune. Institutional adoption has also accelerated, albeit in small doses.

While it may seem that Bitcoin has crossed the chasm, it remains elusive in the wealth management arena, with many firms forbidding their advisors from recommending it. The reasons for this are twofold.

First, the volatility of Bitcoin can make it difficult to hold for many investors. There's an old saying that a bad day for stocks is a bad year for bonds. Similarly, a bad day for Bitcoin might amount to a bad year for stocks.

The second reason boils down to logistics. Custody has proved to be a challenging puzzle to solve in the crypto world, although progress has been made on that front. Many asset managers have sought approval to launch ETFs that hold Bitcoin and other digital assets, but the SEC has yet to budge as of this writing. A few firms have gotten around this hurdle by launching products structured as Delaware statutory trusts that trade on over-the-counter exchanges. The major concerns here are the limitations to accredited investors and the significant premiums and discounts to NAV these products can at times trade at.

For most small investors, the preferred route is still direct ownership of crypto assets through one of the many digital wallet services, like Coinbase. While there are transaction fees on purchases and sales, there are no ongoing management fees. In addition, wallets also enable—for those interested—the ability to borrow against, pay with, or generate income from crypto assets.

The entire digital asset space is evolving at a rapid clip and as is the case with any nascent market, a wide range of outcomes exists, and the risk of loss is substantial. Allocators must enter any allocation with eyes wide open.

The novel design of crypto-powered blockchains are a genuine technological breakthrough. Bitcoin and its brethren represent a massive-scale attempt at reshaping and improving the global financial system. More and more people are betting that it will succeed in at least making a dent.

Collectibles

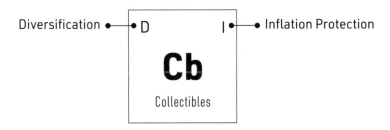

To say that collectibles markets are experiencing a renaissance would be putting it mildly. Some recent transactions in 2021 alone are emblematic of the recent resurgence:

- A highly graded version of Action Comics #1—the first appearance of Superman—sold for $3.25m, making it the most expensive comic book ever sold.
- The prototype pair of Nike Air Yeezy's from hip-hop mogul Kanye West were sold in a private sale for $1.8m, making them the world's most expensive sneakers.
- A LeBron James rookie card set an all-time record for a basketball card, selling for $5.2m in a private transaction. It matched the all-time high for *any* sports card, tying a 1952 Mickey Mantle baseball card that sold earlier in 2021.

For decades, many would-be investors have been effectively boxed out of building collectibles portfolios in their areas of interest simply due to the barriers to entry and high price points. That is no longer the case as investing in collectibles no longer requires purchasing and taking possession of the item in its entirety.

Today, a slew of fintech platforms are aligned in their mission to make collectibles a generally accepted portfolio sleeve, right alongside stocks, bonds, and other alternatives. While high-end collectibles markets have historically been dominated by hobbyists and deep-pocketed collectors, these platforms leverage securitization and fractionalization to allow for small dollar investments into shares of collectible assets versus purchasing them outright.

When you hear the word collectibles, you probably imagine your grandpa going to an antique show or maybe your aunt with a book of rare stamps. Today's collectibles markets are a bit different and span a wide range of interests. You can invest in sneakers, trading cards, classic literature, wine, spirits, classic cars, sports and pop culture memorabilia, watches, handbags, videogames, and an assortment of other items all from the comfort of your iPhone. And you don't need to be a multi-millionaire to participate.

Investing in collectibles sits at the intersection of profits and passion. In addition to their inherent scarcity, collectibles across categories typically contain one or more of the following traits: aesthetics, nostalgia, longevity, and shared affinity.

Every generation has certain cultural touchstones. It is the basis for why collecting as a hobby exists in the first place. The key transformation taking place today is the evolution of collecting from being a hobby towards being an investable marketplace with a level of standardization, fractionalization and liquidity that has never existed before. A massive step forward has been made in creating transparency around prices. Today, there are several entities trying to create large databases of verified transactions. Mutual funds or ETFs focused on collectibles are unlikely due to a liquidity mismatch, but there is the potential for comingled funds in structures like interval funds that permit more illiquid holdings and may bring a wider audience to the asset class.

While the main return driver for collectibles is the amount of disposable income that consumers have, other asset and category specific factors can impact results. As *Not Boring's* Packy McCormick observes, retail investors "expect different things from their investments than professionals do and value assets differently as a result." Younger generations of retail investors often invest based on entertainment, education, and social status. Those may be non-economic reasons for investing in collectibles, but that doesn't make them irrational.

Rare coins represent the largest category by revenue within collectibles, followed by sports memorabilia, antiques, and comics. While there is no one index that encapsulates the collectibles universe, there are a few proxies we can look to. The Knight Frank Luxury Investment Index was created in 2013 and tracks a basket of high-end collectibles. Another, the PWCC100 Index, is focused on sports cards. A study in the *Journal of Alternative Investments* titled "When Rationality Meets Passion: On the Financial Performance of Collectibles" found that collectibles delivered respectable returns (although it varied by category) while also exhibiting low betas and attractive risk characteristics.

Rally, which started with a narrow focus on collectible cars, has since broadened its capabilities across multiple verticals and quickly ensconced itself as the leader of the pack. They have completed or are in process of completing roughly 250 different offerings and total AUM of nearly $30m as of April 2021. Others have had success as well. Otis has branded itself as the "investment platform for culture" and StockX has become the go-to for sneakerheads and streetwear fanatics. Some have opted for a more niche approach, with Vinovest offering fine wine and Mythic Markets describing itself as investing for geeks.

Risk Considerations

Collectibles' main flaw is like that of other non-income producing assets like gold or Bitcoin—there is difficulty in assessing value. Ultimately, the price of any collectible is subject to the whims of supply and demand. When speculative fervor takes hold, it becomes difficult to disentangle assets with inherent value from those being passed around via the greater fool theory.

Other pain points in collectibles are related to tracking, insurance, lack of data, and liquidity. All these issues are being addressed in some fashion. Exchanges have emerged that allow investors to more frequently and efficiently transact. Indices are being built for performance tracking and benchmarking purposes. Storage and insurance solutions are critical to the platforms that custody these assets given the risk of fraud, theft, and damage to these assets.

Taxes are another consideration for collectibles. They are generally tax-inefficient and do not qualify for capital gains treatment in the United States.

The beauty of collectibles is that they can be bought for investment purposes, enjoyment, or both. To paraphrase Maya Angelou, people might forget what they paid for a collectible, but they will never forget how it made them feel. With scarce supply and growing demand, the asset class is likely to continue garnering interest and providing appreciation over long periods of time. It is important for investors to keep in mind that a long-term orientation is required and that there is always the risk of loss. While collectibles have demonstrated diversification to traditional asset classes, they may not act as a hedge during economic downturns when discretionary spending dries up.

Fine Art

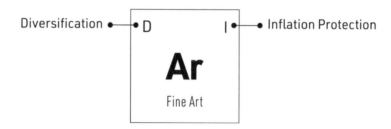

As blogger Nick Maggiulli points out, art was one of the only asset classes in Europe to survive and be preserved through World War II—even as asset classes like stocks and bonds were wiped out as cities lay in ruins. A distinct feature of human culture across continents and borders is our shared appreciation of art. The importance of art throughout history goes beyond its aesthetics, with the value placed on its scarcity and cultural significance standing the test of time. Art is also big business, as U.S. art dealers alone generated $11.8bn in revenues in 2019.

The art world can be intimidating to some, particularly from an investment standpoint. Most people probably assume that it's off limits to them anyway—only reserved for the richest of the rich and the cultural elite. For most of history that has been true, which is unfortunate.

Like most asset classes, there is a great deal of variety within art. It can be broken down into historical periods, as well as type of art (sculptures, paintings, etc.) and various artistic styles (contemporary, impressionism, etc.) While some collectors purchase art purely for display in their home or office, or perhaps for prestige purposes within their circle of friends, others are motivated by the potential for financial returns.

It may surprise some, but art as an asset class has offered substantial returns to those that have been able to access it. The performance of blue-chip art has been impressive, with the Artprice100© index up over 400% since 2000, outperforming the S&P 500. The size of the art market—estimated to be roughly $1.7 trillion as of 2020—is quite substantial. Art has also maintained incredibly low correlations with other asset classes, as seen in Table 9.2.

Table 9.2: Correlation of Art vs. Other Asset Classes (1985–2020)

Asset Class	Correlation with Art
Developed Equities	0.12
Emerging Market Equities	0.25
Investment Grade Fixed Income	0.04
Hedge Funds	0.08
Private Equity	0.06
Real Estate	0.09
Commodities	0.09

Source: Citi Private Bank, Masterworks.io.

The returns of art are driven by attractive supply-demand dynamics. Demand is driven by the secular growth of wealthy investors, with the estimated number of millionaires expected to grow at 6% per annum through 2024. There is also limited supply resulting from artwork being acquired by museums and public collections as well as from donations by the ultra-wealthy. Art is also a global asset, with 64% of collectible wealth held outside of North America.

Like any non-cash flowing asset class, the price of art will fluctuate with the tastes and preferences of consumers and collectors. In addition to the difficulty in valuation, art assets are quite illiquid. Due to the high value of certain pieces and the potential for loss from damage, insurance and storage costs can be quite significant.

The identification, evaluation, and acquisition of artwork requires a great deal of domain expertise. For novices, this means you are likely better off leveraging the resources of a third-party platform when considering art as a component of a diversified portfolio. Most platforms charge a management and/or performance fee for this expertise, which incentivises them to purchase only art they expect to appreciate significantly.

In continuing the pattern of bringing hard-to-access assets to the masses that we have seen for asset classes like real estate and collectibles, companies like Masterworks and Otis are democratizing art. Traditionally, investing in art came with the assumption that you were buying the entire piece. But today, much like you don't need to buy an entire company to participate in corporate America, you don't need to spend millions on a rare painting to partake in the spoils of the art market. In the case of Masterworks, investors need not be accredited and can invest with as little as $10,000, so long as they pass a suitability review with a sales professional. Investors can buy shares in the works of masters, creating digital portfolios that feature the likes of Warhol, Basquiat, Monet, and Banksy.

A great deal of progress has been made in the creation of investment vehicles, securitizations and platforms that are bringing more access, transparency, and data to this market. While the fractional ownership of art through an investment platform doesn't give you the pleasure of displaying the piece in your home, this now unlocked asset class has the potential to being some pleasure to your portfolio. With an uncorrelated return stream, art has generated attractive returns and demonstrated ability to be a solid store of value over time.

A Word on NFTs

If you were to create a Venn diagram of digital assets, collectibles, and fine art, then non-fungible tokens (NFTs) would likely sit at the intersection of all three. According to NFT marketplace OpenSea, NFTs represent "unique, digital items with blockchain managed ownership."

Figure 9.1: Venn Diagram of Digital Assets, Collectibles, Fine Art, and NFTs

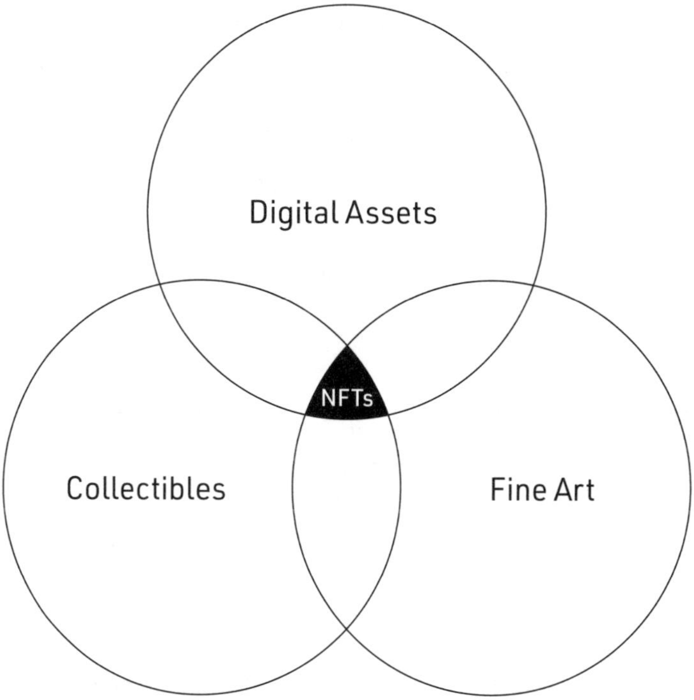

Source: Author.

These pieces of digital art, media, and virtual goods—ranging from songs and videos to GIFs and JPEGs—are free for anyone to view, stream, download, or listen to. It is the ownership rights to those assets, however, that essentially function as rare collectibles. One tweet likened the purchase of NFTs to "angel investing in culture." This application of blockchain technology exploded in popularity in 2021, with an extreme example being the $69m sale price for a JPEG file from artist Beeple.

NFTs are symbolic of the rise of the creator economy. Proponents of the technology point to the improved creator economics that NFTs provide. Venture Capitalist Chris Dixon of Andreessen Horowitz points to three key features of NFTs that change the economics for creators: the removal of rent-seeking intermediaries, granular price tiering that varies with fans' enthusiasm levels, and the conversion of users into owners as a mechanism to lower customer acquisition costs.[24]

Color me skeptical around some of the recent speculation in this space, but if history is a guide the seeds of innovation are often planted in every mania. It is still very early innings and the ecosystem surrounding NFTs will evolve significantly in the coming years. It will be interesting to witness what the next decade holds for NFTs and the problems they are trying to solve.

Shared Home Equity Contracts

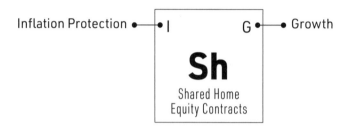

Inflation Protection •—•| G •—• Growth

Sh

Shared Home
Equity Contracts

Shared home equity contracts (SHECs) represent a small but emergent asset class that allows homeowners to monetize the equity in their home by selling away a portion of the equity participation to an investor. These contracts are structured as option agreements, with the homeowner receiving a lump sum and the investor getting a percentage of the current home value and participation in the fluctuation of that value for the duration of the contract.

The SHEC investor gets exposure to tangible real property, with downside protection stemming from the initial purchase being at a discount to the appraised value of the home. The contract itself includes a lien on the home that the homeowner is obligated to abide by—this favors the investor.

There are benefits to the homeowners in these transactions as well. It's well known that many U.S. homeowners are cash poor but house rich. For roughly two-thirds of homeowners, that equity in their primary residence is their largest asset. It could be argued that the historical inability to sell an equity stake in one's home has led to the overleveraging of homeowners. When a SHEC deal closes, the homeowner receives immediate liquidity

---

24   C. Dixon, "NFTs and a Thousand True Fans," Andreessen Horowitz (February 27, 2021),

without having to sell their home or take on any debt. For obvious reasons, those are not terribly desirable options for a lot of people.

This innovative non-debt solution has the potential to unlock an asset class to a broad spectrum of allocators who find equity participation in the residential real estate asset class appealing. The creators of these SHECs are a handful of VC-backed fintech companies like Unison, Noah, and Point. SHECs are currently available in over 20 states and are expected to continue penetration throughout the country as these contract origination platforms scale.

This space is intriguing for several reasons, the first being the sheer size of the residential real estate market. Another compelling rationale is the odd fact that most things can be financed with either equity or debt, except for our primary residences. Lastly, SHECs address the needs of investors and homeowners, creating a mutually beneficial transaction.

There seems to be a great deal of potential demand from consumers who would happily sell a piece of the equity in their home to use it for other purposes or to reduce the concentration in their wealth. The question remains whether there is an equal supply of investors seeking to participate in non-income producing home price appreciation.

The natural capital providers for this type of stable asset class would be pensions and endowments, but the catch-22 is that those entities are potentially less likely to experiment with a new asset class. Another potentially limiting factor is the slow-moving nature (most of the time) of home price appreciation. It could take years in most cases to gauge how you're doing in this asset class. While demand has yet to arrive in scale, given the size of the opportunity and the herd-like behavior of institutions, it might come gradually... then suddenly.

Income Share Agreements

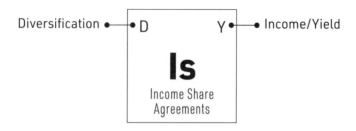

Income share agreements (ISAs) are one of the more novel asset class innovations in recent years. Conceptually they have been around for decades—Yale offered them briefly during the 1970s—but they have only recently picked up steam. Perhaps a natural by-product of the college affordability crisis and the increasing demand for uncorrelated and income-oriented investments, these alternatives to student loans are gaining adoption with nearly 100 American universities and technical academies now offering them.

The mechanics of ISAs work as such: the student enters into an agreement with a school (or other institution), receiving upfront money to attend school in exchange for a share of their income post-graduation. This portion of their income is owed for the life of the ISA, usually a decade or so, or when repayments reach a prespecified cap. In short, a risk transfer takes place from the borrower (student) to the lender (investor). Another way to think about it is the student funding their education via equity in themselves, rather than debt.

ISAs are a long way from being a true threat to the two main ways to fund higher education: government subsidized loans (~$100bn/year) and private debt (~$10bn/year). While some companies offer direct-to-consumer ISAs, most are administered through universities or technical schools. In theory, schools that better prepare their students for the workforce will reap better returns from their programs. ISAs have also been particularly popular at institutions such as Lambda School, which focus on developing coding skills. Yields on ISAs can range from high single digits to low double digits.

The relatively nascent stature of the space has kept large institutions from taking the plunge, but there is certainly an appetite for this uncorrelated asset class from smaller asset managers and family offices. Today, marketplaces such as Edly exist for accredited investors to gain access to diversified, managed pools of ISAs for as little as $5,000. Other applications of ISAs outside the education sphere have also emerged. One example is Big League Advance, a company that has applied the ISA concept towards projecting the future career earnings for minor league baseball players.

With the U.S. student debt burden now greater than $1.5 trillion, the financial struggles facing American higher education are well documented. As Wade Eyerly, chief executive of the Education Insurance Corporation states, "higher education is the only place you would counsel someone you love to borrow 10 to 20 times their net worth and make a single investment [a university degree] with it and hope it works."

Recurring Revenue Streams

A common theme in the depths of the COVID-19 crisis was that companies across industries did whatever they could to cut costs, except for certain software costs that were critical to the operation of their business. Robert Smith, CEO and founder of Vista Equity Partners once quipped: "Software contracts are better than first-lien debt. You realize a company will not pay the interest payment on their first lien until after they pay their software maintenance or subscription fee. We get paid our money first. Who has the better credit? He can't run his business without our software."

The value of recurring revenue is now front and center for many. Companies like Adobe have transformed their business from license models to SaaS models, with recurring revenue moving from less than 10% of overall revenue to over 90% of total revenue. Even Apple, the largest company in the world, benefitted from significant multiple expansion through a smaller— albeit from a much bigger pie—shift towards services and recurring revenue.

With the growing importance of SaaS businesses and recurring revenue models against a backdrop of yield-hungry investors living in a world of zero interest rates, a new asset class has emerged: *recurring revenue streams*. This growing niche within the venture landscape is designed for companies exploring non-traditional, non-dilutive ways to raise capital. Instead of an amortized payment schedule like that of traditional debt, repayments are tied to the monthly revenues of the borrowers.

Companies like Pipe, Capchase, and Clearco have created services that connect companies with monthly or quarterly recurring revenue contracts to investors who bid to purchase them upfront for their annual value. By integrating directly into a company's banking, payment processing and accounting systems, the data scientists working at these companies can analyze the finances, customer-acquisitions costs, and churn rates of startups to effectively rate these businesses. Companies gain visibility into the real-time bids for the annual value of their subscription revenues, which can accelerate the cash flows of long-term contracts.

SaaS companies often offer discounts on annual, upfront payments in the neighborhood of 20–30% in order to incentivise customers and shorten sales cycles, but not many take them up on it. While many variables contribute to the price of a company's subscriptions on these marketplaces, the discounts to their annual value are showing to be significantly less than those afforded to potential customers.

As the cost to start and scale a technology company has plummeted thanks to cloud-based infrastructure, companies are able to achieve revenue sooner in the lifecycle which allows for some flexibility beyond traditional VC funding. This form of financing gives companies more control over their growth plans and can delay their need to tap the VC markets. These discounted cash flows are not without risk, but more and more investors are viewing recurring revenue contracts as assets worthy of being financed.

What's Next for Novel Assets?

The examples in this chapter are but a few of the interesting and promising asset classes that are blossoming before our eyes. Other examples abound.

Technology companies sit on piles of intangible assets that no one has thought to finance before, mainly because these assets never existed before. Today, innovative lenders like CoVenture are creating new verticals altogether, looking at things like Spotify playlists and Airbnb accounts that reside within the platform economies surrounding the largest media and e-commerce giants. Providing financing to technology-enabled businesses and new economy borrowers that don't fit neatly into the standard profiles used by traditional lenders opens new frontiers. As CoVenture co-founder Ali Hamed describes, "Rather than own FB shares, we'd rather own Instagram accounts. Rather than owning Amazon stock, we'd rather own a bunch of third-party selling merchants. And rather than owning Google stock, we'd rather own YouTube libraries."

The Future is Now

It's hard to overstate the importance of technology in shaping our ability to craft and design portfolios. Technology has taken something familiar, i.e. 60/40, and made it easier to implement by orders of magnitude. Now, it has also birthed brand new investment categories while concurrently increasing the access and adoption of others that have been historically hard to reach.

As the preceding chapters have highlighted, the menu of available options to improve diversification in portfolios has broadened significantly. And while the capabilities exist today to build better portfolios than 60/40, we also want to keep one eye on the future and be open minded to what might follow in the footsteps of today's modern alternatives playbook.

The lines between technology and finance continue to blur, as innovative platforms, marketplaces and asset managers continue to chip away at making things possible today that were impossible yesterday. While some technology-enabled assets have crossed the chasm into the mainstream, others find themselves earlier in the adoption curve. As the arc of the investable universe continues to bend towards innovation and democratization, it is exciting to ponder the possibilities that lie ahead for our portfolios.

As fun as it is to daydream about the future, we must act in the present. As we close out this section on our journey through the past, present and future of alternative investments, the time has come to put our knowledge to work. In our next and final section, we roll up our sleeves and get ready to build.

THE ALLOCATOR'S CHEAT SHEET

- Software has eaten the world, and its next meal may be our portfolios.
- Novel asset classes are emerging that seek to continue the trajectory of broadening diversification opportunities and lowering the barriers to entry for previously hard-to-access asset classes.
- In the case of digital assets, advances in computing and cryptography, coupled with the strength of network effects, are causing us to reimagine the concept of money itself, with Bitcoin (digital gold) and Ethereum (programmable money) creating a revolution within finance.
- Asset classes like collectibles and art, once the exclusive domain of hobbyists and the ultra-wealthy, are seeing increased transparency and access with the advent of tech-enabled investment platforms.
- Investments in return streams tied to human capital (ISAs), home price appreciation (SHECs), and recurring revenue streams, are now possible through the innovative efforts of fintech companies.
- As great as the opportunity set is today for investors, the future looks even brighter.

PART III

BUILDING BETTER PORTFOLIOS

CHAPTER 10

Containers and Contents— Matching the Right Structure with the Right Investment

> *"A fish and a bird may fall in love… but the two cannot build a home together."*
>
> **— African proverb**

> *"At times of shock, converting illiquid assets to cash to build flexibility is very expensive. Finding an umbrella in a rainstorm might be impossible or very costly."*
>
> **— Myron Scholes**

YOU WOULDN'T WRAP leftover spaghetti in Saran wrap. Nor would you leave your diamond ring sitting in the glove box of your car. Speaking of cars, you probably wouldn't fill a Jetta with jet fuel. All of this is to say that matching the right contents with the right containers matters.

When an allocator becomes comfortable with a particular asset class or strategy they want to invest in, the next question is which investment vehicle or structure is best suited to access it. Allocators are faced with a variety of fund wrappers to house their investments. Some are appropriate only for certain types of *investors*, and others are appropriate only for certain types of *investments*.

There are many considerations to weigh when evaluating the various containers one can invest in, including:

- Targeted asset class or strategy
- Liquidity, or lack thereof
- Investor qualifications
- Taxation
- Trading
- Fund lifespan
- Costs
- Transparency
- Regulatory protections
- Use of leverage, short selling, and derivatives
- Manager compensation

For traditional asset classes like publicly traded stocks and bonds, open-end mutual funds, ETFs, and separately managed accounts (SMAs) generally check all the right boxes and are sufficient. When we enter the realm of alternative investments, we must dive deeper. Several categories can be effectively managed in daily-liquid, SEC-registered funds whereas others cannot.

In this chapter, we will conduct a thorough review of the main investment structures being used today and how they compare with one another. But first, we will briefly touch on investor accreditations and regulations, and their influence on fund choice.

Investor Accreditation

The Securities and Exchange Commission (SEC) has long maintained that investors in private securities should have a certain level of wealth or income. These thresholds were created with the objective of protecting the interests of individual investors that may not understand the risks involved or that might not be able to bear the financial burden of a loss on these investments.

The two qualifications to understand when evaluating the limitations of certain investment vehicles are **accredited investors** and **qualified purchasers**.

Historically, the accredited investor (AI) definition was limited to an audience meeting certain income or net worth requirements: annual income of at least $200,000 (or $300,000 jointly with spouse) for each of the past two years, or $1m in assets, excluding one's primary residence.

In August of 2020, the SEC expanded the definition of who is eligible to participate in private capital markets. The decades-old, and by many considered stale, definition of an accredited investor was amended. In addition to the two criteria above, several new categories have now been added as qualifiers. For one, individuals with certain professional certifications, designations and credentials designated by the SEC may now be deemed eligible. In addition, anyone holding a Series 7, 65, or 82 license qualifies, as well as those considered to be "knowledgeable employees" of private investment funds. Relying solely on income or net worth, per SEC Chairman Jay Clayton, "disadvantages otherwise financially sophisticated Americans living in lower income/cost-of-living areas."

Qualified purchasers (QPs) must have a net worth of $5m, excluding their primary residence. There is no annual income requirement for QPs. Also included in the definition of QP are individuals or entities investing at least $25m in private capital; a trust sponsored and managed by qualified purchasers; or an entity owned solely by qualified purchasers. The reason certain private funds only allow QPs is that it exempts them from certain onerous SEC regulations.

In 2020, it was estimated that there were approximately 13.6m households in the U.S. that qualified as AI and about 1.5m that qualified as QP.[25]

The Investment Company Act of 1940

The Investment Company Act of 1940 ('40 Act) is an historical piece of legislation that served as the catalyst for the modern era of mutual funds and ETFs. It helped establish trust between investors and asset managers as it relates to things like transparency, independent oversight, and fiduciary duty. Characteristics we take for granted today—like daily NAVs, the use of custodians, leverage limits, disclosure of fees and holdings, simplified tax

---

25 N. Veronis and L. Sexton, "Private Markets Have Become Accessible to Individual Investors," iCapital Network (February 3, 2021).

reporting—are lynchpins of the mutual fund and ETF wrappers governed by the '40 Act.

Liquid Alternatives

Since their creation in 1924, open-end mutual funds have done a world of good for investors. They have helped democratize access to public stock and bond markets, while also providing transparency, regulatory protection, client-friendly tax-reporting and liquidity to end investors. To be sure, this wrapper is not without flaws—no pooled fund structure is perfect. Some critics would point to the lack of intra-day liquidity as a blemish. Others may view that as a feature, not a bug. The main critical design flaw is the propensity of mutual funds to distribute year-end capital gains, which can cause headaches for taxable investors who are punished at the expense of departing shareholders.

ETFs, also characterized as open-end funds registered under the '40 Act, have supplanted mutual funds as the default investment vehicle of choice for many investors. While total ETF assets are still roughly one-third of that of mutual funds, asset flows tell a different story. ETFs have been gathering new assets at a torrid pace, while mutual funds have been slowly bleeding assets. Were it not for the powerful force of inertia, it is likely the gap would close sooner than later.

Relative to mutual funds, ETFs provide not only the intraday liquidity that many seek but also bring increased holdings transparency and added tax benefits thanks to how ETFs create and redeem shares. As much as ETFs have overcome some of the hurdles that mutual funds faced, they also fall short in some respects. For starters, ETFs have no great way to limit capacity or close funds to new assets, which can be detrimental to certain strategies. The ETF format will be relatively more restrictive given limitations on derivatives use. There is also the potential for tax leakage to the extent that derivatives are unable to benefit from in-kind redemption, the feature that makes ETFs such a tax-efficient vehicle in the first place, the same way individual securities are.

As it relates to the use of alternative investments, mutual funds and ETFs can both be great in some cases and lousy in others. This has largely to do with '40 Act regulations around the use of leverage, short sales, derivatives, and illiquid securities. For alternative assets that require little or none of the above, a mutual fund or ETF can make a great deal of sense from a convenience standpoint. In other instances, the limitations of the structures can lead to a watered-down version of a strategy that might be better run in a semi-liquid or illiquid structure.

Where mutual funds and ETFs fall short in their ability to deliver alternatives is when illiquid investments or performance fees are involved. Technically, there can be performance fees levied in mutual funds, but they must follow a fulcrum fee structure where the fees swing equally both ways. From an illiquidity standpoint, mutual funds are capped at holding less than 15% of their value in assets deemed to be illiquid.

Examples of alternative asset classes and strategies that work quite well in mutual funds and ETFs are: catastrophe bonds, managed futures, event-driven, long/short and market neutral equity, alternative risk premia, multi-strategy liquid alternatives, public REITs, public infrastructure, gold, and commodities. Bitcoin would seemingly work quite well in an ETF, assuming that at some point the SEC approves one.

Interval Funds—the Goldilocks Structure?

For a long time, investors in alternatives had a binary choice when it came to liquidity—dip a toe in the shallow end of the pool with daily liquid funds, or do a cannonball off the diving board into the deep end of the pool with long-lockup private vehicles reserved for accredited investors and qualified purchasers. Fortunately, allocators no longer need to be stuck between a rock and a hard place. There are a growing number of fund structures that find a healthy middle ground between the two, with the ability to own substantial illiquid assets while retaining some of the operational, tax reporting, and regulatory benefits that financial advisors find comfort in.

Neither too hot nor too cold, closed-end interval funds (or simply interval funds) are just right when it comes to fund structures that are widely accessible to most investors and also appropriately match the liquidity (or lack thereof) of the underlying holdings in certain alternative investments.

Table 10.1: Structural Characteristics of Interval Funds

	Open-End Fund	Listed Closed-End Fund	Interval Fund	Typical Private Fund
1940 Act Registered	Yes	Yes	Yes	No
Continuously Offered	Yes	No	Yes	No
Daily Valuations	Yes	Yes	Yes	No
1099 Tax Reporting	Yes	Yes	Yes	No
No Performance Fee	Yes	Yes	Yes	No
No Capital Calls	Yes	Yes	Yes	No
Investor Suitability	None	None	Rarely	AI or QP
Investment Minimum	$	$	$$	$$$
Liquidity	Daily	Exchange Traded	Periodic (typically quarterly)	Episodic/ Illiquid
Illiquid Securities	15% Max	No Max Limit	75-95% Max	No Max Limit

Source: BlackRock.

Like mutual funds, interval funds are regulated by the Investment Company Act of 1940. Unlike mutual funds, however, they are subject to episodic liquidity as opposed to daily. Interval funds allow for the provision of certain asset classes that would otherwise be unobtainable in daily-liquid formats. The interval fund has existed since the early 1990s, but it was only a few years ago that it began to really gain traction.

Interval funds exist for myriad investment strategies, but one commonality they all share is their requirement to offer periodic share repurchases at predetermined intervals—hence the name. These intervals are typically quarterly, although that can vary. This has potentially profound impacts for advisors in that it opens the door to a variety of diversification opportunities in markets that are too thinly traded or illiquid to be held within a traditional '40 Act mutual fund or ETF.

Unlike their cousin, listed closed-end funds, interval funds do not undergo an IPO or trade on an exchange. Instead, they look, smell, and feel much more like traditional open-end mutual funds. They are offered continuously, and shares are issued on an ongoing basis. What makes interval funds so intriguing is that they fill a middle ground between daily-liquid, registered funds and private funds that are usually more expensive, less liquid and more complicated from a tax standpoint.

According to the regulations stipulated by the 1940 Act, share repurchases of interval funds must be between 5% and 25% of a fund's outstanding shares. While most funds today offer quarterly repurchases, there is some flexibility around the timing and frequency of them.

Figure 10.1 shows what a typical repurchase timeline looks like for investors in interval funds.

Figure 10.1: Sample Repurchase Timeline for Interval Funds

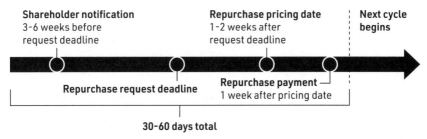

Source: Author.

For allocators introducing interval funds to clients for the first time, it is imperative that a discussion be had with clients around the particulars of the fund structure. Their similarity to mutual funds makes it easy to confuse the two and could lead to a bad experience should there be a surprise if and when they choose to redeem.

While investors should expect to receive full proceeds during normal redemption windows, there always remains the risk that repurchase requests exceed the number of shares being offered in that window. Under such circumstances, a gate will go up and investors will receive shares on a pro-rata basis. Because of this potential uncertainty, investors in interval funds should view them as more illiquid than they seem on the surface and anticipate committing to a multi-year holding period where the underlying asset class(es) are treated as a long-term investment—not a trade. The onus is on the advisor, not the fund company, to ensure that the end investor understands what they own.

Catastrophe reinsurance, derivatives-based strategies, alternative credit, and real assets have been the biggest beneficiaries of the interval fund structure. Asset managers Stone Ridge and Versus Capital are currently the biggest players in this space. Product development has been robust, with both boutique managers as well as brand name firms like PIMCO and BlackRock participating. Assets in interval funds were north of $35bn at the end of 2020, a 12% increase from 2019.

Other Unlisted Fund Structures

While interval funds are the most well-known semi-liquid fund structure, with the largest AUM and number of funds, a handful of other unlisted semi-liquid and illiquid fund types are available and gaining varying levels of traction. Below is a brief description of each, followed by Table 10.2 which comapres some of their key features with those of interval funds.

- **Tender offer funds**: Like interval funds, tender offer funds allow more flexibility to invest in illiquid assets. Instead of the set repurchase schedule that interval funds follow, tender offer funds are more subjective in the liquidity they offer with the fund's board determining when and how much liquidity to provide. They also differ from interval funds in that they are usually for accredited investors or qualified purchasers only, limiting their potential use with smaller clients. NAVs for tender offer funds are priced on at least a monthly basis. Tender offer funds are not required to hold liquid assets, and most have preset terms, or maturities. To date, most registered closed-end funds investing in private equity have opted for this structure.
- **Non-traded REITs**: This structure has seen a bit of a resurgence of late, after overcoming some rightfully deserved reputational damage from over a decade ago. The non-traded REITs of today, relative to their predecessors, have better investor alignment and greater transparency. Funds using this structure can own, originate, and securitize real estate assets. With a focus on high and consistent dividends, they tend to appeal to income-oriented investors. Most non-traded REITs have shifted to quarterly, rather than annual, liquidity terms. While some have been bitten by this fund structure in years past, the presence of higher-quality fund managers should bolster confidence to a degree.
- **Non-traded BDCs**: For investors seeking access to middle-market lending, non-traded BDCs are a potential solution. Approved by Congress in the 1980s, BDCs are designed to help U.S. business raise capital. As more non-bank lenders have stepped in to fill the void left by banks after

the GFC, BDCs have become increasingly popular. There are publicly traded BDCs and non-traded, private BDCs. The public versions can be quite volatile and may trade at a discount or premium to NAV. Private BDCs are not listed on an exchange and are usually available through intermediaries. Investors usually need to be accredited to own non-traded BDCs, and because they are structured as pass-through entities, they must distribute at least 90% of their income annually. While non-traded BDCs have the option to convert to public via IPOs at some point, some managers are recognizing the appeal and demand for evergreen, unlisted vehicles and are responding in-kind.

Table 10.2: Key Features of Unlisted Fund Structures

	Interval funds	Tender offer funds	Non-traded REITs	Non-traded BDCs
Liquidity	Repurchase offers required at specific intervals (quarterly, semi-annually, annually)	Tender offers at the discretion of the board	Possible discretionary repurchase offers—likely illiquid until fund's expiration	Typically discretionary repurchase offers
Regulatory leverage limits	33.3%	33.3%	Technically unlimited	2:1
Registration	1940 Act	1940 Act	1934 Act, 1933 Act	1940 Act
Who can invest	No limitations	Often limited to qualified clients ($2m net worth)	$250k net worth or $70k income	Typically accredited investors
NAV frequency	At least weekly	At least monthly	Typically quarterly	At least quarterly
Performance fees	Yes, if limited to qualified clients	Yes, if limited to qualified clients	Yes	Yes
Liquid assets restriction	Must hold liquid assets from beginning of repurchase offer period to pricing date	No	No	No
Tax reporting	1099	1099	1099	1099

Source: Used with permission from Pacific Investment Management Company, LLC.

Private Investment Funds

Private funds are usually structured as limited partnerships (LPs). Used by private equity and hedge fund managers, LP structures have fewer requirements around transparency and investor protections than products that are regulated by the Investment Company Act of 1940.

Private market LP funds are most often formed as closed-end vehicles, meaning they have a defined life span. Because withdrawals and redemptions are generally not permitted, investors need to be absolutely sure they have the wherewithal to withstand the lengthy lockup period, often in excess of ten years. The closed-end structure is advantageous to the fund manager, providing certainty of capital, optimization of the entry and exit timing of portfolio companies, and the ability to focus on long-term value over short-term concerns.

A private market LP fund has three main parties:

1. The **investment manager**: The investment manager sets up the partnership and handles the day-to-day management and operations. The investment manager typically receives a management fee, which covers overheads and expenses related to investment professionals.
2. The **general partner** (GP): The GP is a vehicle formed by the investment manager that controls the partnership and assumes liability for its financial obligations. The investment manager commits capital to the partnership through the GP and receives its share of the profits.
3. The **limited partners** (LPs): LPs commit capital to the fund, which is called in at various intervals. An LP lacks decision-making authority related to the partnership, but is limited from a liability standpoint to the capital they have committed. This protects them in the event of a lawsuit or bankruptcy.

Figure 10.2 from HarbourVest helps illustrate the various parties involved and how cash flows among them.

Figure 10.2: The Parties Involved and Cash Flows in Private Investment Funds

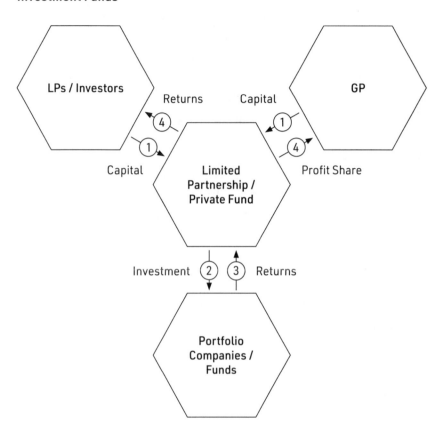

Source: HarbourVest Partners.

LP Governance and Fees

A limited partnership agreement (LPA) is the governing document of the partnership, establishing roles, fund terms, and investment guidelines and restrictions.

Potential LPs should be keenly aware of how fees work in private funds. While traditional funds only have management fees to consider, private funds usually charge both management and performance fees. Management fees can vary but are often between 1–2%—higher than most traditional funds. Management fees can be applied to either committed or called capital, although applying to committed capital seems to be the standard. It is also common for management fees to be reduced following what's known as the investment period, usually the first three to five years of a fund.

Performance fees, also referred to as carried interest (or simply carry), are the share of profits received by the investment manager/GP and the most common level is 20% of profits. Most private funds also have what's known as a hurdle rate, or preferred return. The hurdle refers to a rate of return—often 8%—that a manager must exceed before earning any performance fee. This hurdle rate resets annually, helping to align the interests of LPs and GPs.

Another common feature of private funds is what's known as a "catch-up." When investment distributions are made, the first step is the return of all initial capital to LPs. After that has occurred, all profits go to LPs until the hurdle rate has been met. After the preferred return is reached, the "catch-up" takes hold with the GP receiving 100% of the distribution until it recoups cash equal to the carried interest it would have received had a hurdle not been in place. After the GP is caught-up, the normal, agreed split of profits resumes. This somewhat complex cash flow arrangement is best visualized through what's known as the distribution waterfall, as shown in Figure 10.3.

Figure 10.3: Distribution Waterfall

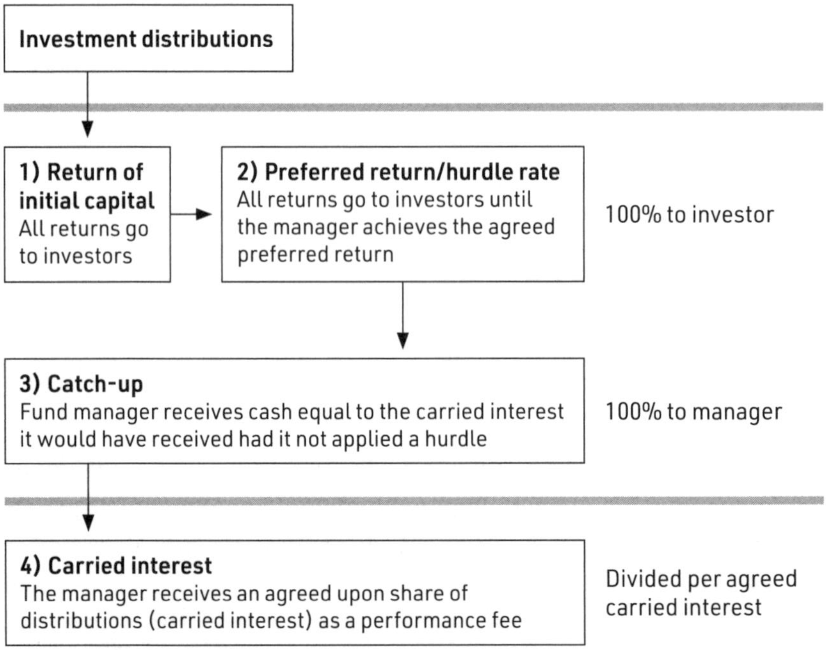

Source: HarbourVest Partners.

Private Fund Lifespans

The lifespan and cash flows of private funds are different in many regards than those of public equity funds. The lifespan of a private fund can be broken down into two distinct periods:

1. **Investment period**: Capital is called from LPs as investments are made into portfolio companies over a three- to five-year period.
2. **Harvest period**: The manager seeks to improve the value of the underlying business over a four- to six-year period with the objective of achieving an exit through an IPO or by selling to another private equity fund or strategic buyer.

Figure 10.4 illustrates this typical lifespan in action, which leads to what is known as the J-curve effect in early years that show losses as capital is called and deployed. While J-curves are largely unavoidable for primary funds, the use of secondary funds and/or direct co-investments can help mitigate the J-curve effect.

Figure 10.4: Lifespan of Private Funds

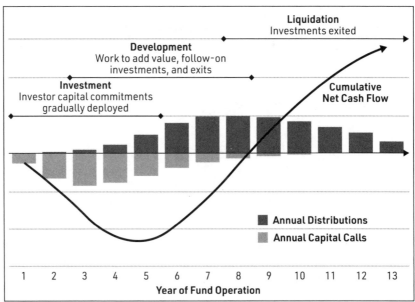

Source: HarbourVest Partners.

This example is specific to private equity. Private funds focused on credit or real estate have different cash flow profiles. Specifically, those strategies generate a higher degree of current income, which can lead to earlier distributions than private equity.

Commitment Pacing

Because private market assets are also typically self-liquidating, investors must develop a thoughtful commitment pacing plan to target and maintain their overall exposure, manage cash flows, and obtain reasonable diversification over time across vintages, managers, strategies and geographies.

Because GPs have discretion over capital calls and distributions, LPs must decide what to do with their uncalled capital and how to allocate money received from distributions. A balance should be struck between committing too much, too soon and too little, too slowly. Investors want to avoid capital calls and distributions that are too sporadic and/or lumpy over time.

A private market portfolio can be thought of as having three distinct buckets: 1) called capital; 2) committed, but uncalled, capital; and 3) uncommitted capital, which represents distributions from prior commitments but that hasn't been re-committed yet. Two strategies that private market investors can consider deploying to optimize their allocation over time are a *target NAV strategy* and a *cash flow matching strategy*. Target NAV is focused on achieving and maintaining a private market allocation that is a specific percentage of the total portfolio; while cash flow matching seeks to have distributions and capital calls recycled while cash flows remain somewhat neutral in each period.

Benchmarking and Performance Reporting

For a variety of reasons, private market funds are not as easy to benchmark as their public market counterparts. Variable cash flows, a lack of clearly defined universes for comparison, and infrequent and lagged valuations are just a few. That's not to say there aren't plenty of indices and benchmarking methodologies available to private market investors—there certainly are. But they each come with limitations that allocators need to be aware of.

Private market investors depend on several public and private benchmarks to inform allocation decisions, monitor performance of their overall program, and assess performance at the manager level relative to objectives and peer groups.

Private Equity Vintage Programs

Much like prevailing conditions can influence the vintage quality of wine, market conditions can have a meaningful impact on the returns of private equity vintages. A PE fund's life effectively begins the year in which it makes its first investment, or its *vintage year*. Despite their illiquidity, private markets are not immune to the cyclical forces that drive public market volatility. Certain PE vintages may do exceedingly well by investing at low valuations in the trough of a cycle, while others might suffer the misfortune and bad timing of launching into the teeth of a late-cycle environment. This effect can be mitigated over time by investing across multiple vintages.

The dispersion of results between the top and bottom managers in private market categories is significantly wider than that of public markets. Your choice of manager(s) may ultimately determine whether you succeed or fail in your private market allocation.

Hedge Fund LPs

While LP structures are common for hedge funds like they are for private market asset classes, there are some modest differences. First, most hedge funds are open-ended, designed to be evergreen in nature with opportunities for investors to contribute and redeem capital at NAV on a periodic basis. Subscriptions and redemptions can be offered monthly, quarterly, annually, or even longer. Lockups are also common, although far less restrictive than those of PE funds—usually one to three years. It's also worth noting that gates can go up at the discretion of the manager to delay, suspend, or prorate withdrawals during periods of tumult.

While the "2 and 20" fee model used to be the standard for hedge funds, fees have been coming down and "1.5 and 15" seems to be more common these days. That said, managers seem more willing to reduce management fees than they do carried interest.

Some hedge funds must outperform a high-water mark or a previously achieved return threshold before they can collect a performance fee. This attribute prevents managers from collecting a performance fee until investors recoup previous losses.

Private Alternative Investment Platforms for Wealth Managers

The historical pain points of private alternatives are being addressed by the emergence of private alternative investment platforms that cater to RIAs and other wealth managers. These platforms take on a variety of responsibilities, including manager sourcing, due diligence, and selection. They also streamline the onboarding, allocation, documentation and reporting of these investments.

Many advisors, without these skills and experience themselves, or without access to a CAIA professional on staff, may find value outsourcing many of the core investment and operational functions that these platforms provide. Advisors may also need alternatives education if they are new to the space, and thankfully some platforms provide thorough educational programs.

Another attractive feature of alternatives platforms is that they bring the investment minimums down to more reasonable levels for affluent investors. The investments themselves still have AI or QP requirements, but a great percentage of investors that meet those requirements still often don't have the assets required to allocate to these funds directly. The lower minimums are achieved via feeder fund structures, by which the platform creates its own fund and then aggregates smaller subscriptions, usually with minimums between $50,000–250,000.

In terms of investment options, these platforms curate a limited menu of funds and managers across the basic food groups of private alternatives: private equity, private credit, real estate, and hedge funds. Some platforms, such as iCapital and CAIS, are quite broad-based in their offering and have a mix of brand-name managers and lesser known, boutique managers. Others, like newcomer Windmuehle Funds, have taken a different approach altogether by focusing exclusively on more esoteric and capacity constrained investments like litigation finance and credit card receivables.

One interesting application a few alternatives platforms have embarked on is the creation of their own series of vintage funds. These funds provide a quicker path to create a diversified private markets program with significantly lower minimums than going direct or through a fund-of-funds.

There's an App for That

Regulation A (Reg A), which was passed as part of the 2012 JOBS Act, allows small- and medium-sized companies (that would have a hard time bearing the cost of SEC registration) to raise capital and also gives non-accredited investors the ability to invest—with limitations—in private companies and assets. Reg A is what allows companies like Rally, Fundrise, and Otis to democratize access to asset classes like collectibles, art, and commercial real estate.

This has led to a groundswell of innovation from fintech companies that are bringing to market alternative investing mobile apps and online platforms, like how Robinhood, Betterment and others have brought stock trading and basic asset allocation into the 21st century. The success and popularity of these platforms is largely a result of their removal of frictions from the user experience. Some examples include the digital signature of subscription documents and the securitization and fractionalization of expensive, unique assets so that more investors can access them at smaller bite sizes. Table 10.3 provides a sample of some of the apps and platforms available today, broken down by category.

Table 10.3: The Rise of Alternative Investing Platforms

Asset Class	Example(s)
Collectibles & Culture	Rally, Otis, Collectable, Mythic Markets, StockX
Art	Masterworks
Real Estate	Fundrise, Cadre, PeerStreet, Roofstock
Farmland	FarmTogether, AcreTrader
Alternative Income	YieldStreet
Startups/Private Companies	AngelList, EquityZen, Seed Invest
Digital Assets	Coinbase, Gemini, BlockFi
Royalties	RoyaltyExchange
Income Share Agreements	Edly
Recurring Revenue Streams	Pipe

Source: Author.

Today's consumers—particularly millennials and younger—are increasingly comfortable using mobile devices and apps to manage their personal finances. According to NYU Professor Scott Galloway, the most valuable real estate in the world are the icons that sit on the home page of our smart phones. With the onslaught of activity and growth within fintech, it becomes easy to imagine a future where these apps and platforms disrupt the fund industry altogether. With supercomputers at our fingertips, the very nature of how we access our investments is subject to change and as allocators we should stand ready to adapt with the times. You never know, the home screen could be the new pie chart:

Figure 10.5: The Fintech Smartphone Home Screen

For illustrative purposes only. Left to right: Betterment, Rally, Fundrise, Yieldstreet. Fundrise and the Fundrise logo are registered trademarks of Fundrise, LLC.

Due Diligence

This goes without saying, but it should be obvious by now that performing due diligence on alternative funds and managers is a different animal than vetting a large cap growth manager or selecting an emerging markets ETF. Even within liquid alternatives, there are more moving pieces and nuances to consider when evaluating strategies, processes, performance dispersion, capacity, and fees.

As you progress from liquid alternatives across the spectrum of illiquidity into interval funds (and their cousins) and finally into private fund territory, there are incrementally more layers of due diligence required and boxes that need to be checked. Importantly, operational due diligence becomes equally important as investment due diligence when you are evaluating private fund managers.

A deep dive into due diligence questions and checklists is beyond the scope of this book, but I would stress that all allocators should have a firm understanding of the due diligence resources at their disposal, either internally or through a trusted third-party, and what they are—and are not—equipped to handle.

Making the Right Choice

It's clear that demand for alternative investments is increasing, most notably from those who have been excluded from such investments in the past. As this is new terrain for many, prudent matching of the containers and contents of an investment is key to success. While it may feel like we're stuck in a paradox of choice with the number of investment vehicles allocators must sift through, we can narrow the funnel by first determining:

- Which alternative asset or strategy we are targeting.
- What liquidity preferences or needs our clients have.
- Whether they meet potential investor qualification standards.

Too much choice can be overwhelming, but at the same time we are now entering what could be a golden age of optionality and democratization that hasn't existed before within alternatives.

While liquid alternatives have disappointed some, there are a growing number of high-quality options across the liquidity spectrum.

Registered funds with episodic liquidity windows, like interval funds, have broadened access to illiquid and diversifying asset classes previously unavailable through mutual funds and ETFs. And investors that qualify for, and are interested in, private funds can now leverage a host of alternative investment platforms that solve for the sourcing, diligence, and operational hurdles that advisors have historically grappled with. Finally, the rapid growth of tech-enabled, direct-to-consumer alternative investing apps and platforms has created opportunities that bypass funds altogether to access diversifying assets more directly.

Deciding what to invest in and how to invest in it is a critical step in the allocation process. But the most important decision lies ahead in the next chapter, where we take aim at building better portfolios by putting all the pieces together.

THE ALLOCATOR'S CHEAT SHEET

- Allocators need to ensure they are matching the right investments (contents) with the appropriate structure (container).
- Mutual funds and ETFs check all the right boxes for traditional asset classes and a select group of liquid alternative investments.
- Interval funds (and other semi-liquid fund wrappers) have emerged in a happy middle ground between '40 Act mutual funds and private funds.
- For accredited investors and/or qualified purchasers interested in private alternatives, caution and judiciousness is warranted given the additional complexities and considerations involved.
- Technology is acting as an accelerant to democratize private investments, with many platforms and apps coming to market in recent years that aim to make the exercise of allocating to illiquid investments more accessible and efficient.

CHAPTER 11

The Allocator as Architect—Designing
and Constructing Modern Portfolios

*"Architecture should speak of its time and place but yearn
for timelessness."*

— ***Frank Gehry***

"Whatever good things we build end up building us."

— ***Jim Rohn***

P ARTS I AND II of this book put a spotlight on the challenges facing 60/40
allocations and evaluated the world of possibilities that exists within
alternative investments to augment traditional portfolios. The previous
chapter stressed the importance of alignment between the investments we
wish to own and the structures best designed to efficiently capture them.
We're inching ever closer towards building better portfolios, but we're not
quite there yet. Critical questions still need to be addressed.

- Which alternative building blocks should be selected?
- What is an appropriate target allocation in the aggregate and at the
  individual strategy level?
- Where should the allocation(s) be sourced from?

Beyond those key questions, there are other important considerations
that warrant attention, both holistically and at the individual client
level. These include asset levels, portfolio objectives, liquidity preferences,

investment costs, fund and manager selection, and the impact of taxes, among other things.

This is where the allocator puts on their architect hat, armed with an abundance of raw materials and the vital expertise needed to construct robust portfolios that will succeed in the context of a client's unique needs and circumstances.

In this chapter, we examine potential alternatives to a traditional 60/40 portfolio using index and backtest data. A handful of sample portfolios are presented based on investment objectives and client types. Various frameworks for sizing, sourcing, and selecting alternatives are identified. The chapter closes with commentary related to important trade-offs and considerations allocators will need to weigh during the portfolio construction process.

Is there a new 60/40?

Yes and no. Yes, from the standpoint that we can and should expand beyond the limitations of 2-D portfolios to include a broad, third dimension of diversifying investments under the alternatives umbrella. Investors seeking balance and using 60/40 as their baseline should generally own less of the "40," perhaps a bit less of the "60," and a decent amount more of "other." But that is where the generalizations end.

To prescribe a specific portfolio would be a disservice and an oversimplification of an inherently nuanced process. At the risk of butchering a Tolstoy quote: conventional portfolios are all alike; every unconventional portfolio is unconventional in its own way. So, while there is no one new 60/40, there are many ways to skin this cat. Arriving at the end allocation should follow a four-step process:

1. Choose what you want to own and understand why you want to own it.
2. Determine how much you are willing and able to hold.
3. Figure out where new allocations should be funded and sourced from.
4. Reconcile any limitations or constraints at the organization or client level.

Despite my regular usage of the word alternatives throughout this book, hopefully its lack of utility as a catchall is evident by now. From real estate to Bitcoin and everywhere in between, there are no shortage of opportunities to select from. Some allocators may be all in and want it all. Others may have a more targeted approach in mind. Regardless, I think a useful framework for identifying what your own alternatives allocation should look like is what Stone Ridge CEO Ross Stevens refers to as the 10/10 (Ten Ten) portfolio. Per Ross, "In its purest, unobtainable form, the 10/10 is ten long-term allocations, each 10% weight, each with a persistent, pervasive, and intuitive risk premium, each uncorrelated with traditional markets, each uncorrelated with each other, each anti-fad."

Figure 11.1 shows a sample 10/10 portfolio using many of the assets discussed in the preceding chapters. This particularly 10/10 could be achieved by both accredited and non-accredited investors alike using mutual funds, ETFs, interval funds, and—in the case of digital assets—direct ownership of coins. Assuming that one day a Bitcoin ETF is approved by the SEC in the U.S., this 10/10 could be owned using exclusively 1940 Act registered investment vehicles.

Figure 11.1: Hypothetical 10/10 Portfolio

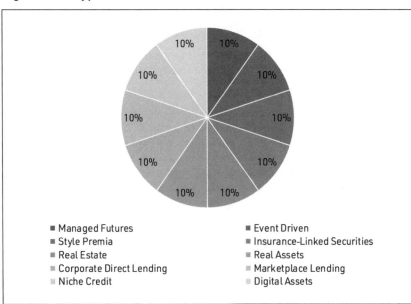

Source: Author.

What I like about the 10/10 framework is that it separates the alternatives allocation as its own pie with ten equal slices. Once this piece of the puzzle is specified, the subsequent decisions about sizing and sourcing in the context of the total portfolio are made simpler. It's important to keep in mind that the 10/10 is just like any other framework in that it's only a jumping off point—you can be flexible and bend the rules.

Suppose you haven't identified ten alternative allocations you want to sink your teeth into. Perhaps you have seven. That leaves you with three slices open for you to allocate additional weight across your highest conviction asset classes. On the flipside, maybe you have twelve or thirteen alternatives you want to make room for. The 10/10 approach could instill some discipline by requiring that you rank your top ten and ditch the runners-up. Alternatively, you could get creative and lump certain exposures together as one line item so that everything still fits. For example, infrastructure, farmland, and timberland are similar, but different. Yet there are diversified real asset strategies that combine them together in one fund. In the context of 10/10, that could take up one slot rather than three.

The 10/10 framework is but one of many approaches that range in complexity and (perceived) optimization. Its beauty is in its simplicity and explicit humility. This sort of thing can be easily overthought and overengineered and we must not forget that eventually it needs to be translated and explained to the client.

Assuming you're confident in your arsenal of alternatives, decisions around sizing and sourcing remain.

Sizing and Sourcing Alternatives

This may sound like a broken record by now, but there is no one-size-fits-all allocation weight that makes sense for all investors. There are too many variables at the individual client level that must be evaluated to determine an appropriate allocation. If you have decided to commit to an alternatives allocation as a strategic component of your portfolio mix, the sweet spot lies somewhere between "enough to make a difference" and "too much that investors can't stick with it." What's become increasingly clear is that the only wrong answer is zero.

I know that's not exactly a satisfactory answer for those who were hoping for a precise declaration, but it's the truth. In my own experience, anything below 10% doesn't move the needle enough to matter and anything above 30% you start to test the boundaries of behavioral risk.

The exact number you land on will ultimately depend on:

- Investor qualifications (AI, QP, etc.)
- Average client size
- Types of alternatives being used
- Tax considerations
- Liquidity considerations
- Existing portfolio/holdings
- Client sophistication level/experience with alternatives
- Age and time horizon
- Cash flow needs

Model portfolios with target weights to various assets work great in a vacuum and can be an excellent starting point, but allocators need to be somewhat malleable—especially those working with larger clients that need (and expect) a more tailored approach.

In addition to sizing the third dimension of the portfolio, allocators must figure out where it will come from—stocks, bonds, or some combination of the two. The outcome will rest on a handful of variables, namely the views of the allocator and/or their client, the composition of the alternatives bucket, and the priority of the objectives the portfolio is trying to achieve.

A client with a high return target is likely to fund most, if not all, of the alternatives allocation from traditional fixed income and will recognize that this choice will likely result in some additional mark-to-market volatility relative to a 60/40. This preference may also end up incorporating a private market allocation within equities.

A portfolio objective more geared towards stability and income generation may tilt heavily towards credit and real assets within the alternatives sleeve. And given a focus on preservation and drawdown control, a larger than usual portion might be funded from stocks.

Lastly, an allocator with a strong conviction that abnormally high inflation is on the horizon is certain to lighten the load on traditional fixed income. In its place is likely to be an emphasis on both inflation-sensitive assets as well as structurally uncorrelated assets that aren't directly influenced by macro factors.

Modern Portfolios in Action

While it's clear that cookie cutter allocation recommendations aren't of great benefit, we still need to examine some hypotheticals. What follows is by no means an explicit endorsement of a particular portfolio and is not representative of an actual investor experience. With all the usual caveats and disclaimers out of the way, I went about constructing a few sample portfolios that we can contrast against a 60/40.

I wanted the samples to be representative of something most individual advisors could access through a financial advisor. For those reasons I excluded asset classes like private equity that aren't truly available to non-AI/QP clients. I did, however, include indices representative of less liquid asset classes where '40 Act interval funds exist.

The indices and backtests used to represent the various alternative chapters are the same as in the chapters from Part II. Specifically, our alternatives allocation within each portfolio will be equal-weighted amongst alternative risk premia, insurance-linked securities, real assets, and alternative credit. For the stock and bond allocations in both the 60/40 as well as the hypothetical portfolios including alternatives, we use the MSCI ACWI to represent global stocks and the Barclays US Aggregate Bond Index as our proxy for fixed income.

I built three hypothetical portfolios with varying degrees of alternatives for different investor objectives and characteristics:

1. **50% stocks/25% alternatives/25% bonds**: This portfolio introduces a meaningful 25% weighting to the alternatives mix and sources the allocation 60% from bonds and 40% from stocks. It is intended to have a similar risk profile as a 60/40 portfolio, but with an objective of higher returns due to the low expected returns offered by traditional fixed income.

2. **60% stocks/20% alternatives/20% bonds**: This portfolio is geared towards an investor willing to tolerate a little higher volatility in the pursuit of higher expected returns. In this example, the alternatives allocation comes exclusively from bonds. Meant to be long horizon in nature, this portfolio can weather the inevitable equity storms, but still requires diversification and is not dependent upon bonds exclusively to get the job done.

3. **40% stocks/30% alternatives/30% bonds**: This portfolio is intended for a more conservative investor who is looking to de-risk significantly from 60/40 but is hesitant to move too much capital into fixed income. In this case, an even higher allocation of 30% to alternatives is targeted, coming two-thirds from stocks and one-third from bonds.

Each portfolio has achieved the desired objectives, as seen in Table 11.1. The 50/25/25 portfolio outperformed the 60/40 with less volatility and a lower max drawdown. The 60/20/20 allocation achieved the highest returns relative to the 60/40, commensurate with its slightly higher risk profile. Lastly, the 40/30/30 portfolio earned returns in line with the 60/40 but with a greater than 20% reduction in volatility and maximum drawdown.

Table 11.1: Three Hypothetical Portfolios with Varying Alternatives Allocations

10/1/2004–12/31/2020	60/40	50/25/25	60/20/20	40/30/30
Annualized Return	7.18%	7.54%	7.65%	7.15%
Volatility	9.53%	8.48%	10.17%	7.40%
Maximum Drawdown	-36.48%	-32.28%	-39.11%	-27.88%

Source: Author.

It's important to remember that this is what would have happened over the last 15 years or so. As we look forward, which we should always do, the bond piece will not have the large tailwind of declining rates to support it and the math of low starting yields is unavoidable. While the future has yet to be written, it is reasonable to assume that introducing substantive allocations to alternatives can result in portfolios that are more robust to a wider spectrum of potential outcomes.

At its core, asset allocation is an exercise in managing trade-offs under a set of constraints. The choices we make, and their perceived benefits and costs, are made on a relative basis to other options we can exercise.

How I Invest My Money

If the three preceding hypothetical portfolios aren't quite tangible enough for you, how about we take a more granular look at someone's real life asset allocation—my own. While I am unable to share the specific funds I own, I can provide a detailed glimpse into how I approach alternatives with my own money.

We'll start with how I assess the role of alternatives broadly, and their target weight in my overall portfolio. My wife and I are in our mid-thirties, with a relatively high tolerance for risk and multiple decades until we retire. Our long time horizon coupled with our ability to stomach volatility and drawdowns points us toward an equity-heavy portfolio to achieve our financial goals. We have no current income needs from the portfolio and no major short- or intermediate-term liabilities that would require us keeping significant liquidity in cash or core bonds. As such, our portfolio does not target any traditional fixed income investments. That does not mean yours shouldn't, as no two investors' circumstances are the same. This is just what works for us.

I mentioned our portfolio is equity-centric, but that does not mean it is equity-only. It would probably be weird if I wrote this book if that was the case, wouldn't it? I am a big believer that true diversification is magic. Period. Because of this, we target a material allocation to diversifying, non-traditional investments across our portfolio. What that target is depends on how we account for one large variable.

The largest asset on our balance sheet is the equity ownership in the company I work for, which is a private registered investment advisor (RIA) firm. The decision to include or exclude that asset as a part of our investment portfolio has a big impact on what our target allocation to alternatives looks like. When included as part of our equity allocation, our portfolio resembles an 85/15 mix of stocks and alternatives. When omitted, the portfolio targets shift to a 75/25 mix of stocks and alternatives. Personally, I like looking at it both ways due to the idiosyncratic nature of the business ownership asset.

Regardless of which total portfolio target is used, the allocation within alternatives looks the same. Figure 11.2 shows my allocation targets across the various categories discussed in Part Two of the book.

Figure 11.2: My Alternatives Target Allocation

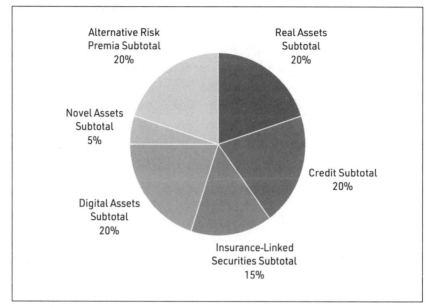

Source: Author.

Some additional details on each:

- **Alternative Risk Premia**: A diversified mix of single-strategy and multi-strategy mutual funds that provide exposure to managed futures, event-driven, style premia, global macro, equity market neutral, and put selling strategies.
- **Real Assets**: I lump real estate into this bucket alongside infrastructure, farmland, and timberland. Currently, the real estate allocation is all in publicly traded REITs. The allocation to the other asset classes is obtained through an interval fund that accesses all three, predominantly in private markets.
- **Alternative Credit**: A roughly equal split across three different interval funds that provide exposure to Corporate Direct Lending, Marketplace Lending, and Niche Credit.
- **Insurance-Linked Securities**: This allocation is spread across a mutual fund and an interval fund to achieve a relative balance between catastrophe bonds and quota shares.

- **Digital Assets**: This is probably the sleeve that differs the most from client portfolios. With no great ways to access Bitcoin and other crypto assets in '40 Act funds as of this writing, I choose to own the assets directly. This is certainly not for everybody, nor is it for the faint of heart. As mentioned in Chapter 9, the volatility of digital assets can be magnitudes higher than that of stocks. I have done my homework, have conviction in the long-term investment thesis, and am comfortable with the risk in my portfolio.
- **Other Novel Assets**: Currently, this is a smaller allocation focused on collectibles through a couple of the apps mentioned in previous chapters. My expectation is that over time this will grow to include asset classes like art and ISAs.

Notably absent from the inventory above is private equity. I mentioned earlier the equity ownership stake in my employer. I also have a smaller direct investment in a private company that operates in an industry I am extremely passionate about—professional wrestling (that's a topic for another book). Given the illiquid and private nature of these and how much they represent of my total wealth, I don't view it as absolutely necessary to own more private equity at this stage of my life. I fully anticipate that will change at some point, but when the time comes I will view it not as an alternative investment but as a component of my strategic equity allocation—not all allocators will agree with that.

I should also mention that other than my investments in crypto and collectibles, the alternative assets in my portfolio are owned inside of retirement accounts through my attempt to optimize asset location and preserve the return streams of my least tax-efficient asset classes.

As cathartic as it was to write about the "why" behind my own portfolio, hopefully it demonstrated how messy things can get in the real world when investing based on unique individual circumstances. With that in mind, we will shift gears and review some best practices to consider when allocating to alternatives.

Alternatives and Liquidity

The subject of liquidity is a Pandora's box with a great deal of nuance that extends beyond this chapter. While liquidity exists on a spectrum and can be viewed through a variety of lenses, in short it simply represents the ability to turn an asset into cash or cash into an asset.

Liquidity is a personal choice, not an edict. For some, illiquidity is a non-starter. They want none of it. To others, it is the preferred path, freeing them from the stomach-turning volatility that public markets can bring to bear. Millions of entrepreneurs wake up each morning accepting illiquidity as they invest in themselves, pouring blood, sweat and tears into what eventually becomes their largest asset. Those lucky enough to see it succeed and even luckier still to be able to one day monetize that asset might have different attitudes towards illiquidity than a W-2 employee whose only investment experience is through daily redeemable funds in their 401(k) plan.

The reality is that most people do not *need* fully liquid portfolios. We have just grown accustomed to investing that way due to common portfolio construction practices and the historic lack of quality illiquid investment choices for most people. High minimums and other factors have kept less liquid asset classes out of reach for most of modern investment history, reserving them only for the pensions, endowments, and uber-wealthy of the world. As we have documented, that has all started to change and there are more and more options today for both accredited and non-accredited investors to access semi-liquid and illiquid investments.

For investors with long-term goals, sacrificing some liquidity may bring multiple benefits. First and foremost, there is the opportunity to earn the illiquidity premium that is associated with private and illiquid investments. While there is no way to pinpoint exactly what that premium is, both theory and practice support its existence. The perhaps understated benefit of illiquidity is that it enforces discipline and a long-term mindset in a way that public markets can't. The temptation to change course and succumb to market volatility are all too present in daily liquid investments. As AQR's Cliff Asness quips, "What if investors are simply smart enough to know that they can take on a lot more risk (true long-term risk) if it's simply not shoved in their face every day (or multi-year period!)?"

Just as illiquidity isn't inherently a negative, neither is liquidity. Liquidity provides optionality, and like any option there can be value to it. It allows you to fine-tune risk in a way that illiquidity does not. Liquidity also allows you to rebalance a portfolio to a degree that illiquidity does not. Conversely, while there may be a behavioral benefit to locking up capital in illiquid investments, it forgoes the optionality and flexibility that liquidity provides and should be compensated as such.

Liquidity gives us a feeling of control over our investments by allowing us to determine when and how we move into and out of them. But the sense of control can come at a cost. By demanding 100% liquidity in a portfolio, we may be forgoing potentially valuable opportunities for return enhancement, income generation, and risk management. We should view illiquidity as the price of admission to gain access to alternative investments with favorable properties. Now seems like the appropriate time for advisors to revisit the antiquated notion that a 100% daily liquid portfolio should be the default choice.

Alternatives and Market Timing

No matter the investment type or strategy, there will always be a subset of allocators enamored with the notion of successfully timing entry and/ or exit. Famed investor Peter Lynch is credited as saying, "Far more money has been lost by investors preparing for corrections, or trying to anticipate corrections, than has been lost in corrections themselves." While Lynch was referring specifically to the stock market and the challenges associated with market timing in that arena, it's natural to wonder whether non-traditional investments may lend themselves better to timing strategies.

Due to the heterogenous nature of alternatives as discussed ad nauseum in this book, a blanket answer will not suffice. With that in mind, here are some considerations:

- **Illiquid assets don't lend themselves well to timing**: The inability to transact easily and the lack of control around cash flow timing makes tactical allocation decisions for private market investments a near impossibility.
- **What's good for the goose is good for the gander**: If timing has been largely unsuccessful in stock markets, interest rates, etc., then we should be skeptical of our ability to time other assets. Even if there is some

signal that a timing strategy might work, whether it can survive post-transaction costs and post-taxes is a different question altogether.

- **Occasionally lean in**: This does not apply to all asset categories, but there are a handful of alternatives that tend to experience higher returns following certain events. Similar to how equity markets usually do better than average when bought at low multiples, strategies like merger arbitrage work best when deal spreads are abnormally high, and reinsurance occasionally offers hard markets following bad loss years when favorable renewal rates follow. Things can get whacky during periods of extreme market dislocations, where spreads and prices may be more indicative of forced liquidations as opposed to efficient market pricing.

While all or nothing decisions rarely work in investing, slight modifications to strategic allocations may provide a release valve for investors with an itch that needs to be scratched. And certain asset classes do exhibit tendencies to perform better when certain conditions are met. More than anything, remain humble with any deviations from your strategic allocation, and don't expect to be rewarded immediately. Remember, the market doesn't care that you made an allocation change.

All else equal, any allocation in the portfolio is best made with an owner's—not a renter's—mentality.

Alternatives and Taxes

Investing is a hard enough exercise before throwing the additional complexities around taxes into the equation. One advantage that many institutions have over individual investors is their favorable tax treatment. Managing one pool of capital that is largely tax-exempt is a different animal than overseeing multiple accounts, each with different tax treatment, for the same household whose marginal tax rate may change over time with corresponding changes to their income and/or the tax code.

There are a number of commonly used tax-management strategies that wealth managers have historically used for taxable investors, such as tax-loss harvesting, gain deferral, the use of tax-efficient asset classes (municipal bonds) and vehicles (ETFs), and asset location.

As it relates to alternatives specifically, asset location may be the strategy with the potential to add the most value, depending on the mix and size of account types and the client's tax bracket. While certainly not a blanket statement, alternatives are generally not the most tax-efficient asset classes and strategies. This owes in large part to either: a) their propensity to pay out high levels of current income taxed at ordinary income rates; or b) the distribution of capital gains that can often show up in higher turnover strategies. Where appropriate, allocators should consider housing tax-inefficient alternatives inside of tax-deferred (or exempt) accounts such as Traditional or Roth IRAs.

Determining which investments best fit into which account types requires decomposing the expected returns of each asset class into the various tax-sensitive components. Expectations and estimates around the following components of return can help contextualize an investment's attributes regarding taxation:

- Ordinary income
- Dividends
- Long-term capital gains
- Short-term capital gains
- Asset class specific tax rates
- Federal tax exemption
- State/local tax exemption
- Foreign income subject to withholding

While tax-loss harvesting (TLH) can be a valuable tax-management technique, there are some additional considerations related to harvesting losses for alternatives. Key to the success of TLH is having a high-quality substitute security to purchase with the proceeds of the position you are liquidating so as not to disrupt the integrity of the overall asset allocation. In traditional asset classes, finding an appropriate match is a relatively straightforward exercise with many options and tighter dispersion between funds in the same category. As discussed earlier, funds in alternative categories see much wider return dispersion between the top and bottom performing funds. This added layer of uncertainty and the potential dearth of decent options in certain categories may make the trade-offs of TLH less compelling.

Managing taxes is a critical component of portfolio management for taxable investors. That said, there is a risk of becoming too overly focused on taxes to the detriment of investment returns and optimal diversification. For taxable investors without the luxury of account type diversification, it's important to not let the tax tail wag the investment dog. Even for those investing with mostly taxable dollars, a tax-inefficient investment can still be a valuable addition to a portfolio if on an after-tax basis it offers enough return and/or diversification relative to existing holdings.

While many alternative investments are subject to material tax-drag for taxable investors, some investment managers offer tax-aware implementation of their strategies to alleviate the impact. For example, tax loss harvesting can be better facilitated by strategies that use both long and short positions, regardless of market direction.

Alternatives and Costs

Alternatives are more expensive than stock and bond index funds. There's no getting around it. In a world where passive market beta is almost free, investors rightfully place a greater degree of scrutiny on investments that at first glance seem pricey.

Like anything in life, there is a place for low cost and a place for higher cost. Sometimes we want a burger from McDonald's and other times we prefer a tasting menu from a fine dining establishment. Of course, all else equal, lower cost is better. The problem with that line of thinking, however, is that all else is rarely equal. Trade-offs must be weighed and evaluated, and the costs of any investment must be contextualized. To help with this conversation, I like to frame costs in terms of what I call the Four C's of Investment Costs: **Capacity**, **Craftsmanship**, **Complexity**, and **Contribution**.

- **Capacity**: The amount of capital a strategy can prudently oversee without degrading its integrity is of paramount importance to its cost. The reason market-cap weighted U.S. large-cap stock index funds are essentially free is because they have near infinite capacity. So, while the expenses as a percentage are infinitesimal, from a dollar standpoint they can create meaningful revenue for an asset manager given the incredibly large base they have to charge it on. Conversely, asset classes like reinsurance aren't as scalable. To offer such a strategy at Vanguard-like fees would not be profitable.

- **Craftsmanship**: For nuanced strategies, implementation and design choices can make all the difference between success and failure when translating something that works on paper into the real world. Fees should be commensurate with the level of detail involved in the development and execution work needed to maximize efficacy and minimize slippage.
- **Complexity**: Assets with a higher degree of embedded intricacy typically require oversight and management from people with specialized talent, knowledge and expertise that are not as plentiful as found in other corners of investing. Higher degrees of compensation naturally accompany useful skills that are in high demand and scarce supply.
- **Contribution**: Investments that are structurally uncorrelated to things people already own and that offer meaningful risk premiums are valuable and thus should command a premium price. The more differentiated and additive to the portfolio, the more willing you should be to pay up.

Figure 11.3 summarizes the main features of low-cost and high-cost assets.

Figure 11.3: Features of Low-Cost and High-Cost Assets

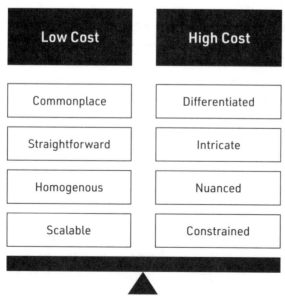

Low Cost	High Cost
Commonplace	Differentiated
Straightforward	Intricate
Homogenous	Nuanced
Scalable	Constrained

Source: Author.

When comparing the expenses of different investment products, we must avoid comparing apples and oranges. The expenses of an S&P 500 ETF should have no bearing on whether a managed futures mutual fund is deemed too expensive. Investment expenses can be looked at in absolute or relative terms. A "smart beta" ETF that costs 25 bps might appear dirt cheap at first glance. But if you look under the hood, you might discover that for all intents and purposes the fund isn't that much different than the broad market—which you can own for 3 bps. In this scenario, you are paying a great deal for the minimal amount of active risk being taken. On the flip side, the price tag for a liquid alternative mutual fund might seem steep at 1.25%, but when measured against a similar hedge fund that charges 2 and 20 it could be a bargain.

Costs can be a tricky subject to navigate with clients. What's important is that you don't overpay for things you can get for much cheaper. When you do decide to pay up, may sure your expected benefits survive the additional costs. As Cliff Asness has stated, "there is no investment product so good gross, that there isn't a fee that could make it bad net."

Alternatives and Due Diligence

Deciding which investments you want exposure to is only half the battle. The matter of choosing which fund or manager provides the best chassis with which to express that allocation decision remains. A great allocation decision can be diminished by poor manager and fund selection.

An extra layer of due diligence is involved for alternative funds, even liquid ones. We've noted already that alternatives in general have wider dispersion within categories than traditional asset classes. Also worth mentioning is the wide range of correlations found within several Morningstar liquid alternatives categories, as evidenced in Figure 11.4. For Long Short Equity and Multi-Alternative, the average three-year correlations to U.S. stocks of funds in those categories is surprisingly high. In the case of Multi Alternative, there are funds with correlations to stocks as high as 0.97 and as low as -0.85.

Figure 11.4: Correlations of Liquid Alternative Categories to Stocks

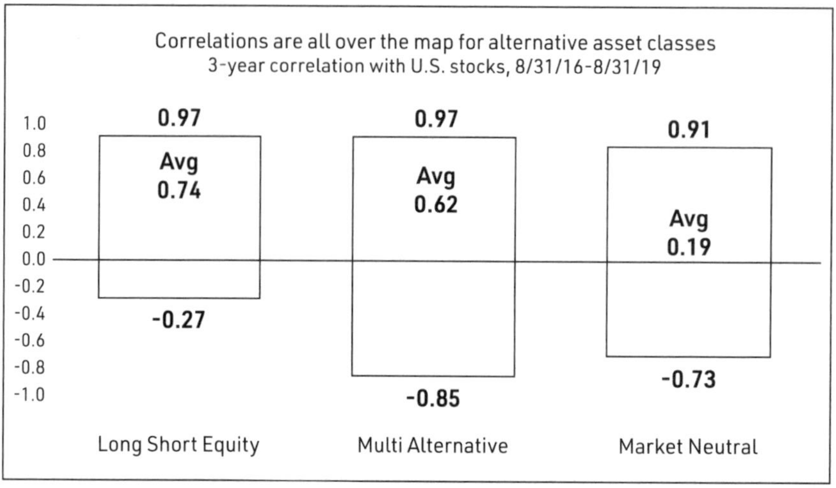

Correlations are all over the map for alternative asset classes
3-year correlation with U.S. stocks, 8/31/16–8/31/19

Source: Morningstar Direct.

Another critical factor in the fund selection is the choice to use a compilation of single strategy funds or a multi-strategy product. This brings up the age-old dilemma between bundling and unbundling. Unbundling of course brings greater control to the allocator in terms of which managers they use, what strategies are involved and in what proportions. This comes with added line item risk, or the risk that at least one thing is always underperforming.

All parents can relate to how difficult it can be to get a young child to eat their vitamins or vegetables. Sometimes, the easiest way to sneak it by them is by mixing it in with other foods. This is analogous to the argument in favor of multi-strategy approaches. Ultimately, allocators will need to weigh their diligence bandwidth and client sensitivity to these issues to make the appropriate decision.

The "One Job" of Asset Allocators

Michael Mauboussin describes the "one job" of equity investors as taking advantage of gaps between expectations and fundamentals. The "one job" of an asset allocator is much different. As portfolio architects, our job is to take the best raw materials at our disposal and design an allocation that can most reliably meet clients' objectives over the widest possible array of market environments. That's it. That's the job.

Balancing long-term wealth accumulation and some reasonable measure of short-term safety is a tall order but not unrealistic. For many years, the 60/40 was able to deliver it. But as Warren Buffett has stated, "what the wise do in the beginning, fools do in the end." Early adopters of traditional 60/40-like portfolios were indeed wise as they sought to diversify, balance risk, rebalance and so forth. Those that implemented that approach decades ago benefitted greatly from a massive tailwind of declining interest rates and generally buoyant equity markets. Relying exclusively on those two levers today is going to make the "one job" of allocators increasingly tougher in the years ahead. Fortunately, as we have seen in this chapter, there are several alternatives.

As we enter the final chapter of the book, the focus shifts towards the most fundamentally important aspect of implementing alternative investments— inspiring the confidence needed for clients to stick with them.

THE ALLOCATOR'S CHEAT SHEET

- Once we have our arms around all the available tools and raw materials at our disposal, we must get to work and build.
- While 60/40 may no longer be the answer, there are many possible new answers.
- There is no one-size-fits-all portfolio.
- The sheer number of asset classes, strategies, structures, fund options, and portfolio construction methods with which to build portfolios can be daunting.
- Advisors and the individuals and families they serve need to have honest discussions around the role that alternatives can play within a portfolio and the various implementation issues to consider when determining appropriate investment types, position sizing, and sourcing.

CHAPTER 12

Sharpening Your Edge—Cultivating the Client Experience Through Courage and Communication

> *"The value of an idea lies in the using of it."*
> — ***Thomas Edison***

> *"Courage is reckoned the greatest of all virtues; because, unless a man has that virtue, he has no security for preserving any other."*
> — ***Samuel Johnson***

> *"To simplify before you understand the details is ignorance. To simplify after you understand the details is genius."*
> — ***James Clear***

G REAT INVESTMENTS (AND by extension great portfolios) are nothing if not paired with equally great investors. The best-laid investment plans can fall apart because of bad investor behavior, poor communication, or mismatches in expectations. In this final chapter of the book, we shift gears to the important task of cultivating a successful investment experience for our clients.

I have witnessed first-hand the common pitfalls and struggles advisors have experienced when allocating to alternatives. Addressing these issues at their core is a two-part process:

1. **Defining** the Allocator's Edge.
2. **Harnessing** the Allocator's Edge.

To sharpen the Allocator's Edge, we must first define what it is. In prior chapters, we identified the ideas and components necessary to build better portfolios. But adopting new portfolios requires a new mindset to go with it. That will be easier for some than others. By quantifying the defining characteristics of the Allocator's Edge, we create an ideal that we can all strive for.

We can then put this into practice in our day-to-day engagements with clients. The investment experience we deliver to the end client is just as important as the underlying investments themselves. This needs to be executed properly. We will close with actionable ideas and tactics related to client communication, education, and expectation setting.

The 60/40 Security Blanket

Meaningful shifts in portfolio construction are challenging not because we lack the tools and methods, but due to the simple fact that it is hard to stray from convention and act independently. Few argue the math confronting traditional portfolios, but fewer act differently because the 60/40 is the collective security blanket we have all clung to.

In 1997, Apple made a splash with their "Think Different" ad campaign, which was widely assumed to be a response to IBM's slogan "Think." Quite ironic, in that the same way "no one ever got fired for buying IBM," allocators rarely get fired for recommending a 60/40.

The Apple ad included the quote:

Here's to the crazy ones.
The misfits.
The rebels.
The troublemakers.
The round pegs in the square holes.
The ones who see things differently.
They're not fond of rules.
And they have no respect for the status quo.

If this resonates with you as an allocator, then congratulations—you may be one of the crazy ones! Many talk the talk of being a contrarian or thinking differently, but few walk the walk. And that is simply because human nature leads us to conform our behavior to that of our peers.

Evolution moves at an indiscernibly slow pace and this trait is hardwired in many of our brains. The social pressure to follow the crowd is all too real and translates into portfolios that all too often resemble those of our peers. As John Maynard Keynes famously stated, "worldly wisdom teaches that it is better for reputation to fail conventionally than to succeed unconventionally."

Edges in Investing

The pursuit of edge in investing is as old as the hills. For generations, investors have sought to capture sustainable excess returns above and beyond those produced by common risk factors. Most edges have been ephemeral, with very few enduring over time. One thing is for certain—competition and technology erode edges.

Researcher Michael Mauboussin documents four historical sources of edge in markets: *behavioral, analytical, informational,* and *technical.* For the latter three, secular forces have been working in concert, chipping away at these edges with reckless abandon:

- The significant reduction of computing and trading costs.
- Increased competition from a large cohort of intelligent, motivated, and well-resourced investors.
- More uniform and fair access to data and information.

Today's markets are dominated by well-trained and highly resourced institutional and professional investors. In fact, research from Morgan Stanley estimates that the number of chartered financial analyst (CFA) charterholders per public company jumped from about 1 in 1976 to 27 in 2019! This is in stark contrast to the composition of markets 50 years ago, when individuals represented roughly 75% of corporate equity ownership.

With analytical, informational, and technical edges few and far between in today's hypercompetitive and high-frequency market landscape, perhaps the last bastion of hope is behavior. As legendary investor Jim O'Shaughnessy quips, "Arbitraging human nature is the last sustainable edge."

Behaving differently than the next person in the crowd puts us in a position to produce a more robust and differentiated investment experience for clients with greater odds of long-term success.

How do we behave differently? We start by imagining the persona best equipped to buck convention.

Defining the Allocator's Edge

The Allocator's Edge is not a specific portfolio per se, but rather a set of characteristics that, if applied cohesively, can improve the odds of achieving unconventional success. If we were to build an allocator from scratch, what traits would we want them to exhibit?

If I were to translate it into an equation, it would be this:

The Allocator's Edge = **S**ensible + **H**umble + **A**utonomous + **R**esolute + **P**ersevering

Hey, what a coincidence—it spells SHARP! Ok, maybe not a coincidence, but I like a good mnemonic device as much as the next guy.

In today's uncertain world, with such lackluster prospects for traditional portfolios, it's hard to imagine five better qualities you would want an allocator to possess to best navigate the challenging road ahead.

- **Sensible**: Armed with logic and data, the sensible allocator approaches her decisions with common sense, practicality, and an evidence-based mindset.
- **Humble**: Lacking clairvoyance, the humble allocator has an appreciation for history, while respecting its limitations. She understands that while we can't predict the future, we can prepare for many possible futures.
- **Autonomous**: Curious, confident, and courageous, the autonomous allocator applies independent thinking with a blatant disregard for traditional portfolio orthodoxy.
- **Resolute**: Purpose-driven to do the right thing by their client, the resolute allocator works tirelessly to meet his goals and objectives with unrivaled tenacity.

- **Persevering**: Patient and process-oriented, the persevering allocator endures through the inevitable rough patches and focuses steadfastly on the long term.

None of us would score a perfect ten on all the above. But that shouldn't keep us from continually striving for excellence in all five areas. Much like incremental returns can compound significantly over decades, so too can incremental habits and behavior changes.

Harnessing the Allocator's Edge

The success of a portfolio is contingent upon the comfort of the investor holding it. The clients most likely to maintain and stick with a portfolio during challenging times are the ones who understand the process behind it the best. This underscores the importance of effective communication, education and transparency between allocator and client.

For those familiar with power laws, my running joke at work is that the 80/20 rule applies to alternative investments. If they account for 20% of the portfolio, they'll be the source of 80% of client questions. While that may sound daunting, responding to these inquiries is not as challenging at it may seem and much of it can be nipped in the bud on the front end through honest, straightforward, and regular communication.

George Bernard Shaw said, "The single biggest problem in communication is the illusion that it has taken place." Often what we deem to be effective communication and education is interpreted by our clients as finance-speak and technical jargon. To bypass this, I have compiled a series of best practices, tactics, and anecdotes to use when translating the benefits of alternative investments in a portfolio in ways that clients can understand.

Establish Principles

All advisors and allocators should have a documented investment philosophy or set of guiding principles that is shared with clients. It doesn't have to be written in stone, but it shouldn't be written in pencil either. These guiding maxims should serve as the foundation for how you manage client assets.

The earlier you introduce these to clients, the more likely they will become familiarized and comfortable with your approach and be less inclined to challenge your recommendations—provided they are in line with your principles.

Once you establish your principles, you can store them wherever you like—your website, the client's portal, their investment policy statement, or in a marketing brochure. It doesn't matter. What matters is that clients are aware they exist and that they are revisited from time to time.

I have a list of 14 principles. Two that I go back to with clients from time to time when discussing alternatives are the ones below:

1. **No investment is an island**: Like all complex systems, portfolios aren't single investments but rather intricate webs of raw materials, each influencing the other. The merits of any particular investment, therefore, must be weighed not only in isolation, but also in the context of how it fits and interacts with the rest of the portfolio.
2. **No silver bullets**: There is no reward without risk, or returns without volatility. The holy grail of all the upside and none of the downside is pure fiction. The secret to success is not to avoid risk, but to take intelligent risks that have historically been compensated.

(All 14 principles can be found in Appendix 3 of the book.)

Set Reasonable Expectations

It's crucial to set reasonable expectations before your clients set unreasonable ones.

Be honest and transparent when reviewing the trade-offs between conventional and unconventional approaches. Don't sugar-coat the challenges facing fixed income and don't overpromise the benefits of alternatives.

"Embrace the suck" is a term used by the military that refers to dealing with bad situations. With more moving parts in a more diversified portfolio, it's best to create an understanding with the end client that every time you meet—whether that be quarterly, semi-annually, or annually—there will always be something in the portfolio that "sucks."

Unconventional portfolios are going to be uncomfortable to hold at times. They will look and behave different than those of our peers. As Howard Marks notes, "Non-consensus ideas have to be lonely. By definition, non-consensus ideas that are popular, widely held or intuitively obvious are an oxymoron. Thus such ideas are uncomfortable; non-conformists don't enjoy the warmth that comes with being at the center of the herd."

Advisors should also set the expectation that the portfolio they hold in ten years may look materially different than the one they hold today. This won't be a function of us changing our stripes or an implication that the decisions we make today are flawed. Rather, it is a tacit recognition that the investable universe will continue to evolve like it always has and that we must be prepared to roll with the punches.

The Double-Edged Sword of Diversification

My three favorite quotes about diversification:

> *"Diversification means always having to say you're sorry."*
> — **Brian Portnoy**

> *"Diversification is a regret-maximizing strategy."*
> — **Jason Hsu**

> *"The bottom line is that since diversification is the only free lunch in investing, you might as well eat a lot of it."*
> — **Larry Swedroe**

To recap: the only free lunch in investing means always saying you're sorry and being full of regret. Doesn't sound like much of a free lunch, does it?

Such is the frustrating nature of diversification.

Don't get me wrong—I absolutely believe in the power of diversification. But diversification can take a long time to bear fruit, as you tend to oscillate between periods of relative and absolute disappointment. We're always going to wish we had more of one thing and less of something else.

Asset manager BlackRock evaluated the experience of owning a diversified portfolio comprised of 40% U.S. stocks, 15% international stocks, 5% small cap stocks, 30% U.S. bonds, 10% high-yield bonds versus that of the S&P 500 over a nearly 20-year period beginning in 2000 and ending in 2019.

What they found was that regardless of the environment, investors had to reckon with either losing money in absolute terms or underperforming in relative terms. Each experience is equipped with its own behavioral quirks. Yet over the full period, the diversified portfolio ended up in roughly the same place while delivering a significantly smoother ride. This stylized example, summarized in Figure 12.1, demonstrates how patience can be a virtue and that investors often have trouble seeing the forest for the trees.

Figure 12.1: Short-Term Absolute or Relative Underperformance, But Long-Term Stability, Brought by Diversification

40% U.S. stocks, 15% international stocks,
5% small cap stocks, 30% U.S. bonds, 10% high yield bonds

Years	S&P 500	Diversified Portfolio		
8/2000-2002	(40.1%)	(18.6%)	✕	"I lost money"
2003-2007	+82.9%	+73.8%	⊖	"I didn't make as much"
2008	(37.0%)	(24.0%)	✕	"I lost money"
2009-2019	+351.0%	+191.7%	⊖	"I didn't make as much"
Total Return	+211.4%	+213.5%	✓	"Diversification wins even when it feels like its losing"
Gr $100K	$311,420	$313,510		

Source: BlackRock.

In some markets, we regret every dollar we put into diversifiers and in others we regret every dollar we didn't put into diversifiers. The 1990s and the 2010s were both challenging decades for diversification. Perhaps not surprisingly, they both coincided with enormous bull markets in U.S. stocks that were accompanied by rising valuations and declining yields. The CAPE ratio for the S&P 500 reached an all-time high of 44.2 in December of 1999. Fast forward to the end of 2020, and despite dropping down to 24.8 in the midst of the COVID-19 bear market, it marched right back up without looking back, finishing the year at the nosebleed level of 33.5 (within the top 2% of historical observations).

Every financial advisor, at some point in their career, has been on the receiving end of a complaint from an unhappy client seeking to abandon diversification (usually right before it is needed most). Much like a global portfolio of stocks and bonds often felt like it was losing relative to an inappropriate benchmark like the S&P 500, a diversified portfolio including a material allocation to alternatives will at times feel foolish versus just owning a 60/40. That doesn't mean it won't be proven the right decision in the end.

The Fox and the Hedgehog

The Ancient Greek poet Archilochus wrote, "the fox knows many things, but the hedgehog knows one big thing." In a hypothetical illustration from AQR, they compare the portfolio of a hedgehog and a fox. The hedgehog owns one strategy with a 0.40 Sharpe ratio. The fox, on the other hand, owns four unique and independent strategies, each with an individual Sharpe of 0.25 but with a combined Sharpe of 0.5 due to the uncorrelated nature of the four components. The two portfolios are illustrated in Figure 12.2.

Figure 12.2: The Sharpe Ratios of the Fox and the Hedgehog

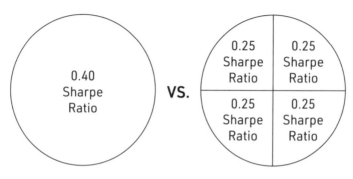

Source: AQR Capital Management.

They then compare the likelihood of at least one strategy being down over various time horizons as well as the likelihood of beating cash over the same time horizons. What they find is that the fox has a slight edge over the hedgehog in beating cash over every time frame, yet is substantially more likely to experience at least one strategy being down.

Said differently, the fox will almost surely lose more battles, but has a higher likelihood of winning the war. This is illustrated in Figure 12.3.

Figure 12.3: Losing More Battles vs. Winning the War

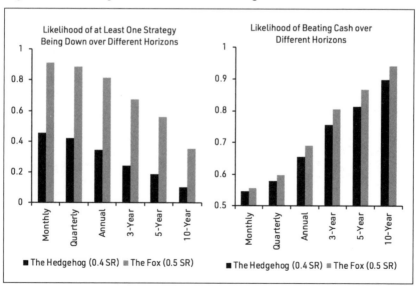

Source: AQR Capital Management.

Setting the Record Straight: Diversifiers vs. Hedges

One of the most common pitfalls encountered when allocating to diversifying strategies is the confusion between non-correlation and negative correlation. For an uncorrelated investment, the stock market doing X over a particular day, week or month should not intuit any degree of confidence in what the diversifying strategy is likely to have done. But that doesn't stop us from trying anyway!

If the underlying return stream is truly unrelated to the market, then the market falling means your return could be positive, negative, or flat. As much as we would all love something that went up every time stocks took a dive, those types of investments often come at a cost, and that cost is negative expected returns. Figure 12.4 is an illustrative example plotting of the returns of public equities against the returns of private equity, equity put buying protection, and a hypothetical diversifying investment. While the put buying protection strategy generates the most *opposite sign* returns, it produces fewer positive returns in aggregate.

Figure 12.4: Diversification is Not a Hedge

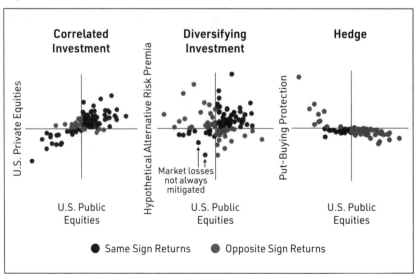

Source: Inspired by AQR. For Illustrative Purposes Only.

Most allocators intuitively like the idea of uncorrelated returns, but most balk at the actual experience of owning uncorrelated return streams. It's important to keep in mind that "uncorrelated" means the results shouldn't bear any relation to what's happening in broader markets.

Make the Unfamiliar Familiar

A phenomenon known as the Lindy Effect states that anything non-perishable has a future life expectancy proportional to its current age. In other words, the longer something exists the more likely it is to continue to exist.

Agriculture, insurance, credit—these asset classes have existed for millennia. In the case of credit, its earliest and most primitive documentation can be traced to ancient Egypt, with letters of credit on clay tablets dating back as far as 3000 B.C. Credit even has historical roots at the philosophical level, as the Athenians widely believed that life itself was a loan from the gods.

Academic research has also documented the existence—and persistence—of investment styles and risk premia such as value, momentum and trend following dating back well over a century. As Robeco's David Blitz notes, "Risks that command a premium should continue to be rewarded with a premium, and mispricing resulting from investor behavior should be persistent as well, since our behavioral tendencies are pretty much hardwired in our DNA."[26]

Allocators should make it their mission to make alternative investments feel less… alternative. As we have discovered in prior chapters, many alternative assets are merely old wine in new bottles. It is only now that they are being unlocked for mainstream adoption. Find ways to incorporate the long histories of these asset classes when introducing them to your clients.

---

26   D. Blitz, "Why I am more bullish than ever on quant," Robeco (November 2020).

Prepare for Long Winters

Time dilation is all too real in the realm of investing—especially when things aren't going your way. Days can feel like weeks, weeks can feel like months, and months can feel like years. In the context of an investor's lifecycle, five to ten years is not that material. Good luck telling that to the investor.

Most investors have a much longer horizon than they give credit to. Even a newly minted retiree has another 20-odd years of life expectancy ahead of them to plan for. Human nature leads us to think of the long term not as point A to point Z, but to each letter of the alphabet along the way. This poses tremendous challenges to our ability to recognize these long horizons as a benefit in our decision-making. Investment portfolios are generally designed to support the spending needs of our future selves decades from now, but you wouldn't know it in how our behavior manifests.

In my experience, alternatives get a much shorter leash for underperformance than traditional investments owing to their novelty and unfamiliarity. We must remember that bad things happen to good processes. More often than not, when something seems broken it is usually just bent. Investors should foster a similar long-term view for non-traditional investments as they would for stocks—the seeds need time to grow.

That doesn't mean you should never consider that something has permanently changed. There is a difference between being disciplined and patient versus being rigid and stubborn. Always keep an open mind, just not so open your brains fall out.

We've all seen the "Death of Equities" cover from *BusinessWeek* in the late 1970s. Of course, it followed a ten-year period of negative returns in stocks. And of course, it was the ultimate buy signal, shortly ahead of the inception of one of the longest bull markets on record. See Figure 12.5.

Figure 12.5: U.S. Equity Risk Premium (Ten-Year Rolling)

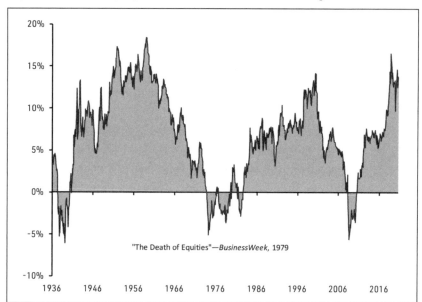

Source: Robeco; Kenneth R. French Data Library.

Today, the value premium (expressed as a long/short portfolio of cheap vs. expensive stocks) is experiencing a similar "lost decade" of negative returns, leading many to declare the death of value. Value has certainly experienced a long winter—but much like equities at the start of the 1980s, the odds seem to favor it simply hibernating as opposed to being gone for good. See Figure 12.6.

Figure 12.6: U.S. Long/Short Value Premium (Ten-Year Rolling)

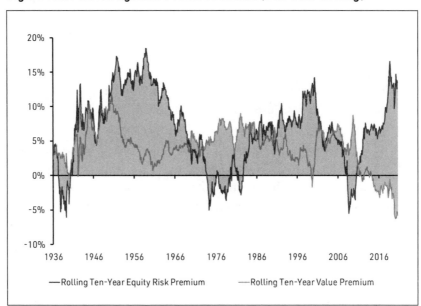

Source: Robeco; Kenneth R. French Data Library.

As cliché and trite as it seems to say, giving any investment with a positive expected return a long enough runway to succeed is paramount to success. As I type this, I can almost hear you saying, "easier said than done." Asset managers, financial advisors, institutional allocators—we are all under immense pressure to deliver short-term results. Even the most long-term oriented among us will recognize that the long term is merely a chain of interconnected short terms, each of which must be lived through by somebody. As allocators, the key thing is making sure we are doing our damnedest to put our constituents in a position to win, and to do whatever is within our power to ensure that journey is as smooth and free of turbulence as possible through our communication, education and responsible setting of expectations.

Jobs to be Done

"Jobs to be Done" is a theory popularized by Clayton Christensen, famous for his work on disruptive innovation. At its core, it recognizes that our lives are full of jobs to be done and we "hire" products to accomplish them. If they do a good job, we're more likely to keep them for the next time. If they fail, odds are they will be "fired."

Portfolios have a variety of potential jobs to be done. The magnitude of those jobs is dependent on the end user. Stocks can perform some jobs well, while failing at others. Same goes for bonds. The ability of investments to succeed at doing a job—whether that be generating income, offering diversification, or protecting against inflation—varies over time. Alternatives are merely another avenue to do another job within a portfolio that cannot be sufficiently accomplished by stocks or bonds.

Football provides a useful analogy here. Offense, defense, and special teams all have specific jobs to be done. And within each of those units, individual players have even more specific jobs. If we think of stocks as our offense, bonds as our defense, then perhaps alternatives are our special teams—picking up slack when the other units are lagging.

Sticking with sports analogies, you could look at the stat sheet of last night's basketball game and assume a player had a bad game because they didn't score any points. But what if that same player had eight rebounds, three steals, and five assists? That player contributed to multiple jobs, even if they didn't rack up any buckets.

Resilience and Antifragility in Asset Allocation

Imagine some of the neighborhood kids are playing baseball outside your house. An errant foul ball comes flying out of nowhere right towards your window. A single-pane window with no grid is likely to shatter to pieces. Now, assume instead you have a triple-pane window with nine grids. Maybe one-pane breaks but the rest remains intact. That's the difference between fragility and resilience.

The difference between fragility and *antifragility* is an entirely different concept altogether. Antifragility results when something gets even stronger after it is stressed. A classic example is the creature of Greek mythology, Hydra, who possesses many heads. As popular lore would have it, when one head was cut off two would grow back in its place.

Most, if not all, of the alternatives covered in this book add some element of resiliency to a portfolio. A small handful of them have exhibited, or may potentially exhibit, antifragile properties. Catastrophe reinsurance, trend following, and Bitcoin are among them.

The concept of antifragility was popularized by Nassim Taleb. Many of the core principles of antifragility can translate to our daily lives as well as the design of our portfolios. *Farnam Street's* Shane Parrish recounts several principles that may resonate with allocators and investors seeking to reduce the fragility of their portfolios:

- Build in redundancy and layers (no single point of failure).
- Experiment and tinker—take lots of small risks.
- Avoid risks that, if lost, would wipe you out completely.
- Keep your options open.
- Focus more on avoiding things that don't work than trying to find out what does work.
- Respect the old—look for habits and rules that have been around for a long time.[27]

Each of these themes has appeared throughout this book. These substantive changes may not make a difference today or tomorrow, but we are playing the long game.

Incremental Upgrades

As fiduciaries and professionals, we should always be seeking ways to upgrade the experience and outcomes for our clients. This goes for guidance around financial planning topics such as estate planning, tax planning and retirement planning. It also relates to the client service we provide and the various components of our technology stacks that touch the client in some way. Clients should similarly understand that we are always looking

---

27   "10 Principles to Live an Antifragile Life," Farnam Street.

for incremental improvements in the way we design and implement their portfolios.

Few iPhone owners noticed any material difference between their iPhone 6 and iPhone 7. But you can best be sure they would be able to see the stark contrast between the first-generation iPhone and the latest. The original iteration of the iPhone and the recently unveiled iPhone 12 both achieve the same core functionality—talk, text, download apps, take pictures, surf the web. Yet if given the chance, exactly zero people would select the original if given a choice between the two. The reasoning is straightforward—today's version has additional features and capabilities AND does all the core stuff better, faster, and more efficiently. The incremental upgrades seem negligible along the way but can be quite substantial when stacked on top of one another.

The More Things Change, the More They Stay the Same

The landing page for Amazon.com back in 1999 contained a grey background, some text and a couple of links.

Welcome to Amazon.com Books!

One million titles, consistently low prices.

(If you explore just one thing, make it our personal notification service. We think it's very cool!)

SPOTLIGHT! – AUGUST 16TH
These are the books we love, offered at amazon.com low prices. The spotlight moves EVERY day so please come often.
ONE MILLION TITLES

Source: Author's impression.

Accounting for what a behemoth of an enterprise Amazon is today, this humble beginning becomes even more inspiring. But as author Morgan Housel has pointed out, "What's neat about this isn't what's changed. It's what's stayed the same." You'll notice at the center of the image the words: *one million titles, consistently low prices*. Amazon has seen many historic successes and some notable failures as well. From Amazon Web Services and Prime to the Fire Phone and Dash Buttons and everything in between, the vision and focus of Jeff Bezos and Co. on selection, price and speed has been astounding. Bezos in his own words:

> "You can build a business strategy around the things that are stable in time. In our retail business, we know that customers want low prices, and I know that's going to be true 10 years from now. They want fast delivery; they want vast selection. It's impossible to imagine a future 10 years from now where a customer comes up and says, 'Jeff I love Amazon, I just wish the prices were a little higher.' Or, 'I love Amazon, I just wish you'd deliver a little slower.' Impossible."

Just as there are timeless strategies that have worked in business for centuries, there are a handful of core objectives and values that will remain evergreen for investors no matter what changes and innovations come our way:

- Meaningful returns are needed to accomplish our financial goals.
- The ability to prudently manage risk is paramount.
- Long term returns are the only ones that matter.
- We will seek diversification across valuable and rewarded risks.
- The ability to transact easily and cost-effectively is a one-way trend.
- Peace of mind, confidence and trust are as important as investment results.
- More transparency is better than less.

Norton Reamer and Jesse Downing, authors of *Investment: A History*, describe investment, at its foundational core, to be "the commitment of resources for future returns." That is as true today as it was centuries ago. Our methods, strategies and actions will progress with the passage of time, but the first principles of investment will remain anchored.

There is No Perfect Portfolio

They say economists suffer from physics envy. Well if that's true, then us allocators probably suffer from a bit of chemistry envy. In chemistry, the same elements combined in the same ratio will always result in the same compound. It doesn't quite work like that with portfolios. The same asset classes combined in the same ratios will not always lead to the same result.

Asset allocation is not a hard science, no matter how bad we want it to be. The perfect portfolio will be forever elusive.

While there is no perfect portfolio to build, that shouldn't stop us from pursuing it. Asset allocation is a bit like putting together a puzzle knowing full well that a few pieces are missing. You trudge ahead anyway and do your absolute best with the materials at your disposal.

Know Your Clients

You know your clients better than I do. Tailor the alternatives experience to them. The profile of your average relationship will help inform which types of asset classes and strategies you ultimately allocate to, in what proportions, and through which vehicle types. Your clients' ages, net worth, tax status, liquidity preferences, attitudes towards risk, technological proficiency and general interest in their portfolio will all play a role in how you ultimately deliver your modified portfolios.

Taking the Leap Forward

Our journey has now reached its conclusion.

It's been said before, but it bears repeating: *there has never been a better time to be an investor.* Advances in portfolio theory, access to information, improvements in transparency, innovation in product development, and significant reductions in costs have created an environment that is conducive to successful investor outcomes.

Though there has never been a better time to be an investor, it does not mean that there has never been an easier time to be an investor. The 24/7 news cycle is constantly nipping at our fingertips and we face an abundance of choice when it comes to selecting our investments. These factors can leave a wide margin for unforced errors to occur. Our biggest challenge as allocators and investors today is staring at us in the mirror.

We have entered a new paradigm of anemic prospects for traditional asset allocation. The prospects of a lost decade ahead for 60/40 portfolios are uncomfortably high. We have seen really expensive stock markets before and incredibly low interest rates before. Seldom have we experienced both concurrently.

Fortunately, there is a growing opportunity to harness a wider array of return streams. The introduction of unique and independent sources of risk into a traditional portfolio can allow investors to maintain their preferred position on the risk curve, but with less uncertainty around the tails and a higher degree of confidence in long-term outcomes.

A future where investors can simultaneously grow and protect their wealth via meaningful diversification and return potential is possible, but it is dependent upon substantive change. Small tweaks and incremental changes will not suffice. The time has come for allocators to be bold and resolute as they forge a new path forward.

The choice facing allocators is best summed up by Seth Godin:

"You can either turn your operation into a cross between McDonald's and Disney, selling the regular kind, pandering to the middle, putting everything in exactly the category they hoped for and challenging no expectations... Or you can do the incredibly hard work of transgressing genres, challenging expectations and seeking out the few people who want to experience something that matters, instead of something that's merely safe."

The Allocator's Edge is there for the taking, and not just for the elite institutions of the world. Innovation and democratization have opened new avenues to reimagine how financial advisors design and implement balanced portfolios on behalf of their clients. Our hindsight no longer remains anchored at 60/40 and the future for allocators need not look like the past. The aperture of our lens is wider than ever before, and the path ahead has been illuminated.

All that remains is the courage to take the leap forward and sharpen the allocator's edge.

THE ALLOCATOR'S CHEAT SHEET

- Alternatives are sure to represent a disproportionate share of questions from clients relative to their weight in the portfolio.
- The investment experience for the end client is just as important as the underlying investments themselves.
- The Allocator's Edge lies in being SHARP–Sensible, Humble, Autonomous, Resolute, and Persevering.
- Clear communications, reasonable expectations, and honest conversations about the sober truth facing 60/40 portfolios and the roles that alternative investments can play will only serve to strengthen client relationships and foster positive outcomes.
- Incremental improvement is the basis for progress in our society and we should continually strive for similar enhancements to our portfolios over time. We must never rest on our laurels or let the insidious nature of complacency rear its ugly head.
- Sharpening the Allocator's Edge won't be easy, but then again, nothing worthwhile ever is.

APPENDICES

APPENDIX 1
Investment Options by Category

F OR ALLOCATORS NEW to alternatives who might not be sure where to begin from a due diligence standpoint, I wanted to provide a list of sample funds and investment options within some of the categories covered within the book. This list is non-exhaustive in nature and is provided for information purposes only. It is not intended to serve as a specific investment recommendation or be considered financial advice. It should not be assumed that any security referenced herein will prove to be profitable. Investors should always consider a fund's risk and investment objectives prior to making an investment.

Alternative Risk Premia

Managed Futures

Fund Name	Ticker	Structure
AQR Managed Futures I	AQMIX	Mutual Fund
PIMCO TRENDS Managed Futures	PQTIX	Mutual Fund
AlphaSimplex Managed Futures Strategy Y	ASFYX	Mutual Fund
Credit Suisse Managed Futures Strategy I	CSAIX	Mutual Fund
American Beacon AHL Managed Futures Strat Y	AHLYX	Mutual Fund
Abbey Capital Futures Strategy I	ABYIX	Mutual Fund

Event-Driven

Fund Name	Ticker	Structure
AQR Diversified Arbitrage	ADAIX	Mutual Fund
Arbitrage I	ARBNX	Mutual Fund
BlackRock Event-Driven Equity	BILPX	Mutual Fund
IQ Merger Arbitrage	MNA	ETF
Water Island Event-Driven Fund	AEDNX	Mutual Fund
Driehaus Event-Driven	DEVDX °	Mutual Fund

Multi-Strategy

Fund Name	Ticker	Structure
AQR Alternative Risk Premia	QRPIX	Mutual Fund
AQR Style Premia Alternative	QSPIX	Mutual Fund
AQR Diversifying Strategies	QDSIX	Mutual Fund
BlackRock Systematic Multi-Strat Instl	BIMBX	Mutual Fund
BlackRock Total Factor	BSTIX	Mutual Fund
GMO Alternative Allocation	GAAGX	Mutual Fund
Stone Ridge Diversified Alternatives	SRDAX	Mutual Fund
Vanguard Alternative Strategies	VASFX	Mutual Fund
Franklin K2 Alternative Strategies Fund	FABZX	Mutual Fund

Insurance-Linked Securities

Insurance-Linked Securities

Fund Name	Ticker	Structure
Stone Ridge High Yield Reinsurance Risk Premium Fund	SHRIX	Mutual Fund
Stone Ridge Reinsurance Risk Premium Interval Fund	SRRIX	Interval Fund
Pioneer ILS Interval Fund	XILSX	Interval Fund

Real Estate and Real Assets

Real Estate

Fund Name	Ticker	Structure
DFA Global Real Estate Securities	DFGEX	Mutual Fund
DFA Real Estate Securities	DFREX	Mutual Fund
DFA International Real Estate Securities	DFITX	Mutual Fund
Vanguard Real Estate Index Fund	VNQI	ETF
Vanguard Global ex-U.S. Real Estate Index Fund	VNQI	ETF
iShares Global REIT	REET	ETF
Versus Capital Multi-Manager Real Estate Income I	VCMIX	Interval Fund
Blackstone Real Estate Income Trust (BREIT)	-	Non-Traded REIT

Real Assets (Infrastructure, Farmland, Timberland, and other Natural Resources)

Fund Name	Ticker	Structure
Versus Capital Real Assets	VCRRX	Interval Fund
First Trust North American Energy Infrastructure	EMLP	ETF
iShares Global Infrastructure	IGF	ETF
Global X U.S. Infrastructure Development	PAVE	ETF
Lazard Global Listed Infrastructure Inst	GLIFX	Mutual Fund
VanEck Vectors Real Asset Allocation	RAAX	ETF
Cohen & Steers Real Assets I	RAPIX	Mutual Fund
GMO Resources Fund	GOFIX	Mutual Fund
FlexShares Morningstar® Global Upstream Natural Resources Index Fund	GUNR	ETF

Alternative Credit

Alternative Credit

Fund Name	Ticker	Structure
Cliffwater Corporate Lending Fund	CCLFX	Interval Fund
Stone Ridge Alternative Lending Risk Premium Fund	LENDX	Interval Fund
Variant Alternative Income Fund	NICHX	Interval Fund
PIMCO Flexible Credit Income Fund	PFLEX	Interval Fund
BlackRock Credit Strategies Instl	CREDX	Interval Fund
Blackstone Private Credit Fund (BCRED)		Non-Traded BDC
Monroe Capital Income Plus Corporation		Non-Traded BDC
Owl Rock Core Income Corp.		Non-Traded BDC

Registered Private Markets Funds

1940 Act-Registered Evergreen Private Markets Funds

Fund Name	Structure
AMG Pantheon Fund	Tender Offer Fund
Conversus StepStone Private Markets	Tender Offer Fund
Hamilton Lane Private Assets Fund	Tender Offer Fund
NB Crossroads Private Markets Access Fund	Tender Offer Fund

Private Alternative Investment Platforms for RIAs/Wealth Management

Platform Name

- iCapital
- CAIS
- Conway Funds
- Proteus
- Windmuehle Funds

APPENDIX 2
Research Rabbit Hole

O NE OF THE most fulfilling aspects of writing this book for a research nerd like me was going down the rabbit hole of books, podcasts, white papers, articles, and blog posts covering the various topics addressed in the text. Since the book's purpose was not designed to go a mile deep into each of these subjects, I wanted to leave a trail of breadcrumbs for those who were interested in exploring the nooks and crannies of alternative investments, asset allocation, and modern portfolio diversification even further.

Asset Allocation

Papers/Articles/Blog Posts

- "Is Alpha Just Beta Waiting to Be Discovered?" (AQR)
- "Running Low: The 2020 Test for Bonds as Hedging Assets" (D. E. Shaw)
- "The Bond Problem" (Man Group)
- "Low Bond Yields and the 60/40 Portfolio" (Abbey Capital)
- "Dare to be Different" (GMO)
- "Grappling with the New Reality of Zero Bond Yields Virtually Everywhere" (Bridgewater Associates)
- "Risk Parity is About Balance" (Bridgewater Associates)
- "The Free Lunch Effect: The Value of Decoupling Diversification and Risk" (Salient Partners)

Books

- *Asset Management: A Systematic Approach to Factor Investing* (Andrew Ang)
- *Your Complete Guide to Factor-Based Investing: The Way Smart Money Invests Today* (Larry Swedroe and Andrew Berkin)
- *Adaptive Markets: Financial Evolution at the Speed of Thought* (Andrew Lo)
- *Adaptive Asset Allocation: Dynamic Global Portfolios to Profit in Good Times—and Bad* (Adam Butler, Michael Philbrick, and Rodrigo Gordillo)
- *Beyond Diversification: What Every Investor Needs to Know About Asset Allocation* (Sebastien Page)
- *Successful Investing Is a Process: Structuring Efficient Portfolios for Outperformance* (Jacques Lussier)
- *Better than Alpha: Three Steps to Capturing Excess Returns in a Changing World* (Christopher Schelling)

Podcasts

- *The Curious Investor:* Face the Factors (S1E2)

Inflation

Papers/Articles/Blog Posts

- "Upside-Down Markets: Profits, Inflation and Equity Valuation in Fiscal Policy Regimes" ("Jesse Livermore," O'Shaughnessy Asset Management)
- "The Inflation Enigma: Balancing Protection and Total Return" (FEG)
- "Fire and Ice: Confronting the Twin Perils of Inflation and Deflation" (AQR)
- "Inflation Regime Roadmap" (Man Group)
- "The Best Strategies for Inflationary Times" (Man Group)

General Alternatives

Papers/Articles/Blog Posts

- "Illuminating the Path Forward: Breaking Free From the 60/40 Portfolio" (Stone Ridge, Oliver Wyman, and Harvard Business School)
- "Alternative Investments: A Primer for Investment Professionals" (CFA Institute Research Foundation & CAIA Association)
- "The Hierarchy of Alpha" (Christopher Schelling)

Podcasts

- *Flirting with Models*: Meb Faber—"Just Survive" (S1E4)
- *The Curious Investor*: Diversify or Hedge? (S2E4)

Books

- *Expected Returns: An Investor's Guide to Harvesting Market Rewards* (Antti Ilmanen)
- *Efficiently Inefficient: How Smart Money Invests and Market Prices Are Determined* (Lasse Heje Pedersen)
- *Pioneering Portfolio Management* (David Swensen)
- *The Investor's Paradox: The Power of Simplicity in a World of Overwhelming Choice* (Brian Portnoy)

Private Equity and Venture Capital

Books

- *VC: An American History* (Tom Nicholas)
- *Patient Capital: The Challenges and Promises of Long-Term Investing* (Victoria Ivashina and Josh Lerner)

Papers/Articles/Blog Posts

- "Public to Private Equity in the United States: A Long-Term Look" (Michael Mauboussin, Morgan Stanley)
- "The PE Secondaries Market Continues to Evolve Rapidly" (Abbott Capital)
- "Do Small Buyout Funds Provide Opportunities for Outperformance?" (Abbott Capital)
- "Building a private markets program at smaller scale" (Meketa)
- "The role of private equity in strategic portfolios" (Vanguard)
- "The Core Role of Private Markets in Modern Portfolios" (BlackRock)
- "The Persistence of PE Performance" (Adams Street Partners)
- "PE Investing at Turning Points in the Market Cycle" (Neuberger Berman)
- "The Importance of Private Markets" (iCapital)
- "Strategic Asset Allocation: Rethinking the Role of Private Markets" (StepStone)

Podcasts

- *First Meeting with Ted Seides*: Dan Rasmussen—Private Equity Risk and Public Equity Opportunity at Verdad Advisers (FM EP.15)
- *Invest Like the Best*: Jerry Neumann—Why Venture is Hard
- *Invest Like the Best*: Brent Beshore—What You Learn About Business

Hedge Funds

Books

- *The Quants: How a New Breed of Math Whizzes Conquered Wall Street and Nearly Destroyed It* (Scott Patterson)
- *When Genius Failed: The Rise and Fall of Long-Term Capital Management* (Roger Lowenstein)
- *The Man Who Solved the Market: How Jim Simons Launched the Quant Revolution* (Gregory Zuckerman)

Podcasts

- *Capital Allocators with Ted Seides:* Adam Blitz—Inside Hedge Fund Allocation (EP.17)

Papers/Articles/Blog Posts

- "Guide to Hedge Funds" (DiMeo Schneider)

Gold and Commodities

Podcasts

- *The Curious Investor*: Commodities: Past, Present, and Futures (S2E2)

Papers/Articles/Blog Posts

- "Gold, the Golden Constant, COVID-19, 'Massive Passives' and Déjà Vu" (Claude Erb, Campbell Harvey, and Tadas Viskanta)
- "Conquering Misperceptions about Commodity Futures Investing" (Claude Erb and Campbell Harvey)
- "The Relevance of Gold as a Strategic Asset" (World Gold Council)

Real Estate

Podcasts

- *Invest Like the Best*: Keith Wasserman—Real Estate Investing
- *Animal Spirits*: Investing in Real Estate with Fundrise

Papers/Articles/Blog Posts

- "How REITs Benefit Asset Allocations" (Cohen & Steers)
- "The Alternative Real Estate Revolution" (CenterSquare)
- "How REITs deliver access to the new economy" (FTSE Russell)

- "Enhancing Real Estate Portfolios: A Holistic Approach Combining Public and Private Investments" (Brookfield)

Real Assets

Papers/Articles/Blog Posts

- "The Triple Play: Adding Timberland, Farmland, and Infrastructure to Portfolios" (Callan)
- "Infrastructure: No Longer a Niche Option" (Callan)
- "Infrastructure" (Meketa)
- "The Right Mix: How Global Listed Infrastructure Complements Private Infrastructure Allocations" (CenterSquare)
- "Introduction to Farmland Investing" (FarmTogether)
- "Agriculture: Ripe for Institutional Investment" (StepStone)
- "Private Real Assets: improving portfolio diversification with uncorrelated market exposure" (Nuveen)
- "Digging In: Assessing the Private Infrastructure Opportunity Today" (Cambridge Associates)
- "Farmland as a Fixed Income Alternative" (Ceres Partners)
- "Timberland and farmland: Real Assets with Complementary Investment Attributes" (Manulife Investment Management)
- "The Case for a Dynamic Allocation to Diversified Real Assets" (Brookfield)

Podcasts

- *First Meeting with Ted Seides*: Jay Girotto—Farmland Opportunity (First Meeting, EP.10)
- *Animal Spirits*: Farmland for the Modern Investor
- *The Meb Faber Show*: Brandon Zick, Ceres Partners, "In Row Crops You're Generating A Lot Of Current Income" (Episode #161)
- *The Meb Faber Show*: David Gladstone, Gladstone Capital, "Farmland Is One of the Most Stable Assets One Can Own" (Episode #114)

Alternative Risk Premia

Podcasts

- *The Curious Investor*: Why Merger Arb Works (S2E5)
- *The Curious Investor*: Gaining Momentum (S2E1)
- *Flirting with Models*: Sandrine Ungari—Alternative Risk Premia (S3E10)
- *Flirting with Models*: Benn Eifert—Volatility Investing (S2E2)
- *Invest Like the Best*: Eric Sorensen—How Quant Evolves
- *Invest Like the Best*: Cliff Asness—The Past, The Present & Future of Quant

Papers/Articles/Blog Posts

- "Two Centuries of Momentum" (Newfound Research)
- "Carry" (Ralph S.J. Koijen, Tobias J. Moskowitz, Lasse Heje Pedersen, and Evert B. Vrugt)
- "Merger Arbitrage Today" (Water Island Capital)
- "Arbitrage: A Brief Introduction" (AQR)
- "Value and Momentum Everywhere" (AQR)
- "Characteristics of Risk and Return in Risk Arbitrage" (Mark Mitchell and Todd Pulvino, *The Journal of Finance*)
- "Will value survive its long winter?" (Robeco)
- "Reports of Value's Death May Be Greatly Exaggerated" (Research Affiliates)
- "A Census of the Factor Zoo" (Campbell Harvey and Yan Liu)
- "Smart Beta, Alternative Beta, Exotic Beta, Risk Factor, Style Premia, and Risk Premia Investing: Data Mining, Arbitraged Away, or Here to Stay?" (Evanston Capital Management)
- "The Impact of Crowding in Alternative Risk Premia Investing" (Nick Baltas, *Financial Analysts Journal*)
- "Understanding the Volatility Risk Premium" (AQR)
- "Asset Allocation Implications of the Global Volatility Premium" (William Fallon, James Park, and Danny Yu, *Financial Analysts Journal*)
- "Are We Living in a Post-Factor World?" (ReSolve Asset Management)

Books

- *Investing with the Trend: A Rules-based Approach to Money Management* (Gregory Morris)
- *Trend Following with Managed Futures: The Search for Crisis Alpha* (Alex Greyserman and Kathryn Kaminski)
- *Dual Momentum Investing: An Innovative Strategy for Higher Returns with Lower Risk* (Gary Antonacci)
- *Quantitative Value: A Practitioner's Guide to Automating Intelligent Investment and Eliminating Behavioral Errors* (Wesley Gray and Tobias Carlisle)
- *Merger Masters: Tales of Arbitrage* (Kate Welling and Mario Gabelli)

Insurance-Linked Securities

Books

- *The Value of Risk: Swiss Re and the History of Reinsurance* (Harold James, Peter Borscheid, David Gugerli, and Tobias Straumann)
- *The Cure for Catastrophe: How We Can Stop Manufacturing Natural Disasters* (Robert Muir-Wood)
- *The Handbook of Insurance-Linked Securities* (Pauline Barrieu, Luca Albertini)

Papers/Articles/Blog Posts

- "Insurance-Linked Securities" (Meketa)
- "Insurance-Linked Securities" (ILS) (Cliffwater)
- "Understanding Reinsurance" (AQR)
- "The Essential Guide to Reinsurance" (Swiss Re)
- "Catastrophe Bonds: Natural Diversification" (Neuberger Berman)
- "Parametric Insurance: Beneficial by Nature" (Neuberger Berman)
- "The Long-Term Case for Insurance Linked Securities" (Amundi Pioneer Asset Management)
- "Cat Bonds Demystified: RMS Guide to the Asset Class" (Risk Management Solutions)

Alternative Credit

Podcasts

- *Invest Like the Best*: Brian Harwitt, Marc Porzecanski, Ali Hamed—Esoteric Credit
- *First Meeting with Ted Seides*: Clarke Futch—Healthcare Royalty Partners (FM.20)

Books

- *Private Debt: Opportunities in Corporate Direct Lending* (Stephen Nesbitt)

Papers/Articles/Blog Posts

- "Where Credit is Due: The Opportunity in 'Alternative' Fixed Income" (Blackstone)
- "Assets-as-a-Service: Credit Investors' Role in a Transforming Economy" (Magnetar Capital)
- "Specialty Finance: An Investor's History" (Magnetar Capital)
- "Credit as a Separate Asset Class" (Cliffwater)
- "US Direct Lending: Comparative Performance Through the Financial Crisis" (Cliffwater)
- "Alternative Credit—The Road Less Traveled" (Ares Capital)
- "Private Credit Primer" (Verus)
- "Private Credit Strategies: An Introduction" (Cambridge Associates)

Digital Assets/Cryptocurrencies

Podcasts

- *Invest Like the Best*: Chris Dixon—The Potential of Blockchain Technology
- *Capital Allocators with Ted Seides*: Crypto for Institutions 1: Eric Peters—The Macro Case for Bitcoin (EP.180)

Papers/Articles/Blog Posts

- "Bitcoin: A Peer-to-Peer Electronic Cash System" (Satoshi Nakamoto)
- "What I think about Bitcoin" (Ray Dalio, Bridgewater Associates)
- "The Case for Digital Assets" (One River Asset Management)
- "In Math We Trust" (One River Asset Management)
- "Bitcoin Investment Thesis: An Aspirational Store of Value" (Fidelity Digital Assets)
- "Illuminating the Path Forward: Bitcoin in Institutional Portfolios" (NYDIG and Oliver Wyman)
- "The Power of Bitcoin's Network Effect" (NYDIG)
- "Ethereum Whitepaper" (Vitalik Buterin)
- "Cryptoassets: The Guide to Bitcoin, Blockchain, and Cryptocurrency for Investment Professionals" (CFA Institute)

Books

- *Cryptoassets: The Innovative Investor's Guide to Bitcoin and Beyond* (Chris Burniske)
- *Digital Gold: Bitcoin and the Inside Story of the Misfits and Millionaires Trying to Reinvent Money* (Nathaniel Popper)

Novel Asset Classes

Podcasts

- *Invest Like the Best*: Jesse Walden—A Primer on NFTs
- *Invest Like the Best*: Rishi Ganti—Esoteric Assets
- *Animal Spirits*: Edly ISA's—Invest in Student Achievement
- *Animal Spirits*: Investing in Art with Masterworks
- *Animal Spirits*: Help with Your Down Payment From Unison

Papers/Articles/Blog Posts

- "NFTs and a Thousand True Fans" (Andreessen Horowitz)
- "The Financialization of Everything" (John Street Capital)
- "The Test of Time: Art as an Investment" (Of Dollars and Data)
- "Software is Eating the Markets" (Not Boring by Packy McCormick)
- "Sneakers as an Alternative Asset Class" (Cowen)
- "A Primer on Investing in Sports Memorabilia" (Collectable)
- "Art as an Asset" (Morgan Stanley)

Books

- *Exotic Alternative Investments: Standalone Characteristics, Unique Risks and Portfolio Effects* (Kevin Mirabile)

Interval Funds and Other Unlisted Investment Structures

Papers/Articles/Blog Posts

- "Frequently Asked Questions About Interval Funds" (Morrison & Foerster LLP)
- "Interval Funds: Addressing the Needs of High-Net-Worth Investors" (Investments & Wealth Institute)
- "An Introduction to Interval Funds" (BlackRock)
- "Access Points for the Masses: Analyzing the alternative asset ecosystem" (PitchBook)
- "Private Markets Have Become Accessible to Individual Investors" (iCapital)
- "Transfer of power: A new epoch for retail investors is just beginning" (*The Economist*)

APPENDIX 3
Investment Principles

A CORE SET OF investment principles can serve as a compass and an anchor when making investment decisions on behalf of clients. Particularly during turbulent times, having a catalog of deeply rooted principles is paramount to long-term success.

The 14 principles below, in no particular order, truly encapsulate how I think about constructing thoughtful portfolios designed to maximize clients' odds of achieving their desired long-term outcomes.

Principle One | Grey Matters

Active versus passive, traditional versus alternative, cheap versus expensive—all examples of black and white thinking that are too simplistic for the complexity of investing. When context matters, respect the grey zone.

Principle Two | Markets are Smart

Financial markets are very efficient. Not perfectly so, of course, but enough to eliminate any low-hanging fruit. The market is collectively smarter than any of us are individually. We must demonstrate humility in our actions and understand that edges in investing are few and far between.

Principle Three | Focus on Factors

If asset classes are food, then factors are the underlying nutrients. Macro factors—such as interest rates, inflation, liquidity, credit, and economic growth—and style factors—such as value, momentum, quality, volatility and size—are the building blocks of returns.

Principle Four | No Investment is an Island

Like all complex systems, portfolios aren't single investments but rather intricate webs of raw materials, each influencing the other. The merits of any particular investment, therefore, must be weighed not only in isolation, but also in the context of how it fits and interacts with the rest of the portfolio.

Principle Five | Minimize Frictions

Tax drag, trading costs and anything else that deters from efficiency should be closely scrutinized because over time, these frictions can accumulate and become costly to the investor. It's what you keep, not what you earn, that matters.

Principle Six | Markets Change, People Don't

Economies go through expansions and recessions. Markets go boom and bust. The root cause in each instance is different, but the human element is constant: fear, greed, hope, envy. Markets are continually evolving, but human nature is unlikely to change.

Principle Seven | Expectations over Forecasts

The stock market crashes from time to time. The stock market is going to crash next year. The former is an expectation, the latter is a forecast. Expectations are grounded in history and examined through a probabilistic lens. Forecasts require a crystal ball. Better to be vaguely right than precisely wrong.

Principle Eight | Data Drives Decisions

Stories are incredibly powerful. Statistics can feel cold and impersonal. Unfortunately, for investors, letting the narrative overwhelm the numbers is a recipe for disaster. The best investors apply a dispassionate and objective lens to their analysis.

Principle Nine | Diversification is Magic

Diversification comes in many flavors—sectors, asset classes, geography, styles, and strategies. It is often referred to as the only free lunch in investing. A truly diversified portfolio has no single point of failure and is robust and resilient to any number of unknown future outcomes. The result of true diversification is a whole greater than the sum of its parts.

Principle Ten | No Silver Bullets

There is no reward without risk or returns without volatility. The holy grail of all of the upside and none of the downside is pure fiction. The secret to success is not to avoid risk, but to take intelligent risks that have historically been compensated.

Principle Eleven | Let Compounding Run Wild

The power of long-term compounding cannot be overstated. There is a reason it is referred to as the Eighth Wonder of the World. It is why time in the market is vastly more important than timing the market. Investment decisions should be made with an "own" not "rent" mentality.

Principle Twelve | Dare to be Different

Above average results don't come to those who always run with the crowd. A differentiated approach will feel uncomfortable at times, but that is by design. Choose unconventional success over conventional failure.

Principle Thirteen | Strong Beliefs Loosely Held

Conviction is healthy but rigidity can be limiting. A healthy dose of skepticism is a virtue. Regularly challenge preconceived beliefs and have a willingness to give up your sacred cows.

Principle Fourteen | Stand on the Shoulders of Giants

Decades of academic research and real-world experience have led to ground-breaking innovations and a deeper understanding of what makes markets tick. There has never been a better time to be an investor.

ACKNOWLEDGMENTS

I thank my lucky stars every day to have been blessed with such an incredible family, both immediate and extended. To my parents, Dave and Nancy, your guidance and unconditional love throughout my life laid the foundation for a life and career I feel so fortunate to have. Thank you for always encouraging me to follow my passions and challenge myself. Mom, thank you for reading every blog post (even if you didn't understand half of them) and for always being my biggest fan.

I am blessed to still have three wonderful grandparents in my life— Barbara "GG" Gauer, Howard Huber, and Carol Huber. Thank you for all your love and support throughout my life.

To my brother Dave Huber Jr. and my sister Trish Myers—you don't get to pick your siblings, but I wouldn't have picked any different. I love you and your families so much.

Danielle Huber, Brad Myers, Frank Phillips, Cathie Phillips, Frankie Phillips—while not by blood, you are every bit as much family to me. I hope I have made you all proud.

Despite writing my own investing blog and being an avid collector of investing and finance books, I never had plans to write one of my own… until Craig Pearce came along. Craig, thank you for helping me realize what I was capable of and for never giving up on me. I could not have asked for a better editor and am so grateful for you and the team at Harriman House for making this dream a reality.

To all my colleagues at Savant Wealth Management, thank you for inspiring me every day in the work you do on behalf of our clients.

To our "Sherpa" and CEO, Brent Brodeski—thank you for your leadership and vision.

To our COO, Kevin Hrdlicka—thank you for your support and for keeping all of us focused on our mission and core values.

To our Director of Research, Gina Beall—I can't imagine a better co-pilot for our investment team. Thank you for being such a joy to work with every single day.

To our Senior Investment Research Analyst, Eamon Verdone—I am so envious of your talents and so appreciative of your help. You are our Swiss army knife.

To our Communications Manager, Martha Conlon—thank you for always being a champion of my content efforts. Without you, there would be no blog. And without the blog, there would be no book.

Before we merged with Savant almost two years ago, I spent almost my entire career at Huber Financial Advisors (HFA). I am proud to say that many of the same co-workers from my early days at HFA are still with me today as part of Team Savant. It's been an incredible journey with you all.

I owe a special debt of gratitude to Rob Morrison, former President of Huber Financial and current Chief Strategy and Innovation Officer at Savant. Your mentorship and friendship throughout my career have been instrumental in shaping who I am today. You have always had my back and I will always have yours.

For those that don't know, the "Huber" in Huber Financial Advisors was not me, but my father Dave Huber. Dad, you already got one mention, but you deserve another. Some people wouldn't dream of working with family. I can't imagine it any other way. While I have carved my own path, I have done so by following in your footsteps. You are my hero and everything I strive to be as a professional, a friend, a husband, and a father.

Speaking of heroes, a heartfelt thank you to my investment hero Cliff Asness for his gracious contribution to this book. If a genie would have granted me a wish to have any one person to write the foreword to this book, it would have been Cliff. I still pinch myself occasionally to believe this happened. You are about as authentic as they come in this industry, and I so appreciate that about you.

Two of the greatest professional decisions I have ever made were activating my Twitter account and starting my own blog. These two mediums have collectively changed my life and career in ways that are hard to fathom. The relationships spawned from these endeavors have brought immense value and joy into my life. It's hard to think of a cooler thing about the internet age than the ability to transform online acquaintances into IRL friendships.

There are a handful of industry friends who went above and beyond the call of duty in providing honest feedback and thorough reviews of the various manuscript drafts. This book is better because of your generous contributions of time and your valuable insights.

Brian Portnoy has been my sounding board and confidant since day one, when this book was merely a figment of my imagination. I walk away from every conversation with Brian feeling like I have learned something. Thank you for your honesty, wisdom, and friendship.

Corey Hoffstein is the smartest person I know. Full stop. He's also one of the kindest. I am forever grateful for your contributions to this book.

Ted Seides, thank you for overdelivering in every sense of the word. You exceeded all my expectations with your generosity of time and thoughtfulness.

Special thanks are also owed to Shannon Saccocia, Matt Kadnar, Bill Kelly, Ali Hamed, Meb Faber, Michael Batnick, Peter Lazaroff, Christie Hamilton, Ross Stevens, and Chris Schelling for their support, feedback, edits, and endorsement of *The Allocator's Edge*.

There are many others whose acts of kindness helped get this project to its ultimate end state. I owe a sincere debt of gratitude to Jason Mersey, Guillaume Auvray, Pat Kearns, Peter Nakada, J. B. Hayes, Mike Miller, Casey Frazier, Bill Coumas, Brian Rhone, Stephen Nesbitt, and Greg Cipolaro for their assistance.

Writing a book is an insane thing to do. Thank you to my friend Jed Skae for helping me figure out how to stay sane during the process.

To my sweet little birdie, Hannah. As fulfilling as it was to write a book, there is nothing more fulfilling in this life than being your dad. You never fail to make me smile or laugh, especially when I need it most.

There's no other way to close this section than by thanking my amazing wife Christie. Simply put, this book would not have happened without you. Your support, encouragement, critiques, honesty, and tough love when I needed it were the fuel that got me to the finish line. Many of the hours spent on this project were hours that could have been spent with you and Hannah—I can't wait to make up for that lost time. Thank you for allowing me to be selfish and indulge in this dream of mine. Now it's your turn!

INDEX

Note: Page numbers in *italic* refer to Figures; Page numbers 1n2 indicate Notes (Page 1 Note 2)